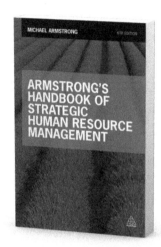

Armstrong's Handbook of Strategic Human Resource Management

Also available by Michael Armstrong

Armstrong's Handbook of Management and Leadership
Armstrong's Handbook of Human Resource Management Practice
Armstrong's Essential Human Resource Management Practice
Armstrong's Handbook of Reward Management Practice
Armstrong's Handbook of Performance Management
How to Manage People
How to be an Even Better Manager
Human Capital Management (with Angela Baron)
The Reward Management Toolkit (with Ann Cummins)
Evidence-Based Reward Management (with Duncan Brown and Peter Reilly)

www.koganpage.com

SIXTH EDITION

Armstrong's Handbook of Strategic Human Resource Management

Michael Armstrong

KoganPage

LONDON PHILADELPHIA NEW DELHI

First published in Great Britain and the United States in 1992 as *Human Resource Management: Strategy and Action*
Second edition published as *Strategic Human Resource Management: A Guide to Action* 2000
Third edition 2006
Fourth edition 2008
Fifth edition published as *Armstrong's Handbook of Strategic Human Resource Management* 2011
Sixth edition 2016

2nd Floor, 45 Gee Street
London
EC1V 3RS
United Kingdom

1518 Walnut Street, Suite 900
Philadelphia PA 19102
USA

4737/23 Ansari Road
Daryaganj
New Delhi 110002
India

© Michael Armstrong, 1992, 2000, 2006, 2008, 2011, 2016

ISBN   978 0 7494 7682 3
E-ISBN 978 0 7494 7683 0

British Library Cataloguing-in-Publication Data

A CIP record for this book is available from the British Library.

Library of Congress Cataloging-in-Publication Data

Names: Armstrong, Michael, 1928- author. | Armstrong, Michael, 1928-
   Strategic human resource management.
Title: Armstrong's handbook of strategic human resource management / Michael Armstrong.
Other titles: Strategic human resource management
Description: 6th Edition/ | Philadelphia : Kogan Page Ltd, 2016. | Revised edition of the author's
   Armstrong's handbook of strategic human resource management, 2011. | Includes
   bibliographical references.
Identifiers: LCCN 2015040424 (print) | LCCN 2015042912 (ebook) | ISBN 9780749476823 |
   ISBN 9780749476830 ()
Subjects: LCSH: Personnel management.
Classification: LCC HF5549 .A89784 2016 (print) | LCC HF5549 (ebook) | DDC 658.3/01–dc23
LC record available at http://lccn.loc.gov/2015040424

Typeset by AMNET
Print production managed by Jellyfish
Printed and bound by CPI Group (UK) Ltd, Croydon CR0 4YY

CONTENTS

Introduction   1

PART ONE The framework
of strategic HRM   3

01   **Human resource management**   5

Introduction   6
The concept of HRM   6
The HR architecture   11
The context of HRM   16
The impact of HRM on organizational performance   17
The ethical dimension   18
HRM in SMEs   19
References   22

02   **Strategic management**   26

Introduction   26
Strategic management   27
The meaning of strategy   27
Characteristics of strategy   28
The content of strategy   28
Business model innovation   28
Developing strategy   30
Implementation of strategy   32
References   34

03   **Strategic human resource management**   36

Introduction   36
SHRM defined   37
The nature of SHRM   37
Aims of SHRM   39
The conceptual framework of SHRM   40
The problem with SHRM   45
References   48

04   The strategic role of HR   50

Introduction   50
The strategic nature of HR   51
The strategic business partner model   52
The strategic role of HR directors   54
The strategic role of heads of HR functions   55
The strategic role of HR business partners   56
The strategic contribution of HR advisors or assistants   56
References   58

PART TWO   HRM strategy in general   59

05   The nature of HR strategy   61

Introduction   61
What is HR strategy?   62
The features of HR strategy   63
Evaluating HR strategy   67
References   69

06   Developing HR strategy   71

Considerations affecting the development of HR strategy   71
Approaches to the development of HR strategy   73
Formulating HR strategy   75
References   82

07   Delivering HR strategy   84

Introduction   84
The 'say–do' gap   85
Ensuring the effective delivery of HR strategy   86
The role of line managers in implementing HR strategy   89
The partnership role of HR in implementing strategy   89
References   92

PART THREE   HRM strategies related to organizational capability and organizational and individual performance   93

08   Organization development strategy   95

Introduction   95
Organization development defined   96

Organization development activities   96
Organization development strategy defined   100
Formulating and implementing organization development
    strategy   100
Culture change   101
References   103

09   Human capital management strategy   105

Introduction   105
Aims of HCM   106
The role of HCM strategy   107
The link between HCM and business strategy   108
Developing an HCM strategy   111
References   116

10   Knowledge management strategy   117

Introduction   117
The process of knowledge management   118
Sources and types of knowledge   118
Approaches to the development of knowledge management
    strategies   119
Strategic knowledge management issues   120
Components of a knowledge management strategy   121
References   123

11   Corporate social responsibility strategy   124

Introduction   124
CSR defined   125
The rationale for CSR   125
Strategic CSR defined   126
CSR activities   127
Role of HR   129
Developing a CSR strategy   129
References   132

12   Organizational performance strategy   133

Introduction   133
The process of managing organizational performance   134
The strategic approach to managing organizational
    performance   135
Organizational capability   138
Developing a high-performance culture   138
How HR strategies enhance organizational performance   145
References   147

13 Individual performance management strategy 148

Introduction 148
The nature of a performance management system 149
Performance management activities 151
Limitations of the model 153
Implementation problems 155
The nature of performance management strategy 156
References 157

PART FOUR HRM strategies dealing with specific aspects of HRM 159

14 Employee engagement strategy 161

Introduction 161
What is engagement? 162
Why is engagement important? 163
What are the factors that influence employee engagement? 163
The nature and content of employee engagement strategy 164
References 168

15 Resourcing strategy 170

Introduction 171
The rationale for strategic resourcing 171
The strategic HRM approach to resourcing 171
Integrating business and resourcing strategies 172
Bundling resourcing strategies and activities 173
The components of employee resourcing strategy 173
Workforce planning 174
Employee value proposition 177
Resourcing plans 178
Retention strategy 180
Flexibility strategy 184
Diversity and inclusion strategy 184
References 187

16 Talent management strategy 189

Talent management defined 189
Strategic talent management 190
What is talent? 190
Talent management strategy 192
References 197

17   Learning and development strategy   198

Introduction   198
Strategic learning and development philosophy   199
Elements of learning and development   201
Strategy for creating a learning culture   202
Organizational learning strategy   202
Individual learning strategy   203
References   207

18   Reward strategy   209

Introduction   209
Reward strategy defined   210
Why have a reward strategy?   210
Characteristics of reward strategy   211
The basis of reward strategy   211
The content of reward strategy   215
Guiding principles   217
Developing reward strategy   219
Effective reward strategies   220
Reward strategy and line management capability   221
The problem with the concept of reward strategy   222
References   225

19   Employee relations strategy   226

Introduction   226
The employment relationship   227
The nature of employment relations strategy   230
Partnership agreement strategy   231
Employee voice strategy   231
Trade union recognition strategy   232
References   234

PART FIVE The international scene   235

20   Strategic international HRM   237

Introduction   237
Strategic international HRM (SIHRM)   238
SIHRM issues   238
Approaches to SIHRM   243
References   245

21   International HRM strategies   247

Introduction   247
Resourcing strategy   248
International talent management   250
International performance management   252
International reward management   253
Managing expatriates   255
References   257

Author Index   259
Subject Index   262

Introduction

Strategic human resource management (SHRM) was defined by Armstrong and Long (1994: 38) as 'an approach to making decisions on the intentions of the organization concerning people which are an essential component of the organization's corporate or business strategy'. Human resource management (HRM) strategies focus on specific plans on what needs to be changed and what needs to be done and are produced within the SHRM framework.

SHRM is built on the concepts of HRM and strategic management and these are therefore dealt with in turn in the first two chapters of Part 1 of this book. The third chapter in Part 1 explains how this linked approach takes place. An important aspect of SHRM is that it indicates the need for HR specialists to act strategically, as explained in the fourth chapter of Part 1.

The second part of the book deals with the nature of HRM strategies and how they can be developed and implemented. It is explained that they are governed or at least influenced by the overall approach adopted to strategic HRM. They could be regarded as manifestations of SHRM in action.

The third part of the book describes HRM strategies dealing with broad issues of organizational capability and organizational and individual performance, while the fourth part examines strategies concerned with specific aspects of HRM. Finally, the fifth part considers SHRM and HRM strategies in the international arena.

The relationships between these parts is illustrated in Figure 0.1.

FIGURE 0.1 Plan of the book

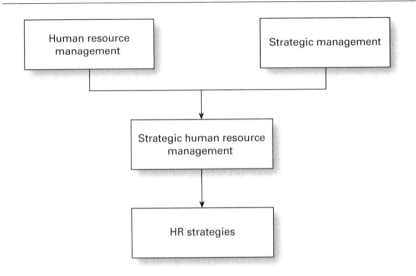

Reference

Armstrong, M and Long, P (1994) *The Reality of Strategic HRM*, IPM, London

PART ONE
The framework of strategic HRM

Human resource management

KEY CONCEPTS AND TERMS

Added value
Contextual model of HRM
European model of HRM
5-P model of HRM
Hard HRM
Harvard framework
HRM architecture
HR philosophy
Human resource management (HRM)
Matching model of HRM
Resource-based theory
Soft HRM
Strategic alignment
Strategic human resource management (SHRM)

LEARNING OUTCOMES

On completing this chapter you should be able to define these key concepts. You should also know about:

- the fundamental concept of HRM and how it developed;
- the goals of HRM;
- the philosophy of HRM;
- models of HRM;
- the HRM architecture;
- the impact of HRM on organizational performance;
- the ethical dimension of HRM;
- HRM in small and medium-sized enterprises (SMEs).

Introduction

Human resource management (HRM) is concerned with all aspects of how people are employed, managed and developed in organizations. As Boxall (2013: 13) pointed out: 'Human resources include the knowledge, skills, networks and energies of people and, underpinning them, their physical and emotional health, intellectual capabilities, personalities and motivations.' HRM is delivered through the human resource (HR) architecture of systems and structures, the HR function and, importantly, line management.

Some people criticize the notion of referring to people as resources as if they were any other factor of production. Osterby and Coster (1992: 31) argued that: 'The term "human resources" reduces people to the same category of value as materials, money and technology – all resources, and resources are only valuable to the extent they can be exploited or leveraged into economic value.' People management is sometimes preferred as an alternative but HRM, in spite of its connotations, is the term that is most commonly used.

HRM emerged in the 1980s as a philosophy of how people should be managed. As Hendry and Pettigrew (1990: 20) observed: 'What HRM did at this point was to wrap around some of the observable changes, while providing a focus for challenging deficiencies – in attitudes, scope, coherence and direction – of existing personnel management.' They also commented (1990: 25) that HRM can be perceived as a 'perspective on personnel management and not personnel management itself'. HRM can therefore be regarded as a concept and this is discussed in the first section of this chapter. But HRM is manifested in a set of practices. These are examined in the second section of this chapter and include the overarching framework of strategic human resource management (see Chapter 3) within which HR strategies are formulated and implemented (see Part 2). Four other aspects of HRM are dealt with in this chapter: first, the implications of the context in which HR takes place; second, the impact that HRM makes on organizational performance; third, its ethical dimension; and fourth, the special considerations affecting HRM in small to medium-sized enterprises (SMEs).

The concept of HRM

HRM as originally conceived had a conceptual framework consisting of a philosophy underpinned by a number of theories drawn from the behavioural sciences and from the fields of strategic management, human capital management and industrial relations. The HRM philosophy has been heavily criticized by some academics as being managerialist and manipulative but this criticism has subsided, perhaps because it became increasingly evident that the term HRM had been adopted as a synonym for what used to be called personnel management. As noted by Storey (2007: 6): 'In its generic broad and popular sense it [HRM] simply refers to any system of people management.'

HRM practice today is no longer governed by the original philosophy, if it ever was. It is simply what HR people and line managers do.

HRM defined

Human resource management is defined as a strategic, integrated and coherent approach to the employment, development and well-being of the people working in organizations. It was defined more pragmatically by Boxall and Purcell (2003: 1) as 'all those activities associated with the management of employment relationships in the firm'. A more comprehensive definition was offered by Watson (2010: 919):

> HRM is the managerial utilization of the efforts, knowledge, capabilities and committed behaviours that people contribute to an authoritatively co-ordinated human enterprise as part of an employment exchange (or more temporary contractual arrangement) to carry out work tasks in a way that enables the enterprise to continue into the future.

The goals of HRM

The goals of HRM are to:

- support the organization in achieving its objectives by developing and implementing HR strategies that are integrated with the business strategy (strategic HRM);
- contribute to the development of a high-performance culture;
- ensure that the organization has the talented, skilled and engaged people it needs;
- create a positive employment relationship between management and employees and a climate of mutual trust;
- encourage the application of an ethical approach to people management.

The philosophy of HRM

The following explanation of HRM philosophy was made by Legge (1989: 25), whose analysis of a number of HRM models identified the following common themes:

> That human resource policies should be integrated with strategic business planning and used to reinforce an appropriate (or change an inappropriate) organizational culture, that human resources are valuable and a source of competitive advantage, that they may be tapped most effectively by mutually

consistent policies that promote commitment and that, as a consequence, foster a willingness in employees to act flexibly in the interests of the 'adaptive organization's' pursuit of excellence.

Storey (2001: 7) noted that the beliefs of HRM included the assumptions that it is the human resource that gives competitive edge; that the aim should be to enhance employee commitment; that HR decisions are of strategic importance; and that therefore HR policies should be integrated into the business strategy.

Underpinning theories of HRM

The original notion of HRM had a strong theoretical base. Guest (1987: 505) commented that: 'Human resource management appears to lean heavily on theories of commitment and motivation and other ideas derived from the field of organizational behaviour.' However, resource-based theory expressed as 'the resource-based view' has had the greatest influence on HRM. This theory states that competitive advantage is achieved if a firm's resources are valuable, rare and costly to imitate. It is claimed that HRM can play a major part in ensuring that the firm's human resources meet these criteria.

Models of HRM

Over the years a number of models (as summarized below) have defined what HRM is and how it operates. Of these, the matching model and the Harvard framework have been the most influential.

The matching model of HRM

Fombrun, Tichy and Devanna (1984) proposed the 'matching model', which indicated that HR systems and the organization structure should be managed in a way that is congruent with organizational strategy. This point was made in their classic statement that: 'The critical management task is to align the formal structure and human resource systems so that they drive the strategic objectives of the organization' (1984: 37). Thus they took the first steps towards the concept of strategic HRM.

The Harvard model of HRM

Beer *et al* (1984) produced what has become known as the 'Harvard framework'. They started with the proposition that: 'Human resource management (HRM) involves all management decisions and actions that affect the nature of the relationship between the organization and employees – its human resources' (1984: 1). They believed that: 'Today... many pressures are demanding a broader, more comprehensive and more strategic perspective with regard to the organization's human resources'

(1984: 4). They also stressed that it was necessary to adopt 'a longer-term perspective in managing people and consideration of people as a potential asset rather than merely a variable cost' (1984: 6). Beer and his colleagues were the first to underline the HRM tenet that it belongs to line managers. They suggested that HRM had two characteristic features: 1) line managers accept more responsibility for ensuring the alignment of competitive strategy and HR policies; 2) HR has the mission of setting policies that govern how HR activities are developed and implemented in ways that make them more mutually reinforcing.

Contextual model of HRM

The contextual model of HRM emphasizes the importance of environmental factors by including variables such as the influence of social, institutional and political forces that have been underestimated in other models. The model advocates integrating the HRM system in the environment in which it is developed. According to Martin-Alcázar, Romero-Fernandez and Sánchez-Gardey (2005: 638): 'Context both conditions and is conditioned by the HRM strategy.' A broader set of stakeholders is involved in the formulation and implementation of HR strategies. This is referred to by Schuler and Jackson (2000: 229) as a 'multiple stakeholder framework'. These stakeholders may be external as well as internal, and both influence and are influenced by strategic decisions.

The 5-P model of HRM

As formulated by Schuler (1992) the 5-P model of HRM describes the way that HRM operates under the five headings of:

- *HR philosophy*: a statement of how the organization regards its human resources, the role they play in the overall success of the business, and how they should be treated and managed.
- *HR policies*: these provide guidelines for action on people-related business issues and for the development of HR programmes and practices based on strategic needs.
- *HR programmes*: these are shaped by HR policies and consist of co-ordinated HR efforts intended to initiate and manage organizational change efforts prompted by strategic business needs.
- *HR practices*: these are the activities carried out in implementing HR policies and programmes. They include resourcing, learning and development, performance and reward management, employee relations and administration.
- *HR processes*: these are the formal procedures and methods used to put HR strategic plans and policies into effect.

European model of HRM

Brewster (1993) described a European model of HRM as follows:

- Environment – established legal framework.
- Objectives – organizational objectives and social concern; people as a key resource.
- Focus – cost/benefits and environment analysis.
- Relationship with employees – union and non-union.
- Relationship with line managers – specialist/line liaison.
- Role of HR specialist – specialist managers: ambiguity, tolerance, flexibility.

The main distinction between this model and what Brewster referred to as 'the prescribed model' was that the latter involves deregulation (no legal framework), no trade unions and a focus on organizational objectives but not on social concern.

The hard and soft HRM models

Storey (1989: 8) distinguished between the 'hard' and 'soft' versions of HRM. He wrote that: 'The hard one emphasizes the quantitative, calculative and business-strategic aspects of managing human resources in as "rational" a way as for any other economic factor. By contrast, the soft version traces its roots to the human-relations school; it emphasizes communication, motivation and leadership.'

However, it was pointed out by Keenoy (1997: 838) that 'hard and soft HRM are complementary rather than mutually exclusive practices'. Research in eight UK organizations by Truss *et al* (1997) indicated that the distinction between hard and soft HRM was not as precise as some commentators have implied.

HRM today

As a description of people management activities in organizations the term HRM is here to stay, even if it is applied diversely or only used as a label to describe traditional personnel management practices. Emphasis is now placed on the need for HR to be strategic and businesslike and to add value, that is, to generate extra value (benefit to the business) by the expenditure of effort, time and money on HRM activities. There have been plenty of new interests and developments including human capital management, engagement, talent management, competency-based HRM, e-HRM, high performance work systems, and performance and reward management. But these have not been introduced under the banner of the HRM concept as originally defined.

HRM has largely become something that organizations *do* rather than an aspiration or a philosophy, and the term is generally in use as a way of describing the process of managing people. A convincing summary of what HRM means today, which focuses on what HRM *is* rather than on its philosophy, was provided by Boxall, Purcell and Wright (2007), representing the new generation of commentators.

SOURCE REVIEW   The meaning of HRM – Boxall, Purcell and Wright (2007: 1)

Human resource management (HRM), the management of work and people towards desired ends, is a fundamental activity in any organization in which human beings are employed. It is not something whose existence needs to be radically justified: HRM is an inevitable consequence of starting and growing an organization. While there are a myriad of variations in the ideologies, styles and managerial resources engaged, HRM happens in some form or other. It is one thing to question the *relative* performance of particular models of HRM… It is quite another thing to question the necessity of the HRM process itself, as if organizations cannot survive or grow without making a reasonable attempt at organizing work and managing people.

The HR architecture

HRM is delivered through the HR architecture of the HR system, the HR function and, importantly, line management. As explained by Becker, Huselid and Ulrich (2001: 12): 'We use the term HR architecture to broadly describe the continuum from the HR professionals within the HR function, to the system of HR related policies and practices, through the competencies, motivation and associated behaviours of the firm's employees.' It was noted by Hird, Sparrow and Marsh (2010: 25) that: 'this architecture is seen as a unique combination of the HR function's structure and delivery model, the HR practices and system, and the strategic employee behaviours that these create'.

The HR system

The HR system consists of the interrelated and jointly supportive HR practices, which together enable HRM goals to be achieved. Boselie, Dietz and Boon (2005: 73) pointed out that in its traditional form HRM can be viewed as 'a collection of multiple discrete practices with no explicit or discernible link between them. The more strategically minded system approach views HRM as an integrated and coherent bundle of mutually reinforcing practices.'

As illustrated in Figure 1.1, the HRM system brings together *HR philosophies* that describe the overarching values and guiding principles adopted in managing people and, taking account of the internal and external contexts in which the organization operates, develops *HR strategies* that define the direction in which HRM intends to go; *HR policies* that provide guidelines defining how these values, principles and strategies should be applied and implemented in specific areas of HRM; *HR processes* that comprise the formal procedures and methods used to put HR strategic plans and policies into effect; linked *HR practices* that consist of the approaches used in managing people; and *HR programmes* that enable HR strategies, policies and practices to be implemented according to plan.

The role and organization of the HR function

Members of the HR function provide insight, leadership, advice and services on matters affecting the management, employment, learning and development, reward and well-being of people, and the relationships between management and employees. Importantly, they contribute to the achievement of organizational effectiveness and success.

The basic role of the HR function is to deliver HRM services. But it does, or should do, much more than that. Increasingly, the role of HR is seen to be business-oriented, contributing to the achievement of sustained competitive advantage. Becker and Huselid (1998: 97) argued that HR should be 'a resource that solves real business problems'. But one of the issues explored by Francis and Keegan (2006) in their research was the tendency for a focus on business performance outcomes to obscure the importance of employee well-being in its own right. They quoted the view of Ulrich and Brockbank (2005: 201) that 'caring, listening to, and responding to employees remains a centrepiece of HR work'. It can also play a key part in the creation of an environment that enhances engagement by enabling people to make the best use of their capacities, to realize their potential to the benefit of both the organization and themselves, and to achieve satisfaction through their work.

HR activities can be divided into two broad categories: 1) transformational (strategic) activities that are concerned with developing organizational effectiveness and the alignment and implementation of HR and business strategies; and 2) transactional activities, which cover the main areas of HR service delivery – resourcing, learning and development, reward and employee relations.

The ways in which HR operates vary immensely. As Sisson (1990) commented, HR management is not a single homogeneous occupation – it involves a variety of roles and activities that differ from one organization to another and from one level to another in the same organization. Tyson (1987) claimed that the HR function is often 'balkanized' – not only is there a variety

FIGURE 1.1   The HRM System

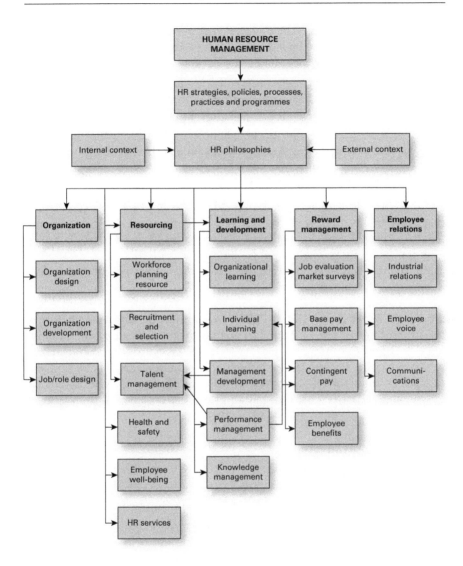

of roles and activities but these tend to be relatively self-centred, with little passage between them. Hope-Hailey *et al* (1997: 17) believed that HR could be regarded as a 'chameleon function', in the sense that the diversity of practice established by their research suggests that 'contextual variables dictate different roles for the function and different practices of people management'.

The notion of delivering HRM through three major areas (sometimes called 'the three-legged stool model') – emerged from the HR model produced by Ulrich (1997,1998), although Ulrich has stated that is not actually his idea at all but an interpretation of his writing. The areas are:

- *Centres of expertise*: these specialize in the provision of high-level advice and services on key HR activities such as talent management, leadership development and reward.
- *Strategic business partners*: these work with line managers to help them reach their goals through strategy formulation and execution. They are often 'embedded' in business units or departments.
- HR *shared service centres*: these handle all the routine 'transactional' services across the business, which include such activities as recruitment, training, absence monitoring and advice on dealing with employee issues such as discipline and absenteeism.

But there are difficulties with the model. Gratton (2003: 18) commented that: 'this fragmentation of the HR function is causing all sorts of unintended problems. Senior managers look at the fragments and are not clear how the function as a whole adds value.' And as Reilly (2007) observed, there are problems in introducing the new model. These included difficulties in defining roles and accountabilities, especially those of business partners, who, according to an HR director interviewed by Reilly, risk being 'hung, drawn and quartered by all sides'. At the same time, the segmented nature of the structure gives rise to 'boundary management' difficulties, for example when it comes to separating out transactional tasks from the work of centres of expertise. The model can also hamper communication between those engaged in different HR activities. Other impediments were technological failure, inadequate resources in HR and skills gaps.

STRATEGIC HRM IN ACTION

HR organization at the National Australia Bank Group

HR at the National Australia Bank Group has a number of centres of expertise, business partners, solutions consultants, project managers, a shared services centre, and telephone advisory service for employees (the people advisory helpline):

- *Centres of expertise*
  Centres of expertise cover areas such as reward, employment policy, talent management, culture management, diversity and performance. The staff in the centres are specialists in their respective fields, while the other parts of HR can be found in the HR service centre (with the exception of recruitment, which is conducted by line managers).

- *Business partners*
  Business partners attend business unit leadership team meetings; they set the company's people strategies and deliver the HR requirements emerging from various projects. They tend to work in the areas of talent, performance, leadership, diversity and culture, and their job is to facilitate the implementation of corporate people initiatives with the relevant specialist HR partners. Unlike shared services staff, they only get involved in HR's daily operational matters if projects escalate and extra help is required.

- *Solutions consultants*
  Solutions consultants deal with operational queries referred to them from the people advisory helpline – mainly issues of case management and other more complex enquiries. They are a key point of contact for people leaders on matters of policy and procedure, although they do participate in some transaction work as well.

- *Project staff*
  Project staff work on projects that emerge from strategic discussions.

SOURCE: IRS (2010) *Employment Trends*, June, pp 15–16

The HR role of line managers

HR can initiate new policies and practices but it is line managers who have the main responsibility for implementing them. In other words, HR proposes but the line disposes. Guest (1991: 159) observed that: 'HRM is too important to be left to personnel managers.'

If line managers are not inclined favourably towards what HR wants them to do then they won't do it or, if compelled to against their will, they will be half-hearted about it. Following their research, Guest and King (2004: 421) commented that 'better HR depended not so much on better procedures but better implementation and ownership of implementation by line managers'.

As noted by Purcell *et al* (2003), high levels of organizational performance are not achieved simply by having a range of well-conceived HR policies and practices in place. What makes the difference is how these policies and practices are implemented. That is where the role of line managers in people management is crucial: 'managers… play a vital role in making involvement happen, in communicating, in being open to allow employee concerns to be raised and discussed, in allowing people space to influence how they do their job, and in coaching, guiding and recognizing performance and providing help for the future' (Purcell *et al*, 2003: 40). Purcell and his colleagues emphasized that dealing with people is perhaps the aspect of their work in which line managers can exercise the greatest amount of discretion – and they can use that discretion by not putting HR's ideas into practice. As they pointed out, it is line managers who bring HR policies to life.

A further factor affecting the role of line managers is their ability to do the HR tasks assigned to them. People-centred activities – such as defining roles (job design), interviewing, reviewing performance, providing feedback, coaching, identifying learning and development needs, and deciding how their staff should be rewarded – all require special skills. Some managers have the skills; many don't. Performance management systems and performance-related pay schemes can easily fail because of untrained line managers. The implementation of policies to enhance engagement levels depends largely on line managers.

The context of HRM

The design and operation of an HR system takes place within the context of the internal and external environments of the organization. These exert considerable influence on the HR architecture.

The external environment

The external environment consists of social, political, legal and economic developments and competitive pressures. Global competition in mature production and service sectors is increasing. This is assisted by easily transferable technology and reductions in international trade barriers. Customers are demanding more as new standards are reached through international competition. Organizations are reacting to this competition by becoming 'customer focused', speeding up response times, emphasizing quality and continuous improvement, accelerating the introduction of new technology, operating more flexibly and 'losing cost'. The pressure has been for businesses to become 'lean and mean', downsizing and cutting out layers of management and supervision. They reduce permanent staff to a core of essential workers, increase the use of peripheral workers (subcontractors, temporary staff) and zero-hours contracts, and they 'outsource' work to external service providers. These pressures can be considerable in an economic downturn.

The internal environment

The following aspects of the internal environment will affect HR policy and practice:

- the type of business or organization – private, public or voluntary sector; manufacturing or service;

- the size of the organization;
- the extent to which it operates internationally;
- the age or maturity of the organization;
- the technology or key activities of the business will determine how work is organized, managed and carried out;
- the type of people employed, eg professional staff, knowledge workers, technicians, administrators, production workers, sales and customer service staff;
- the size of the organization – HR in SMEs will differ from that in larger and more complex businesses;
- the financial circumstances of the organization, especially in economic downturns;
- the organization's culture – the established pattern of values, norms, beliefs, attitudes and assumptions that shape the ways in which people behave and things get done;
- the political and social climate within the organization.

The impact of HRM on organizational performance

The message of the resource-based view is that HRM delivers added value and helps to achieve sustainable competitive advantage through the strategic development of the organization's rare, hard-to-imitate and hard-to-substitute human resources. Guest (1997: 269) argued that: 'The distinctive feature of HRM is its assumption that improved performance is achieved through the people in the organization.' If, therefore, appropriate HR policies and practices are introduced, it can also be assumed that HRM will impact on the firm's performance.

Much research has been carried out, which has shown that there is a correlation between good HRM practice and organizational performance. Notable examples in the UK are Guest *et al* (2000a), Patterson *et al* (1997), Purcell *et al* (2003), Thompson (2002) and West *et al* (2002). But Guest *et al* (2000b) observed that such research left uncertainties about cause and effect. And Ulrich (1997: 304) pointed out that: 'HR practices seem to matter; logic says it is so; survey findings confirm it. Direct relationships between performance and attention to HR practices are often fuzzy, however, and vary according to the population sampled and the measures used.' Guest (2011: 11) summed up his article on HRM and performance with the comment that: 'After hundreds of research studies we are still in no position to assert with any confidence that good HRM has an impact on organization performance.'

Any belief that HRM improves organizational performance is likely to be based on three propositions: 1) that HR practices can make a direct impact on employee characteristics such as engagement, commitment, motivation and skill; 2) if employees have these characteristics it is probable that organizational performance in terms of productivity, quality and the delivery of high levels of customer service will improve; and 3) if such aspects of organizational performance improve, the financial results achieved by the organization will improve. This can be described as the HR value chain.

The propositions highlight the existence of an intermediate factor between HRM and financial performance. This factor consists of the HRM outcomes in the shape of employee characteristics affected by HR practices. Therefore, HRM does not make a direct impact on financial performance.

The ethical dimension

HRM has an ethical dimension – that of exercising concern for the interests (well-being) of employees, bearing in mind Schneider's (1987: 450) view that 'organizations are the people in them… people make the place'. Beer *et al* (1984: 13) emphasized that: 'It is not enough to ask how well the management of human resources serves the interests of the enterprise. One should ask how well the enterprise's HRM policies serve the well-being of the *individual employee*' (original emphasis). Ulrich (1997: 5) argued that HR professionals should 'represent both employee needs and implement management agendas'. Boxall, Purcell and Wright (2007: 5) contended that: 'While HRM does need to support commercial outcomes (often called "the business case"), it also exists to serve organizational needs for social legitimacy.'

Ideally, an ethical approach would involve:

- treating people equally in terms of the opportunities for employment, learning and development provided for them;
- treating people according to the principle of procedural justice (Adams, 1965; Leventhal, 1980) – that is to say, the ways in which people are managed are fair, consistent and transparent;
- treating people according to the principles of distributive justice, ie rewards are distributed to them according to their contribution, and they receive what was promised to them;
- treating people according to the principles of natural justice, ie individuals know the standards they are expected to achieve and the rules to which they are expected to conform, are given a clear indication of where they are failing or what rules have been broken and, except in cases of gross misconduct, are given a chance to improve before disciplinary action is taken;
- taking account of the views of employees on matters that affect them;
- being concerned with the well-being of employees as well as the pursuit of commercial gain;
- offering as much security of employment as possible;

- providing a working environment that protects the health and safety of employees and minimizes stress;
- acting in the interests of providing a reasonable balance for employees between their life and their work;
- protecting employees against harmful practices at work such as bullying, harassment and discrimination.

But ethical behaviour on the part of employers may not be regarded as important and certainly does not necessarily happen. It was asserted by Winstanley and Woodall (2000: 6) that 'the ethical dimension of HR policy and practice has been almost ignored in recent texts on HRM, where the focus has shifted to "strategic fit" and "best practice" approaches'. Grant and Shields (2002) stated that the emphasis typically placed on the business case for HRM suggests a one-sided focus on organizational outcomes at the expense of employees.

HRM in SMEs

SMEs are usually defined as companies with up to 250 employees. Clearly they vary widely, as does the approach to HR they adopt. However, people management activities tend to be informal in small firms, especially in the earlier stages of their development. Research conducted by Miller (2015) established that there were four stages of SME growth. As a company moves through each change there are different HR requirements that emerge, which may lead to the appointment of full-time or part-time HR professionals or the extended use of external agencies and consultants:

- *Stage 1, start-up*

  In this initial stage, business people matters tend to be dealt with by the owner, with no formal HR role. Overall the business is characterized by informality, with an emergent strategy, fluid structures and flexible job roles. The owner takes responsibility for hiring, looking for someone who 'fits' with what the company is all about. The people-related requirements tend to be minimal, centred on pay and contracts, with the rate for the job set by the owner.

- *Stage 2, emerging enterprise*

  In a growing business the owner will have to delegate more, and people issues become more important. Someone may be appointed to look after HR matters, possibly on a part-time basis, for any of the following reasons:

  - The business has reached a size where policies and procedures are needed to guide work and create a sense of fairness.
  - The owner feels that people issues are taking up too much of his or her time.

- People management is seen as vital for growth and to achieve the company's vision.
- There is a specific people issue that needs to be addressed, for example tribunal cases, skills shortages, high turnover.

But the owner may decide simply to outsource HR work such as recruitment and to seek advice from consultants on any serious people problem.

- *Stage 3, consolidation*

   As the business develops and expands it may appoint a full-time HR specialist who will introduce more sophisticated practices in areas such as recruitment, talent management, or reward or performance management in order to meet the needs of the business for talented high-performing employees.

- *Stage 4, established business*

   Fully established businesses will set up an HR department under a generalist manger with specialized assistants, for example one focusing on recruitment and talent management, and another dealing with learning and development.

The research by Miller found that attaching workforce numbers to the stages did not reveal any particular pattern. SMEs tended to develop more formal HR practices and a dedicated HR manager or function at different workforce sizes, depending on the people requirements of the business, the leader's view on people management and the industry the business operates in.

However, Marlow, Taylor and Thompson (2010) established through their research in six growing SMEs that although there was some formalization of HR, some owners still retained informal control over employment matters. They commented that SMEs did not necessarily move from informality to formality, and that it could be argued that in a small firm there may be advantages in maintaining an informal approach to people management.

STRATEGIC HRM IN ACTION

Improving HR services at the Royal Bolton Hospital

The Royal Bolton Hospital became a foundation trust in October 2008, and serves around 263,000 people in the Bolton area. In 2011 it employed around 3,600 staff.

In 2005 the newly appointed head of HR found that the function was traditional and hierarchical and had a poor customer perspective. A significant cultural shift was needed to move to a 'can-do' attitude and realize the potential within the function, so that it added value to the business and to patients. In 2006 HR services were restructured, adopting a business partner model linked to the divisions within the trust.

In 2008, the Strategic Health Authority (NHS North West) worked with the Institute for Employment Studies to develop a model of world-class HR and organizational development for health trusts in the region. World-class HR was defined in terms of six criteria: aligning and integrating with the business; proactively leading the people agenda; achieving the desired results for the business; having a compelling employee proposition; getting the basics right; and supporting people management.

An exercise was conducted with the executive board and staff to identify what HR should continue doing, what to improve, what to develop and what to stop doing. A peer review by another health trust and a staff customer survey identified the following issues: time to recruit, inconsistency in HR advice, and insufficient communication.

It was clear that the credibility of HR was based on getting the basics right, so that became a priority. The HR team was then set the challenge of changing customer perception. The realigned team structure was further embedded to provide more support for managers. The Employee Services Centre team streamlined its processes and, in particular, increased communication within the recruitment process.

The customer survey was repeated in 2010 and showed significant improvements in HR customer perceptions on the six world-class factors when compared with 2008. In 2010, 60 per cent of management and clinician respondents rated their HR function as 'better' or 'much better' than before. People indicators across the trust, including attendance statistics, also showed improvement during the same period.

SOURCE: *People Management* (2011) February, p 31

KEY LEARNING POINTS

- HRM is concerned with all aspects of how people are employed, managed and developed in organizations. HRM is delivered through the HR architecture of systems and structures, the HR function and, importantly, line management.
- Human resource management can be defined as a strategic, integrated and coherent approach to the employment, development and well-being of the people working in organizations.

- The goals of HRM are to:
  - support the organization in achieving its objectives by developing and implementing HR strategies that are integrated with the business strategy (strategic HRM);
  - contribute to the development of a high-performance culture;
  - ensure that the organization has the talented, skilled and engaged people it needs;
  - create a positive employment relationship between management and employees, and a climate of mutual trust;
  - encourage the application of an ethical approach to people management.
- The main message of HRM philosophy is that human resource policies should be integrated with strategic business planning and used to reinforce an appropriate (or change an inappropriate) organizational culture.
- Resource-based theory expressed as 'the resource-based view' has had the greatest influence on the concept of HRM.
- The matching model and the Harvard framework have been the most influential models of HRM.
- HRM is delivered through the HR architecture of the HR system, the HR function and, importantly, line management.
- There are three propositions on the impact that HRM makes on performance: 1) that HR practices can have a direct impact on employee characteristics such as engagement, commitment, motivation and skill; 2) if employees have these characteristics it is probable that organizational performance will improve; and 3) if such aspects of organizational performance improve, the financial results achieved by the organization will improve.
- HRM has an ethical dimension – that of exercising concern for the interests (well-being) of employees.
- In SMEs people management activities tend to be informal in the earlier stages of development. Professional HR support is more likely in the later stages.

References

Adams, J S (1965) Injustice in social exchange, in *Advances in Experimental Psychology*, ed L Berkowitz, Academic Press, New York

Becker, B E and Huselid, M A (1998) High performance work systems and firm performance: a synthesis of research and managerial implications, *Research on Personnel and Human Resource Management*, **16**, pp 53–101

Becker, B E, Huselid, M A and Ulrich, D (2001) *The HR Score Card: Linking people, strategy, and performance*, Harvard Business School Press, Boston MA

Beer M, Spector B, Lawrence P, Quinn Mills D and Walton, R (1984) *Managing Human Assets*, The Free Press, New York

Boselie, P, Dietz, G and Boon, C (2005) Commonalities and contradictions in HRM and performance research, *Human Resource Management Journal*, 15 (3), pp 67–94

Boxall, P F (2013) Mutuality in the management of human resources: assessing the quality of alignment in employment relationships, *Human Resource Management Journal*, 23 (1), pp 8–17

Boxall, P F and Purcell, J (2003) *Strategy and Human Resource Management*, Palgrave Macmillan, Basingstoke

Boxall, P F, Purcell, J and Wright, P (2007) Human resource management: scope, analysis and significance, in *Oxford Handbook of Human Resource Management*, ed P Boxall, J Purcell and P Wright, pp 1–16, Oxford University Press, Oxford

Brewster, C (1993) Developing a 'European' model of human resource management, *The International Journal of Human Resource Management*, 4 (4), pp 765–84

Fombrun, C J, Tichy, N M and Devanna, M A (1984) *Strategic Human Resource Management*, Wiley, New York

Francis, H and Keegan A (2006) The changing face of HRM: in search of balance, *Human Resource Management Journal*, 16 (3), pp 231–49

Grant, D and Shields, J (2002) In search of the subject: researching employee reactions to human resource management, *Journal of Industrial Relations*, 44 (3), pp 313–34

Gratton, L A (2003) The humpty dumpty effect: a view of a fragmented HR function, *People Management*, 5 January, p 18

Guest, D E (1987) Human resource management and industrial relations, *Journal of Management Studies*, 24 (5), pp 503–21

Guest, D E (1991) Personnel management: the end of orthodoxy, *British Journal of Industrial Relations*, 29 (2), pp 149–76

Guest, D E (1997) Human resource management and performance: a review of the research agenda, *The International Journal of Human Resource Management*, 8 (3), pp 263–76

Guest, D E (2011) Human resource management and performance: still searching for some answers, *Human Resource Management Journal*, 21 (1), pp 3–13

Guest, D E and King, Z (2004) Power, innovation and problem-solving: the personnel managers' three steps to heaven?, *Journal of Management Studies*, 41 (3), pp 401–23

Guest, D E, Michie, J, Sheehan, M and Conway, N (2000a) *Employee Relations, HRM and Business Performance: An analysis of the 1998 workplace employee relations survey*, CIPD, London

Guest, D E, Michie, J, Sheehan, M, Conway, N and Metochi, M (2000b) *Effective People Management: Initial findings of future of work survey*, CIPD, London

Hendry, C and Pettigrew, A (1990) Human resource management: an agenda for the 1990s, *International Journal of Human Resource Management*, 1 (1), pp 17–44

Hird, M, Sparrow, P and Marsh, C (2010) HR structures: are they working?, in *Leading HR*, ed P Sparrow, A Hesketh, M Hird and C Cooper, pp 23–45, Palgrave Macmillan, Basingstoke

Hope-Hailey, V, Gratton, L, McGovern, P, Stiles, P and Truss, C (1997) A chameleon function?, HRM in the '90s, *Human Resource Management Journal*, 7 (3), pp 5–18

Keenoy, T (1997) HRMism and the images of re-presentation, *Journal of Management Studies*, **34** (5), pp 825–41

Legge, K (1989) Human resource management: a critical analysis, in *New Perspectives in Human Resource Management*, ed J Storey, pp 19–40, Routledge, London

Leventhal, G S (1980) What should be done with equity theory?, in *Social Exchange: Advances in theory and research*, ed G K Gergen, M S Greenberg and R H Willis, Plenum, New York

Marlow, S, Taylor, S and Thompson, A (2010) Informality and formality in medium sized companies: contestation and synchronization, *British Journal of Management*, **21**, pp 954–66

Martin-Alcázar, F, Romero-Fernandez, P M and Sánchez-Gardey, G (2005) Strategic human resource management: integrating the universalistic, contingent, configurational and contextual perspectives, *Journal of International Human Resource Management*, **16** (5), pp 633–59

Miller, J (2015) *What Does the Future of HR in an SME Look Like?*, CIPD, London

Osterby, B and Coster, C (1992) Human resource development – a sticky label, *Training and Development*, April, pp 31–32

Patterson, M G, West, M A, Lawthom, R and Nickell, S (1997) *Impact of People Management Practices on Performance*, Institute of Personnel and Development, London

Purcell, J, Kinnie, K, Hutchinson, S, Rayton, B and Swart, J (2003) *Understanding the People and Performance Link: Unlocking the black box*, CIPD, London

Reilly, P (2007) Facing up to the facts, *People Management*, 20 September, pp 43-45

Schneider, B (1987) The people make the place, *Personnel Psychology*, **40** (3), pp 437–53

Schuler, R S (1992) Strategic HRM: linking people with the needs of the business, *Organizational Dynamics*, **21**, pp 19–32

Schuler, R S and Jackson, S E (2000) *Strategic Human Resource Management*, 2nd edn, Blackwell, Oxford

Sisson, K (1990) Introducing the Human Resource Management Journal, *Human Resource Management Journal*, **1** (1), pp 1–11

Storey, J (1989) From personnel management to human resource management, in *New Perspectives on Human Resource Management*, ed J Storey, pp 1–18, Routledge, London

Storey, J (2001) Human resource management today: an assessment, in *Human Resource Management: A critical text*, ed J Storey, 2nd edn, pp 3–20, Thompson Learning, London

Storey, J (2007) What is human resource management?, in *Human Resource Management: A critical text*, ed J Storey, pp 3–19, Thompson Learning, London

Thompson, M (2002) *High Performance Work Organization in UK Aerospace*, The Society of British Aerospace Companies, London

Truss, C, Gratton, L, Hope-Hailey, V, McGovern, P and Stiles, P (1997) Soft and hard models of human resource management: a re-appraisal, *Journal of Management Studies*, **34** (1), pp 53–73

Tyson, S (1987) The management of the personnel function, *Journal of Management Studies*, **24** (5), pp 523–32

Ulrich, D (1997) *Human Resource Champions*, Harvard Business School Press, Boston MA

Ulrich, D (1998) A new mandate for human resources, *Harvard Business Review*, January–February, pp 124–34

Ulrich, D and Brockbank, W (2005) *The HR Value Proposition,* Harvard Press, Cambridge MA

Watson, T J (2010) Critical social science, pragmatism and the realities of HRM, *The International Journal of Human Resource Management*, 21 (6), pp 915–31

West, M A, Borrill, C S, Dawson, C, Scully, J, Carter, M, Anclay, S, Patterson, M and Waring, J (2002) The link between the management of employees and patient mortality in acute hospitals, *International Journal of Human Resource Management,* 13 (8), pp 1299–310

Winstanley, D and Woodall, J (2000) The ethical dimension of human resource management, *Human Resource Management Journal*, 10 (2), pp 5–20

02 Strategic management

Introduction

In this chapter strategic management is described as a way of managing a business that stresses the need to think and act strategically, ie to be concerned with where the business is going and how it is going to get there. In a sense it is a mindset – 'this is how we do things around here'. But it is also about getting things done – converting visions into reality. Strategic human resource management (SHRM) adopts a strategic management approach when intentions are being defined on how HRM strategy should be developed.

Strategic management

As stated by Boxall and Purcell (2003: 44): 'Strategic management is best defined as a process. It is a process of strategy making, of forming and, if the firm survives, reforming its strategy over time.' Strategic management was described by Johnson, Scholes and Whittington (2005: 6) as 'understanding the strategic position of an organization, making strategic choices for the future, and turning strategy into action'. The purpose of strategic management was expressed by Kanter (1984: 288) as being to 'elicit the present actions for the future and become action vehicles – integrating and institutionalizing mechanisms for change'.

The key strategic management activity identified by Thompson and Strickland (1996: 3) is: 'deciding what business the company will be in and forming a strategic vision of where the organization needs to be headed – in effect, infusing the organization with a sense of purpose, providing long-term direction, and establishing a clear mission to be accomplished'. Truss, Mankin and Kelliher (2012: 49) emphasized the action-orientated nature of strategic management. They defined it as 'the process that enables organizations to turn strategic intent into action'.

The focus is on identifying the organization's mission and strategies, but attention is also given to the resource base required to make it succeed. Managers who think strategically will have a broad and long-term view of where they are going. But they will also be aware that they are responsible, first, for planning how to allocate resources to opportunities that contribute to the implementation of strategy, and second, for managing these opportunities in ways that will add value to the results achieved by the firm.

To summarize, strategic management deals with both ends and means. As an end it describes a vision of what something will look like in the future. As a means, it shows how it is expected that the vision will be realized. To understand how strategic management functions it is necessary to appreciate the meaning of strategy, as discussed below.

The meaning of strategy

Strategy is the approach selected to achieve specified aims in the future. As defined by Chandler (1962: 13) it is: 'The determination of the long-term goals and objectives of an enterprise, and the adoption of courses of action and the allocation of resources necessary for carrying out those goals.' The formulation and implementation of corporate strategy is a process for developing a sense of direction, making the best use of resources and ensuring strategic fit. It is also about business model innovation, as explained later in this chapter.

Characteristics of strategy

Strategy has three fundamental characteristics. First, it is forward looking. It is about deciding where you want to go and how you mean to get there. In this sense a strategy is a declaration of intent: 'This is what we want to do and this is how we intend to do it.' Strategies define longer-term goals but they also cover how those goals will be attained. They guide purposeful action to deliver the required result. A good strategy is one that works, one that in Abell's (1993: 1) phrase, ensures that organizations adapt to changing demands and circumstances by 'mastering the present and pre-empting the future'. As Boxall (1996: 70) explained: 'Strategy should be understood as a framework of critical ends and means.'

The second characteristic of strategy is the recognition that the organizational capability of a firm (its capacity to function effectively) depends on its resource capability (the quality and quantity of its resources and their potential to deliver results). This is called the resource-based view.

The third characteristic of strategy is that it aims to achieve strategic fit – the need when developing functional strategies such as HR to achieve congruence between them and the organization's business strategies within the context of its external and internal environment.

The content of strategy

Hambrisk and Fredrickson (2001) explained that a complete business strategy needs to cover five points:

1 Where the organization will be active – what type of products and services it will offer, what markets it will serve.
2 How it will operate – where it will operate or get its products and services.
3 How it will win – what its competitive advantage will be.
4 What its moves will be – how it will change and grow.
5 How it will be profitable – what business model it will follow (as discussed below).

Business model innovation

Strategy is concerned with defining and developing the business model of an organization – a picture of the business that explains how it achieves competitive advantage and makes money. Business model innovation is the process followed by an organization to introduce a new business model or change an existing one in order to improve its performance.

STRATEGIC HRM IN ACTION

Examples of corporate strategies

The following are three examples of how strategies can be expressed formally. The first two were set out in the recent reports of the companies and, typically, are expressed in very broad terms. The third is an internal document developed by a charity. This expresses the strategy in the form of a balanced score card, a technique conceived by Kaplan and Norton (1992) for providing a balanced description of what an organization is intending to do, ie its strategy, and for measuring its performance, which in the example below is a balanced score card that consists of four related perspectives.

GKN

'GKN delivers innovative technologies that help our customers stay ahead in their markets and enable us to maintain our competitive edge, ensuring we remain in higher value markets. We work with our customers to develop new technologies, driven by global trends such as fuel efficiency, the low-carbon agenda, electrification, urbanization and population growth. At the same time, we aim to be an employer of choice with a high-performance culture, motivated people and outstanding leaders, always ensuring that safety is paramount in all our locations.'

W H Smith

- Develop new formats and channels in the UK and internationally.
- Managing our offer to reflect changing needs of our customer.
- Maximizing returns from our space.
- Optimizing efficiency.
- Focused use of cash.
- The right people and skills.
- Operating responsibly.

Balanced score card in an international charity

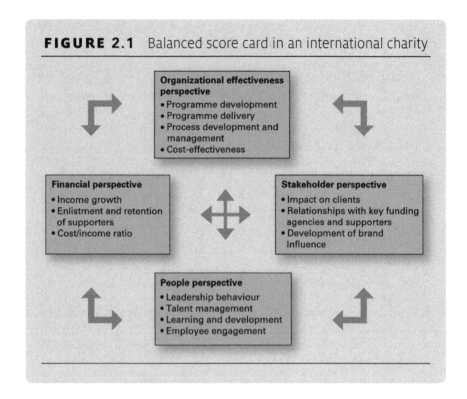

FIGURE 2.1 Balanced score card in an international charity

Developing strategy

Developing strategy is a matter of creating a sense of direction and purpose and ensuring strategic fit. It used to be regarded as a logical, step-by-step affair, which was described by Whittington (1993) as the classical approach – strategy formulation as a rational process of deliberate calculation. Conceptually this involves the following:

1 Define the mission.

2 Set objectives.

3 Conduct internal and external environmental scans to assess internal strengths and weaknesses and external opportunities and threats (a SWOT analysis).

4 Analyse existing strategies and the business model to determine their relevance in the light of the internal and external appraisal. This may include gap analysis, which will establish the extent to which environmental factors might lead to gaps between what could be achieved if no changes were made and what needs to be achieved. The analysis would also cover resource capability, answering the question: 'Have we sufficient human or financial resources available now or which can readily be made available in the future to enable us to achieve our objectives?'

5 Define in the light of this analysis the distinctive capabilities of the organization.

6 Define the key strategic issues emerging from the previous analysis. These will be concerned with such matters as product-market scope, delivering value to customers, enhancing shareholder value and resource capability, and the need to change the business model.

7 Determine corporate and functional strategies for achieving goals and competitive advantage, taking into account the key strategic issues. These may include business strategies for growth or diversification, business model innovation, broad generic strategies for innovation, quality or cost leadership or specific corporate/functional strategies concerned with product-market scope, technological development or talent management.

8 Prepare integrated strategic plans for implementing strategies.

9 Implement the strategies.

10 Monitor implementation and revise existing strategies or develop new strategies as necessary.

But this model assumes that the development of corporate strategy is a logical, step-by-step affair, the outcome of which is a formal written statement that provides a definitive guide to the organization's intentions. Many people still believe and act as if this were the case, but it is a misrepresentation of reality. In practice the formulation of strategy may not be as rational and linear a process as some writers describe it or as some managers attempt to make it. There are limitations to the totally logical model of management that underpins the concept of strategic human resource management. In the words of Mabey, Salaman and Storey (1998: 74): 'The reality is… that strategies may not always be easy to discern, that the processes of decision making may be implicit, incremental, negotiated and compromised.'

Sparrow *et al* (2010: 4) asserted succinctly that: 'Strategy is not rational and never has been.' Strategy formulation can best be described as 'problem solving in unstructured situations' (Digman, 1990: 53) and strategies will always be formed under conditions of partial ignorance. Quinn (1980: 9) stated that a strategy may simply be 'a widely held understanding resulting from a stream of decisions'. He believed that strategy formulation takes place by means of 'logical incrementalism', ie it evolves in several steps rather than being conceived as a whole. Pettigrew and Whipp (1991: 26) observed that: 'strategy does not move forward in a direct linear way, nor through easily discernable sequential phases. Quite the reverse; the pattern is much more appropriately seen as continuous, iterative and uncertain.'

Another difficulty is that strategies are often based on the questionable assumption that the future will resemble the past. Some years ago, Heller (1972: 150) had a go at the cult of long-range planning: 'What goes wrong', he wrote, 'is that sensible anticipation gets converted into foolish numbers:

and their validity always hinges on large loose assumptions.' Faulkner and Johnson (1992: 17–18) said of long-term planning that:

> It was inclined to take a definitive view of the future, and to extrapolate trend lines for the key business variables in order to arrive at this view. Economic turbulence was insufficiently considered, and the reality that much strategy is formulated and implemented in the act of managing the enterprise was ignored. Precise forecasts ending with derived financials were constructed, the only weakness of which was that the future almost invariably turned out differently.

Strategy formulation is not necessarily a deterministic, rational and continuous process, as was emphasized by Mintzberg (1987). He noted that, rather than being consciously and systematically developed, strategy reorientation happens in what he calls brief 'quantum loops'. A strategy, according to Mintzberg, can be deliberate – it can realize the intentions of senior management, for example to attack and conquer a new market. But this is not always the case. In theory, he says, strategy is a systematic process: first we think, then we act; we formulate then we implement. But we also 'act in order to think'. In practice, 'a realized strategy can emerge in response to an evolving situation' and the strategic planner is often 'a pattern organizer, a learner if you like, who manages a process in which strategies and visions can emerge as well as be deliberately conceived' (Mintzberg, 1987: 68, 73). This concept of 'emergent strategy' conveys the essence of how in practice organizations develop their business and HR strategies.

Boxall and Purcell (2003: 34) suggested that: 'it is better if we understand the strategies of firms as *sets of strategic choices* some of which may stem from planning exercises and set-piece debates in senior management, and some of which may emerge in a stream of action'. Research conducted by Tyson (1997: 280) confirmed that, realistically, strategy:

- has always been emergent and flexible – it is always 'about to be', it never exists at the present time;
- is not only realized by formal statements but also comes about by actions and reactions;
- is a description of a future-oriented action that is always directed towards change;
- is conditioned by the management process itself.

Implementation of strategy

'Implementation entails converting the strategic plan into action and then into results' (Thompson and Strickland, 1996: 20). Dreaming up a strategy is fairly easy; getting it to work is hard. Kanter (1984: 305) noted that: 'Many companies, even very sophisticated ones, are much better at generating impressive plans on paper than they are at getting "ownership" of the plans so that they actually guide operational decisions.'

Such changes impact on people. They involve employees in planning and implementing them. They are therefore the concern of the HR function as well as operational management. HR has a major role in ensuring that innovation or change is carried out effectively through people. HR needs to be involved in planning the change and implementing it by developing and facilitating the introduction of appropriate HR strategies.

STRATEGIC HRM IN ACTION

ARM's business model

ARM is involved in designing chips for mobile phones and a growing number of other small, low-powered devices, ranging from digital cameras to tablet computers. But it does not actually make any of the 6 billion or so chips based on its designs that are produced each year. Instead, its business model is to earn revenues from licensing its design technology to semiconductor manufacturers and from royalties paid each time an ARM-based chip is sold. This model means that ARM has never had to bear the costs of building and operating its own factories. At the same time, its customers are able to avoid having to design chips for their own products from scratch by outsourcing much of their research and development work to ARM. The business strategy is essentially about building a partnership of many hundreds of customers.

The continued success of the business depends on people working effectively together to produce innovative designs. HR activity in ARM is largely about connecting employees – spread across 30 far-flung sites – with each other, with their customers and with other external partners across different time zones, national boundaries and cultures. That means delivering effective communications and learning and development programmes, and acting with agility.

SOURCE: Arkin, A (2011) Cash in the chips, *People Management*, May, pp 36–39

KEY LEARNING POINTS

The process of developing and implementing strategy is called strategic management.

- Strategic management deals with both ends and means. As an end it describes a vision of what something will look like in the future.

As a means, it shows how it is expected that the vision will be realized.

- Strategy is the approach selected to achieve specified aims in the future.
- Strategy has three fundamental characteristics: 1) it is forward looking; 2) it recognizes that the organizational capability of a firm (its capacity to function effectively) depends on its resource capability (the quality and quantity of its resources and their potential to deliver results; 3) it aims to achieve strategic fit.
- A business strategy needs to cover five points:
  - where the organization will be active;
  - how it will operate;
  - how it will win;
  - what its moves will be;
  - how it will be profitable.
- Developing strategy is a matter of creating a sense of direction and purpose and ensuring strategic fit.
- In practice the formulation of strategy may not be a rational or linear process.
- Implementing strategy entails converting the strategic plan into action and then into results.

References

Abell, D F (1993) *Managing with Dual Strategies: Mastering the present, pre-empting the future*, Free Press, New York

Boxall, P F (1996) The strategic HRM debate and the resource-based view of the firm, *Human Resource Management Journal*, **6** (3), pp 59–75

Boxall, P F and Purcell, J (2003) *Strategy and Human Resource Management*, Palgrave Macmillan, Basingstoke

Chandler, A D (1962) Strategy *and Structure*, MIT Press, Boston MA

Digman, L A (1990) *Strategic Management – Concepts, Decisions, Cases*, Irwin, Chicago

Faulkner, D and Johnson G (1992) *The Challenge of Strategic Management*, Kogan Page, London

Hambrisk, D C and Fredrickson, J W (2001) Are you sure you have a strategy?, *Academy of Management Executive*, **15** (4), pp 48–59

Heller, R (1972) *The Naked Manager*, Barrie & Jenkins, London

Johnson, G, Scholes, K and Whittington, R (2005) *Explaining Corporate Strategy*, 7th edn, FTPrentice Hall, Harlow

Kanter, R M (1984) The *Change Masters*, Allen & Unwin, London

Kaplan, R S and Norton, D P (1992) The balanced scorecard: measures that drive performance, *Harvard Business Review*, January–February, pp 71–79

Mabey, C, Salaman, G and Storey, J (1998) *Human Resource Management: A strategic introduction*, 2nd edn, Blackwell, Oxford

Mintzberg, H T (1987) Crafting strategy, *Harvard Business Review*, July–August, pp 66–74

Pettigrew, A and Whipp, R (1991) *Managing Change for Competitive Success*, Blackwell, Oxford

Quinn, J B (1980) *Strategies for Change: Logical incrementalism*, Irwin, Ontario

Sparrow, P, Hesketh, A, Hird, M and Cooper, C (2010) Introduction: performance-led HR, in *Leading HR*, ed P Sparrow, A Hesketh, M Hird, and C Cooper, pp 1–22, Palgrave Macmillan, Basingstoke

Thompson, A A and Strickland, A J (1996) *Strategic Management, Concepts and cases*, 9th edn, Irwin, Chicago

Truss, C, Mankin, D and Kelliher, C (2012) *Strategic Human Resource Management*, Oxford University Press, Oxford

Tyson, S (1997) Human resource strategy: a process for managing the contribution of HRM to organizational performance, *The International Journal of Human Resource Management*, 8 (3), pp 277–90

Whittington, R (1993) *What is Strategy and Does it Matter?*, Routledge, London

Strategic human resource management

Introduction

Strategic human resource management (SHRM) uses strategic management approaches (as described in Chapter 2) to develop and implement HRM policies and practises (as examined in Chapter 1). SHRM combines the processes of human resource management and strategic management.

The aim of this chapter is to define the nature of SHRM and analyse its conceptual framework as provided by the concepts of strategic fit and the resource-based view, and the notions of best practice, best fit and 'bundling'.

SHRM defined

SHRM is an approach to managing people that deals with how the organization's goals will be achieved through its human resources by means of integrated HR strategies, policies and practices. It is based on the following propositions:

- The human resources of an organization play a strategic role in its success.
- HR strategies and plans should be integrated with business strategies and plans.
- Human capital is a major source of competitive advantage.
- It is people who implement the business strategy.
- A systematic approach should be adopted to planning and implementing HR strategies.

There are many definitions of SHRM. For example, SHRM has been described in general terms by Schuler (1992: 30) as 'all those activities affecting the behaviour of individuals in their efforts to formulate and implement the strategic needs of the business'. Mabey, Salaman and Storey (1998: 25) introduced the key notion of capability when they defined SHRM as the process of 'developing corporate capability to deliver new organizational strategies'. The HR activities aspect of SHRM was emphasized by Wright and McMahan (1992: 298) when they defined it as: 'The pattern of planned human resource deployments and activities intended to enable an organization to achieve its goals.' Alvesson (2009: 52) also focused on goal achievement but incorporated the role of employment relationships when he wrote that SHRM is concerned with 'how the employment relationships for all employees can be managed in such a way as to contribute optimally to the organization's goal achievement'. Schuler and Jackson (2007: 5) concentrated on integration when they stated that SHRM is about 'systematically linking people with the firm'. Boxall, Purcell and Wright (2007: 3) referred to the significance of overall HR strategies when they stated that strategic human resource management 'focuses on the overall HR strategies adopted by business units and companies'.

The nature of SHRM

SHRM provides the foundation for developing and implementing approaches to people management, which enable the organization to achieve its objectives and take into account the changing context in which the firm operates and its longer-term requirements. It can be regarded as a perspective on the way in which strategic decisions are made that have a major and long-term impact on the behaviour and success of the organization and enable critical issues or success factors related to people to be addressed As Lengnick-Hall and Lengnick-Hall (1988: 454) argued: 'Achieving competitive advantage through human resources requires that these activities be managed from a strategic perspective.'

One of the earlier but still most helpful descriptions of SHRM was made by Hendry and Pettigrew (1986: 4) who suggested that it had four meanings:

1 The use of planning.
2 A coherent approach to the design and management of HR systems based on an employment policy and manpower strategy and often underpinned by a 'philosophy'.
3 Matching HRM activities and policies to some explicit business strategy.
4 Seeing the people of the organization as a 'strategic resource' for the achievement of 'competitive advantage'.

The rationale for SHRM is the perceived advantage of having an agreed and understood basis for developing and implementing approaches to people management, and that takes into account the changing context in which the firm operates and its business plans and priorities. As Dyer and Holder (1988: 13) remarked, SHRM should provide 'unifying frameworks which are at once broad, contingency based and integrative'.

Strategic HRM and HRM

One of the characteristics of HRM is that it is strategic, so what is the difference between HRM and strategic HRM? An answer to this question was provided by Truss and Gratton (1994: 666) who wrote that: 'We should perhaps regard SHRM as an overarching concept that links the management and development of people within the organization to the business as a whole and its environment, while HRM could be viewed as an organizing activity that takes place under this umbrella.'

Strategic HRM and HRM strategies

What is the difference, if any, between SHRM and HRM strategy? The answer to this question is that SHRM is an overall approach that provides guidance on how key issues of human resource management can be dealt with strategically in the sense that they support the achievement of corporate goals. But SHRM only becomes real when it produces actions and reactions that can be regarded as strategic, either in the form of overall or specific HR strategies or strategic behaviour on the part of HR professionals working alongside line managers. SHRM provides the conceptual framework within which individual strategies can be devised and implemented.

STRATEGIC HRM IN ACTION

The Peabody Trust

This is how the chief executive of the Peabody Trust explained the organization's approach to strategic HRM:

> First of all you have your business strategy, which includes at management team level a review of what we expect our HR to deliver. We define what the strategy means in terms of its implications for us as individuals and for our employees. We decide what changes we have to effect and how we are going to communicate with and motivate the staff group to achieve those changes. The management team needs to be clear on what our vision for our people is, what we see our people doing, what we think they have to learn and what practices they nee to change to effect the strategy we want. When you have answered those questions, then you can start to decide what the strategy is. The key to this is that all our directors have to contribute. The most important thing is the corporate understanding and responsibility for HR strategy.
>
> A good HR strategy is one that actually makes people feel valued. It makes them knowledgeable about the organization, and makes them feel clear about where they sit as a group, a team or individual. It must show that what they do either together or individually fits into the strategy. Importantly, it should indicate how people are going to be rewarded for their contribution and how they might be developed and grow in the organization.

SOURCE: Armstrong, M and Baron, A (2002) *Strategic HRM: The route to improved business performance*, CIPD, London

Aims of SHRM

The fundamental aim of strategic HRM is to generate strategic capability by ensuring that the organization has the skilled, committed and well-motivated employees it needs to achieve sustained competitive advantage. It has two further aims: first, to achieve fit or integration – fitting or aligning HR strategies vertically with business strategies and integrating HR strategies with one another; and second, to provide a sense of direction in an often turbulent environment so that the business needs of the organization, and the individual and collective needs of its employees, can be met by the development and implementation of coherent and practical HR policies and programmes.

When considering the aims of SHRM, account should be taken of ethical considerations – the interests of all the stakeholders in the organization, employees in general as well as owners and management, and the responsibilities of the organization to the wider community. In Storey's (1989) terms, soft strategic HRM will place greater emphasis on the human relations aspect of people management, stressing continuous development, communication, involvement, security of employment, the quality of working life and work–life balance. On the other hand, hard strategic HRM will emphasize the yield to be obtained by investing in human resources in the interests of the business. SHRM should attempt to achieve a proper balance between the hard and soft elements. All organizations exist to achieve a purpose and they must ensure that they have the resources required to do so, and that they use them effectively. But they should also take into account the human factors contained in the concept of soft strategic HRM. In the words of Quinn Mills (1983) they should plan with people in mind, taking into account the needs and aspirations of all the members of the organization. The problem is that hard considerations in many businesses will come first, leaving soft ones some way behind.

Organizations must also consider their responsibilities to society in general on the grounds that because they draw resources from society they must give something back to society. The exercise of corporate social responsibility (CSR), defined by McWilliams, Siegel and Wright (2006: 1) as 'actions that appear to further some social good beyond the interests of the firm and that which is required by law', may be regarded as outside the scope of HRM. But because CSR relates to ethical actions in the interests of people, there is a strong link, and it is therefore an aspect of organizational behaviour that can legitimately be included in the strategic portfolio of HR specialists.

The conceptual framework of SHRM

SHRM is underpinned by a wide range of concepts and theories, as descried below.

The resource-based view

The resource-based view (RBV) expresses the belief that it is the range of resources in an organization, including its human resources, that produces its unique character and creates competitive advantage. The RBV is based on the ideas of Penrose (1959), which were expanded by Wernerfelt (1984). It was suggested by Barney (1991) that resources that are valuable, rare, inimitable and non-substitutable will lead to competitive advantage. He later defined human resources as including 'all the experience, knowledge, judgement, risk-taking propensity and wisdom of individuals associated with a firm' (Barney, 1995: 50). It was stated by Hamel and Prahalad (1989) that competitive advantage is obtained if a firm can obtain and develop human resources that enable it to learn faster and apply its learning more effectively than its rivals.

Unique talents among employees – including superior performance, productivity, flexibility, innovation and the ability to deliver high levels of personal customer service – are ways in which people provide a critical ingredient in developing an organization's competitive position. As Boxall (1996) put it, they provide human capital advantage. People are the key to managing the pivotal interdependencies across functional activities and the important external relationships. It can be argued that one of the clear benefits arising from competitive advantage based on the effective management of people is that such an advantage is hard to imitate. An organization's HR strategies, policies and practices are a distinctive blend of processes, procedures, personalities, styles, capabilities and organizational culture. These provide what Boxall (1996) referred to as human process advantage. He pointed out that: 'The resource-based view of the firm provides a conceptual basis, if we needed one, for asserting that key human resources are sources of competitive advantage' and that the strategic goal emerging from the resource-based view will be to 'create firms which are more intelligent and flexible than their competitors' (Boxall, 1996: 66).

Resource-based strategy is therefore concerned with the enhancement of the human or intellectual capital of the firm. Ulrich (1998: 126) commented that: 'Knowledge has become a direct competitive advantage for companies selling ideas and relationships. The challenge to organizations is to ensure that they have the capability to find, assimilate, compensate and retain the talented individuals they need.'

The significance of the resource-based view of the firm is that it highlights the importance of a human capital management approach to HRM. This provides the justification for investing in people through resourcing, talent management and learning and development programmes as a means of enhancing competitive advantage.

Strategic fit

The concept of strategic fit is fundamental to SHRM. Schuler (1992:18) stated that: 'Strategic human resource management is largely about integration and adaptation. Its concern is to ensure that: 1) human resources (HR) management is fully integrated with the strategy and strategic needs of the firm (vertical fit); 2) HR policies cohere both across policy areas and across hierarchies (horizontal fit); and 3) HR practices are adjusted, accepted and used by line managers and employees as part of their everyday work.'

Perspectives on strategic HRM

Delery and Doty (1996: 802–03) identified three HRM perspectives:

1 *The universalistic perspective*: some HR practices are better than others and all organizations should adopt these best practices. There is a universal relationship between individual 'best' practices and firm performance.

2 *The contingency perspective*: in order to be effective, an organization's HR policies must be consistent with other aspects of the organization. The primary contingency factor is the organization's strategy. This can be described as 'vertical fit'.

3 *The configurational perspective*: 'In order to be effective, an organization must develop an HR system that achieves both horizontal and vertical fit. Horizontal fit refers to the internal consistency of the organization's HR policies or practices, and vertical fit refers to the congruence of the HR system with other organizational characteristics such as firm strategy. An ideal configuration would be one with the highest degree of horizontal fit' (Delery and Doty, 1996: 804).

An alternative way of presenting these perspectives was suggested by Richardson and Thompson (1999). They proposed adopting the commonly used terms of 'best practice' and 'best fit' approaches for the universalistic and contingency perspectives, and 'bundling' as the third approach. This followed the classification made by Guest (1997) of fit as an ideal set of practices, fit as contingency and fit as bundles.

The 'best practice' approach

This 'universalist' approach is based on the assumption that there is a set of best HRM practices and that adopting them will lead to superior organizational performance. They are universal in the sense that they are best in any situation.

The following well-known list of best practices was produced by Pfeffer (1994):

1 Employment security.
2 Selective hiring.
3 Self-managed teams.
4 High compensation contingent on performance.
5 Training to provide a skilled and motivated workforce.
6 Reduction of status differentials.
7 Sharing information.

The 'best practice' rubric was attacked by Cappelli and Crocker-Hefter (1996: 7), who commented that the notion of a single set of best practices has been overstated: 'There are examples in virtually every industry of highly successful firms that have very distinctive management practices. We argue that these distinctive human resource practices help to create unique competencies that differentiate products and services and, in turn, drive competitiveness.'

In accordance with contingency theory, which emphasizes the importance of interactions between organizations and their environments so that what organizations do is dependent on the context in which they operate, it is difficult to accept that there is any such thing as universal best practice. What works well in one organization will not necessarily work well in another because it may not fit its strategy, culture, management style, technology or working practices. However, a knowledge of what is assumed to be best practice can be used to inform decisions on what practices are most likely to fit the needs of the organization, as long as it is understood *why* a particular practice should be regarded as a best practice and what needs to be done to ensure that it will work in the context of the organization. Perhaps it is best to think of 'good practice' rather than 'best practice'.

The 'best fit' approach

The 'best fit' approach emphasizes that HR strategies should be related to the context, circumstances of the organization and its type. There is a choice of models, namely: life cycle, competitive strategy and strategic configuration.

The life-cycle model

The life-cycle model is based on the theory that the development of a firm takes place in four stages: start-up, growth, maturity and decline. This is in line with product life-cycle theory. The basic premise of this model was expressed by Baird and Meshoulam (1988: 117) as follows:

> Human resource management's effectiveness depends on its fit with the organization's stage of development. As the organization grows and develops, human resource management programmes, practices and procedures must change to meet its needs. Consistent with growth and development models it can be suggested that human resource management develops through a series of stages as the organization becomes more complex.

Best fit and competitive strategies

Three strategies aimed at achieving competitive advantage were identified by Porter (1985):

1 *Innovation*: being the unique producer.
2 *Quality*: delivering high-quality goods and services to customers.
3 *Cost leadership*: the planned result of policies aimed at 'managing away' expense.

It was contended by Schuler and Jackson (1987) that to achieve the maximum effect it is necessary to match the role characteristics of people in an organization with the preferred strategy.

Strategic configuration

Another approach to best fit is the proposition that organizations will be more effective if they match one of the ideal types defined by theories such as those produced by Mintzberg (1979) and Miles and Snow (1978). This increased effectiveness is attributed to the internal consistency or fit between the patterns of relevant contextual, structural and strategic factors. The typology of organizations produced by Mintzberg (1979) classified them into five categories: simple structure, machine bureaucracy, professional bureaucracy, divisionalized form and adhocracy. Miles and Snow (1978) identified four types of organizations, classifying the first three types as 'ideal' organizations:

1 *Prospectors*, which operate in an environment characterized by rapid and unpredictable changes.

2 *Defenders*, which operate in a more stable and predictable environment than prospectors and engage in more long-term planning.

3 *Analysers*, which are a combination of the prospector and defender types. They operate in stable environments, like defenders, and also in markets where new products are constantly required, like prospectors.

4 *Reactors*, which are unstable organizations existing in what they believe to be an unpredictable environment. They lack consistent, well-articulated strategies.

Comments on the concept of best fit

The 'best fit' model seems to be more realistic than the 'best practice' model. As Dyer and Holder (1998: 31) pointed out: 'The inescapable conclusion is that what is best depends.' It can therefore be claimed that best fit is more important than best practice.

But there are limitations to the concept of best fit. Paauwe (2004: 37) argued that: 'It is necessary to avoid falling into the trap of contingent determinism [ie acting as if the context absolutely determines the strategy]. There is, or should be, room for making strategic choices.'

There is a danger of mechanistically matching HR polices and practices with strategy. It is not credible to claim that there are single contextual factors that determine HR strategy, and internal fit cannot therefore be complete. As Boxall (2007: 61) contended: 'It is clearly impossible to make *all* HR policies reflective of a chosen competitive or economic mission.'

Purcell (1999: 35) refers to the concept of 'idiosyncratic contingency', which 'shows that each firm has to make choices not just on business and operational strategies but on what type of HR system is best for its purposes'. He commented that: 'The search for a contingency or matching model of

HRM is also limited by the impossibility of modelling all the contingent variables, the difficulty of showing their interconnection, and the way in which changes in one variable have an impact on others, let alone the need to model idiosyncratic and path dependent contingencies' (Purcell, 1999: 37).

Bundling

'Bundling' or 'configuration' is the development and implementation of several HR practices together so that they are interrelated and mutually supportive and therefore complement and reinforce each other. This is the process of horizontal integration or internal fit, which is also referred to as the use of 'complementarities'. Richardson and Thompson (1999) concluded that a firm with bundles of associated HR practices should perform better, providing it also achieves high levels of fit with its competitive strategy.

MacDuffie (1995: 204) explained the concept of bundling as follows:

> Implicit in the notion of a 'bundle' is the idea that practices within bundles are interrelated and internally consistent, and that 'more is better' with respect to the impact on performance, because of the overlapping and mutually reinforcing effect of multiple practices.

His research in US automotive assembly plants established that 'innovative HR practices affect performance not individually but as interrelated elements in an internally consistent HR bundle' (MacDuffie, 1995: 197).

The process of bundling HR strategies is an important aspect of the concept of SHRM. In a sense, SHRM is holistic; it is concerned with the organization as a total entity and addresses what needs to be done across the organization as a whole. It is not interested in isolated programmes and techniques, or in the ad hoc development of HR practices.

The difficulty with the bundling approach is that of deciding which is the best way to relate different practices together. There is no evidence that one bundle is generally better than another.

The problem with SHRM

SHRM as described above appears to be a logical and systematic process but this is something of an illusion. As noted in Chapter 2, strategy formulation can best be described as 'problem solving in unstructured situations' (Digman, 1990: 53) and strategies will always be formed under conditions of partial ignorance. It should also be noted that the integration of HR and business strategies will only be possible if there are clearly defined business strategies. But this is not always the case. As Mabey, Salaman and Storey (1998: 520) commented: 'Much SHRM literature assumes a naive, over-rationalist view of organizational decision making.' It ignores both the political realities and the inability of senior managers to make SHRM decisions.

STRATEGIC HRM IN ACTION

The Children's Society

Strategic HRM at the Children's Society is based on the business plan of the human resources division, which states that the division worked with managers and staff to secure the following outcomes:

- the development of the organization in support of delivering the corporate plan and change management leadership;
- the development and continuous improvement of the human resources strategy for the society;
- the promotion of an employee relations climate that facilitates the aims of the Children's Society to be a force for change in the lives of children and young people;
- the effective use of staff resources within the Children's Society;
- the commissioning of learning and development programmes appropriate to business and employee needs.

The objectives and activities of the HR function are intrinsically linked to the outcomes that other parts of the Children's Society are seeking to realize. The priorities are informed by the corporate plan and the need to maintain effective support services to managers in the deployment of the human resources of the society. The aims are to mirror the core values set out in that plan and to develop the processes needed to enable the organization to achieve its goals.

SOURCE: Armstrong, M and Baron, A (2002) *Strategic HRM: The route to improved business performance*, CIPD, London

KEY LEARNING POINTS

- *Strategic HRM (SHRM) defined*

  SHRM is an approach to managing people, which deals with how the organization's goals will be achieved through its human resources by means of integrated HR strategies, policies and practices. It is based on the fundamental proposition that the human resources of an organization play a strategic role in its success.

- *The conceptual basis of strategic HRM*
  - 'Strategic HRM is the interface between HRM and strategic management'. It takes the notion of HRM as a strategic, inte-

grated and coherent approach and develops that in line with the concept of strategic management (Boxall, 1996).

- An organization's human resources are of critical strategic importance.
- A firm's HRM practices are instrumental in developing the strategic capability of its pool of human resources.

• *The aim of strategic HRM*

To generate organizational capability by ensuring that the organization has the skilled, engaged, committed and well-motivated employees it needs to achieve sustained competitive advantage.

• *Implications of the resource-based view*

The creation of firms that are 'more intelligent and flexible than their competitors' (Boxall, 1996) by hiring and developing more talented staff and by extending the skills base.

• *The three HRM 'perspectives' of Delery and Doty (1996)*

- Universalistic perspective: some HR practices are better than others and all organizations should adopt these best practices.
- Contingency: in order to be effective, an organization's HR policies must be consistent with other aspects of the organization.
- Configurational: relating HRM to the 'configuration' of the organization in terms of its structures and processes.

• *The concepts of 'best practice' and 'best fit'*

- The concept of best practice is based on the assumption that there is a set of best HRM practices that are universal in the sense that they are best in any situation, and that adopting them will lead to superior organizational performance. This concept of universality is criticized because it takes no account of the local context.
- The concept of best fit emphasizes that HR strategies should be congruent with the context and circumstances of the organization. Best fit can be perceived in terms of vertical integration or alignment between the organization's business and HR strategies.
- It is generally accepted that best fit is more important than best practice.

• *The significance of bundling*

The process of bundling HR strategies is an important aspect of the concept of strategic HRM, which is concerned with the organization as a total system or entity and addresses what needs to be done across the organization as a whole.

References

Alvesson, M (2009) Critical perspectives on strategic HRM, in *The Routledge Companion to Strategic Human Resource Management*, ed J Storey, P M Wright and D Ulrich, pp 52–67, Routledge, Abingdon

Baird, L and Meshoulam, I (1988) Managing two fits of strategic human resource management, *Academy of Management Review*, **13** (1), pp 116–28

Barney, J B (1991) Firm resources and sustained competitive advantage, *Journal of Management*, **17** (1), pp 99–120

Barney, J B (1995) Looking inside for competitive advantage, *Academy of Management Executive*, **9** (4), pp 49–61

Boxall, P F (1996) The strategic HRM debate and the resource-based view of the firm, *Human Resource Management Journal*, **6** (3), pp 59–75

Boxall, P F (2007) The goals of HRM, in *The Oxford Handbook of Human Resource Management*, ed P Boxall, J Purcell and P Wright, pp 48–67, Oxford University Press, Oxford

Boxall, P F, Purcell J and Wright P (2007) Human resource management: scope, analysis and significance, in *The Oxford Handbook of Human Resource Management*, ed P Boxall, J Purcell and P Wright, pp 1–18, Oxford University Press, Oxford

Cappelli, P and Crocker-Hefter, A (1996) Distinctive human resources are firms' core competencies, *Organizational Dynamics*, **24** (3) Winter, pp 7–22

Delery, J E and Doty, H D (1996) Modes of theorizing in strategic human resource management: tests of universality, contingency and configurational performance predictions, *Academy of Management Journal*, **39** (4), pp 802–35

Digman, L A (1990) *Strategic Management: Concepts, decisions, cases*, Irwin, Chicago

Dyer, L and Holder, G W (1988) Strategic human resource management and planning, in *Human Resource Management: Evolving roles and responsibilities*, ed L Dyer, Bureau of National Affairs, Washington DC

Dyer, L and Holder, G W (1998) Strategic human resource management and planning, in *Human Resource Management: Evolving roles and responsibilities*, ed L Dyer, pp 1–46, Bureau of National Affairs, Washington DC

Guest, D E (1997) Human resource management and performance: a review of the research agenda, *The International Journal of Human Resource Management*, **8** (3), pp 263–76

Hamel, G and Prahalad, C K (1989) Strategic intent, *The Harvard Business Review*, May–June, pp 63–76

Hendry, C and Pettigrew, A (1986) The practice of strategic human resource management, *Personnel Review*, **15** (5) pp 2–8

Lengnick-Hall, C A and Lengnick-Hall, M L (1988) Strategic human resource management: a review of the literature and a proposed typology, *Academy of Management Review*, **13** (3), pp 454–70

Mabey, C, Salaman, G and Storey, J (1998) *Human Resource Management: A strategic introduction*, Blackwell, Oxford

MacDuffie, J P (1995) Human resource bundles and manufacturing performance, *Industrial Relations Review*, **48** (2), pp 199–221

McWilliams, A, Siegel, D S and Wright, P M (2006) Corporate social responsibility: strategic implications, *Journal of Management Studies*, **43** (1), pp 1–12

Miles, R E and Snow, C C (1978) *Organizational Strategy: Structure and process*, McGraw Hill, New York

Mintzberg, H T (1979) *The Structuring of Organizations*, Prentice-Hall, Englewood Cliffs, NJ

Paauwe, J (2004) *HRM and Performance: Achieving long term viability*, Oxford University Press, Oxford

Penrose, E (1959) *The Theory of the Growth of the Firm*, Blackwell, Oxford

Perkins, S J and Shortland, S M (2006) *Strategic International Human Resource Management*, Kogan Page, London

Pfeffer, J (1994) *Competitive Advantage Through People*, Harvard Business School Press, Boston

Porter, M E (1985) *Competitive Advantage: Creating and Sustaining Superior Performance*, The Free Press, New York

Purcell, J (1999) Best practice or best fit: chimera or cul-de-sac, *Human Resource Management Journal*, **9** (3), pp 26–41

Quinn Mills, D (1983) Planning with people in mind, *Harvard Business Review*, November–December, pp 97–105

Richardson, R and Thompson, M (1999) *The Impact of People Management Practices on Business Performance: A literature review*, Institute of Personnel and Development, London

Schuler, R S (1992) Strategic human resource management: linking people with the strategic needs of the business, *Organizational Dynamics*, **21** (1), pp 18–32

Schuler, R S and Jackson, S E (1987) Linking competitive strategies with human resource management practices, *Academy of Management Executive*, **9** (3), pp 207–19

Schuler, R S and Jackson, S E (2007) Overview of SHRM, in *Strategic Human Resource Management*, 2nd edn, ed R S Schuler and S Jackson, Blackwell, Oxford

Storey, J (1989) From personnel management to human resource management, in *New Perspectives on Human Resource Management*, ed J Storey, pp 1–18, Routledge, London

Truss, C and Gratton, L (1994) Strategic human resource management: a conceptual approach, *International Journal of Human Resource Management*, **5** (3), pp 663–86

Ulrich, D (1998) A new mandate for human resources, *Harvard Business Review*, January–February, pp 124–34

Wernerfelt, B (1984) A resource-based view of the firm, *Strategic Management Journal*, **5** (2), pp 171–80

Wright, P and McMahan, G (1992) Theoretical perspectives for human resource management, *Journal of Management*, **18** (2), pp 295–320

04 The strategic role of HR

KEY CONCEPTS AND TERMS

Business model
Business partner
Outside-in approach to strategy formulation
Service delivery
Strategic business partner
Transactional activities

LEARNING OUTCOMES

On completing this chapter you should be able to define these key concepts. You should also understand:

- the strategic nature of HR;
- the strategic partner model;
- the strategic role of HR directors;
- the strategic role of heads of HR functions;
- the strategic role of HR business partners;
- the strategic contribution of HR advisors or assistants.

Introduction

Strategic human resource management (SHRM) is put into effect through the strategic behaviour of HR specialists working with their line management colleagues to ensure that the business goals of the organization are achieved and its values are put into practice. This chapter starts with an overview of the strategic nature of HR and continues with a review of the strategic business partner model. It concludes with analyses of the strategic roles of HR directors, HR business partners and HR advisors or assistants.

The strategic nature of HR

The work of HR practitioners can be divided into two main activity areas: transactional and strategic. Transactional activities consist of the service delivery aspects of HR – recruitment, training, dealing with people issues, legal compliance and employee services. HR strategic activities support the achievement of the organization's goals and values and involve the development and implementation of forward-looking HR strategies such as talent management and performance management, which are integrated with one another and aligned to business objectives. Importantly, strategic HR practitioners work with their line management colleagues in the continuous formulation and execution of the business strategy. But HR practitioners must not pursue business objectives at the expense of the ethical considerations spelt out in Chapter 1.

It is necessary to get right the balance between strategic and transactional activities. The Chartered Institute of Personnel and Development (CIPD), in its anxiety to enhance the standing of the HR profession, sometimes gives the impression that the only thing that counts is 'being strategic'. Forget about the boring transactional stuff. Kanter (1984: 294) thought that '"strategic" is clearly an overused word'. Alvesson (2009: 57) noted that HR people are redefining themselves 'from being administrators and managers to becoming "strategists"'; he felt that: 'Sometimes one gets the impression that there is very little "non-strategic" HRM going on.'

HR must get its transactional service delivery activities right – that is what it is there to do, day by day, and its reputation with line managers largely depends on this. As an HR specialist commented to Caldwell (2004: 203): 'My credibility depends on running an extremely efficient and cost-effective administrative machine... If I don't get that right, and consistently, then you can forget about any big ideas.' Another person interviewed during Caldwell's research referred to personnel people as 'reactive pragmatists', a realistic view in many organizations. Syrett (2006: 63) commented that: 'Whatever strategic aspirations senior HR practitioners have, they will amount to nothing if the function they represent cannot deliver the essential transactional services their internal line clients require.'

But in accordance with the resource-based view, which emphasizes the importance of human capital in achieving competitive advantage, the credibility of HR professionals, especially at the highest level, also depends on their ability to make a strategic contribution that ensures the organization has the quality of skilled and engaged people it needs. Sparrow *et al* (2010: 88) observed that: 'HR must be fully responsive to the strategy and business model of the business. HR is not a rule to itself. It is not "HR for HR", but HR (as broadly defined across the competing stakeholders whom HR has to satisfy) for the business.' The strategic nature of HR has been expressed in the strategic business partner model, as described below.

The strategic business partner model

HR practitioners share responsibility with their line management colleagues for the success of the enterprise. In 1985, Shaun Tyson, anticipating Dave Ulrich by 13 years, described HR practitioners as business managers who have the capacity to identify business opportunities, to see the broad picture and to understand how their role can help to achieve the company's business objectives. They integrate their activities closely with top management and ensure that they serve a long-term strategic purpose. They anticipate needs, act flexibly and are proactive.

The notion of strategic partner was introduced by Dyer and Holder (1988), not Dave Ulrich as is generally assumed. They described the role as follows:

SOURCE REVIEW   The strategic partner role for HR
                     Dyer and Holder (1988: 31–32)

The recommended role for the HR function is that of 'strategic partner'. This role typically has four aspects:

1   Top HR executives co-operate with their line counterparts in formulating HR strategies.

2   Top HR executives fully participate in all business strategy sessions as equals to chief financial officers and other top executives, thus permitting early evaluation of proposals from an HR perspective.

3   HR executives work closely with line managers on an ongoing basis to ensure that all components of the business strategies are adequately implemented.

4   The HR function itself is managed strategically.

Ulrich and Lake (1990) popularized the idea of the HR strategic business partner. They argued (1990: 95–96) that:

> To ensure that management practices become a means for gaining a sustained competitive advantage, human resource professionals need to become strategic business partners and gear their activities to improving business performance. To do this they require a good working knowledge of the organization and its strategies. In assessing the role of human resources in an organization, management needs to determine the extent to which these professionals meet the following criteria:
>
> 1 Spend time with customers and clients – diagnosing, discussing and responding to needs.
> 2 Actively participate in business planning meetings and offer informed insights on strategic, technological and financial capabilities.
> 3 Understand business conditions.
> 4 Demonstrate competence in business knowledge particularly customer relations, delivery of world-class management practices and management of change.

Schuler and Jackson (2007: xiv) made a similar point when they wrote: 'Today, human resource professionals are being challenged to learn more about the business, its strategy, its environment, its customers, and its competitors.'

The notion of strategic business partner was taken up enthusiastically within the HR profession and its professional body in the UK, the CIPD, which explained in 2007 that the task of strategic business partners was to work closely with business leaders to influence strategy and steer its implementation.

Note that none of these comments indicated any awareness that HR should be aware of ethical as well as business considerations and act accordingly. However, to do Ulrich justice, he did write later that HR professionals should 'represent both employee needs and implement management agendas' (Ulrich, 1997: 5).

The term 'strategic business partner' has been shortened in common parlance to 'business partner'. Conceptually, HR business partners work closely with line managers and are probably embedded in a business unit or a line function. They fully understand the strategies and activities of their unit or function and appreciate the role they can play as partners to the line managers with whom they work in ensuring that business goals are achieved. Business partners are there to enable those line managers to achieve their objectives through their people.

However, the concept does not always work, especially when it is installed as a fashionable approach without considering how well it will match the way in which the business operates. Another problem is that the qualities required by HR business partners are demanding – and people with those qualities may be hard to find. As quoted by Stephens (2015: 36), Stuart Woollard, director of King's College London's HRM learning centre claimed that: 'The implicit promise of an HR business partner role is to contribute to the value of an organization through facilitating more effective human capital management.' In reality, he says: 'Business partners have become part of a dominant HR structure that remains reactive, procedurally focused and transaction-orientated.' Stephens noted that research carried out by the CIPD in 2013 showed that the credibility of the business partner concept was fragile when it found that a misalignment existed between what business partners thought were the priorities for the business and those reported by business leaders.

The strategic role of HR directors

The strategic role of HR directors is to promote the achievement of the organization's goals and values by: 1) developing and implementing HR strategies that are integrated with the business strategy and are coherent and mutually supportive; 2) ensuring that a strategic approach is adopted, which provides that HR activities support the business and add value; and 3) taking into account the ethical dimension of HRM. To carry out this role HR directors need to:

- understand the strategic goals of the organization;
- appreciate the business imperatives and performance drivers relative to these goals;
- understand the business model of the organization (how it makes money) and play a part in business model innovation;
- comprehend how sustainable competitive advantage can be obtained through the human capital of the organization and know how HR practices can contribute to the achievement of strategic goals;
- be aware of the critical factors governing organizational success so that they can encourage and contribute to the development of initiatives designed to improve overall organizational performance such as smart working;
- contribute to the development of the business strategy on an 'outside-in' basis (Wright, Snell and Jacobsen, 2004) starting from an analysis of the customer, competitor and business issues the organization faces – the HR strategy then derives directly from these challenges to create solutions, add value and ensure that the organization has the distinctive human capital required to make an impact;
- contribute to the development for the business of a clear vision and a set of integrated values;
- ensure that senior management understands the HR implications of its business strategy;

- see the big picture, including the broader context (the competitive environment and the business, economic, social, legal factors that affect it) in which the organization operates;
- think in the longer term of where HR should go and how to get there;
- understand the kinds of employee behaviour required to execute successfully the business strategy;
- believe in and practice evidence-based management;
- be capable of making a powerful business case for any proposals on the development of HR strategies;
- fully embrace ethical considerations when developing and implementing HR strategy.

The strategic role of heads of HR functions

The strategic role of heads of HR functions is fundamentally the same for their function as that of HR directors for the whole organization. They promote the achievement of the organization's business goals by developing and implementing functional strategies that are aligned with the business strategy and integrated with the strategies for other HR functions, and adopt a strategic approach in the sense of ensuring that HR activities support the business, add value and are ethical. To carry out this role, heads of HR functions should:

- understand the strategic goals of the organization as they affect their function;
- appreciate the business imperatives and performance drivers relative to these goals;
- help senior management to understand the implications of its strategy for the HR function;
- know how HR practices in the function can contribute to the achievement of the strategic goals;
- ensure that their activities provide added value for the organization;
- be aware of the broader context (the competitive environment and the business, economic, social, legal factors that affect it) in which the function operates;
- think in terms of the bigger and longer-term picture of where HR strategies for the function should go and how to get there;
- believe in and practice evidence-based management;
- be capable of making a powerful business case for any proposals on the development of HR strategies for the function;
- fully embrace ethical considerations when developing and implementing HR strategy for their function.

The strategic role of HR business partners

The strategic role of HR business partners is to promote the achievement of the business goals of the organizational unit or function in which they operate. In doing so, they need to take account of ethical considerations. To carry out this role they should:

- understand the business and its competitive environment;
- understand the goals of their part of the business and the plans to attain them;
- ensure that their activities provide added value for the unit or function;
- build relationships founded on trust with their line management clients;
- provide support to the strategic activities of their colleagues;
- align their activities with business requirements;
- believe in and practice evidence-based management;
- be proactive, anticipating requirements, identifying problems and producing innovative and evidence-based solutions to them;
- see the broad picture and rise above the day-to-day detail;
- fully take into account ethical considerations when performing their business partner role.

The strategic contribution of HR advisors or assistants

The role of HR advisors or assistants is primarily that of delivering effective HR services within their function or as a member of an HR service centre. While they will not be responsible for the formulation of HR strategies they may contribute to them within their own speciality. They will need to understand the business goals of the departments or managers for whom they provide services in order to ensure that these services support the achievement of those goals. They should also fully take into account ethical considerations when performing their role.

STRATEGIC HRM IN ACTION

The strategic role of HR at Smiths Industries

The HR director of Smiths Industries commented on the strategic role of HR as follows:

> I do not believe that you can have stand-alone HR strategies. You have to develop strategies that are an integral part of the business objectives.

I don't see HR standing alone in an ivory tower. Everything we do has to have a value-added benefit for the business. If it doesn't have a positive benefit for the business, we don't do it. If you can make a business case, then it will be supported.

There are issues where it is appropriate for the HR director to lead, but in the main we try to go for an integrated approach. If we are re-organizing a business to respond to a particular market situation, then we would be developing strategies to help the managing director of that business to get to where he or she needs to be.

SOURCE: Armstrong, M and Baron, A (2002) *Strategic HRM: The route to improved business performance*, CIPD, London

KEY LEARNING POINTS

The work of HR practitioners is divided into two main areas: transactional activities and strategic activities.

- The credibility of HR professionals, especially at the highest level, also depends on their ability to make a strategic contribution to ensure that the organization has the quality of skilled and engaged people it needs. But HR must also get right its transactional service delivery activities.

- Human resource professionals need to become strategic business partners concerned with improving business performance. But they should not pursue business objectives at the expense of ethical considerations.

- The strategic role of HR directors is to promote the achievement of the organization's goals and values by: 1) developing and implementing HR strategies that are integrated with the business strategy and are coherent and mutually supportive; 2) that a strategic approach in the sense of ensuring that HR activities support the business and add value is adopted throughout the HR function; and 3) taking into account the ethical dimension of HRM.

- The strategic role of heads of HR functions is fundamentally the same for their function as that of HR directors for the whole organization.

- The role of HR advisors or assistants is primarily that of delivering effective HR services within their function or as a member of an HR service centre. While they will not be responsible for the formulation of HR strategies they may contribute to them within their own speciality.

References

Alvesson, M (2009) Critical perspectives on strategic HRM, in *The Routledge Companion to Strategic Human Resource Management*, ed J Storey, P M Wright and D Ulrich, pp 52–67, Routledge, Abingdon

Caldwell, R (2004) Rhetoric, facts and self-fulfilling prophesies: exploring practitioners' perceptions of progress in implementing HRM, *Industrial Relations Journal*, **35** (3), pp 196–215

Chartered Institute of Personnel and Development (2007) *HR Business Partnering*, CIPD, London

Dyer, L and Holder, G W (1988) Strategic human resource management and planning, in *Human Resource Management: Evolving roles and responsibilities*, ed L Dyer, pp 1–46, Bureau of National Affairs, Washington DC

Kanter, R M (1984) The *Change Masters*, Allen & Unwin, London

Schuler, R S and Jackson, S E (2007) *Strategic Human Resource Management*, Blackwell, Oxford

Sparrow, P, Hesketh, A, Hird, M, Marsh, C and Balain, S (2010) Using business model change to tie HR into strategy: reversing the arrow, in *Leading HR*, ed P Sparrow, A Hesketh, M Hird and C Cooper, pp 68–89, Palgrave Macmillan, Basingstoke

Stephens, C (2015) Are HR partners a dying breed?, *People Management*, February, pp 36–37

Syrett, M (2006) *Four Reflections on Developing a Human Capital Measurement Capability: What's the Future for Human Capital?*, CIPD, London

Tyson, S (1985) Is this the very model of a modern personnel manager?, *Personnel Management,* May, pp 22–25

Ulrich, D (1997) *Human Resource Champions*, Harvard Business School Press, Boston MA

Ulrich, D and Lake, D (1990) *Organizational Capability: Competing from the inside out*, Wiley, New York

Wright, P M, Snell, S A and Jacobsen, H H (2004) Current approaches to HR strategies: inside-out versus outside-in, *Human Resource Planning*, **27** (4), pp 36–46

PART TWO
HRM strategy in general

The nature of HR strategy

LEARNING OUTCOMES

On completing this chapter you should be able to define these key concepts. You should also understand:

- what HR strategy is and its purpose;
- the main types of HR strategies;
- how to evaluate the effectiveness of an HR strategy.

Introduction

HR strategy specifies what the organization is proposing to do about people management generally or in particular areas of HRM. It may be defined formally as part of a strategic HRM process, which leads to the development of overall or specific HR strategies for implementation by HR *and*, vitally, line managers. But it should be noted that an organization that has developed an HR strategy will not be practising strategic HRM unless that HR strategy has relevance to the organization's success. Wright and McMahan (1999: 52) stated that HRM can only be considered to be strategic if 'it enables an organization to achieve its goals'.

As noted in Chapter 3, HR strategy is governed or at least influenced by the overall approach adopted to strategic HRM. It could be regarded as the manifestation of SHRM in action.

However, HR strategy, like any other aspects of business strategy, can come into existence through an emergent, evolutionary and possibly unarticulated process influenced by the business strategy as it develops and changes in the internal and external environment. Pettigrew and Whipp (1991: 30) emphasized that strategy 'far from being a straightforward, rational phenomenon, is in fact interpreted by managers according to their own frame of reference, their particular motivations and information'. But there are still strong arguments for a systematic approach to identifying strategic directions, which can provide a framework for decision making and action, as examined in this chapter.

What is HR strategy?

HR strategy sets out what the organization intends to do about its human resource management policies and practices and how they should be integrated with the business strategy and each other. Tyson and Witcher (1994: 21) defined HR strategies as 'the intentions and plans for using human resources to achieve business objectives'. HR strategies were described by Dyer and Reeves (1995: 656) as 'internally consistent bundles of human resource practices', and in the words of Boxall (1996: 61) they provide 'a framework of critical ends and means'. Richardson and Thompson (1999: 3) suggested that: 'A strategy, whether it is an HR strategy or any other kind of management strategy must have two key elements: there must be strategic objectives (ie things the strategy is supposed to achieve), and there must be a plan of action (ie the means by which it is proposed that the objectives will be met).' HR strategy sets out aspirations, which have to be expressed as intentions, which then have to be converted into actions. Purcell (2001: 72) made the point that: 'Strategy in HR, like in other areas, is about continuity and change, about appropriateness in the circumstances, but anticipating when the circumstances change. It is about taking strategic decisions.'

HR strategies may set out intentions and provide a sense of purpose and direction, but they are not just long-term plans. They can be immediately relevant. It is necessary to bear in mind the dictum of Fombrun, Tichy and Devanna (1984) that business and managers should perform well in the present in order to succeed in the future.

HR strategies should be distinguished from HR policies. Strategies are dynamic. They provide a sense of direction, and answer the question 'How are we going to get from here to there?' Policies are more about the here and now. They define 'the way things are done around here'. Of course they evolve but this may not be a result of a strategic choice. It is when a deliberate decision is made to change policies that a strategy for achieving this change has to be formulated.

Perhaps the main argument for articulating HR strategies is that unless you know where you are going, you will not know how to get there or know when you have arrived.

The features of HR strategy

Because all organizations are different, all HR strategies are different. There is no such thing as a standard strategy, and research into HR strategy conducted by Armstrong and Long (1994) and Armstrong and Baron (2002) revealed many variations.

HR strategy may not be deliberate. It was pointed out by Mintzberg (1987: 67) that: 'An organization can have a pattern (a realized strategy) without knowing it, let alone making it explicit.' He produced the principle of 'emergent strategy', stating that: 'A realized strategy can emerge in response to an evolving situation' (1987: 68). As Mintzberg, Quinn and James (1988) suggested, strategies can simply exist in the 'collective minds' of the people on whom they make an impact. The fact that they have not been articulated may not matter as long as people in the organization share the same perspective through their intentions or their actions.

Mintzberg's concept of 'emergent strategy' rings true, but Grant (1998) has argued that the Mintzberg approach, which downplays the role of systematic analysis and emphasizes the role of intuition and vision, fails to provide a clear basis for reasoned choices. However, Mintzberg (1987: 69) accepted that 'purely emergent strategy making precludes control'. He took the realistic position that there is no such thing as a purely deliberate strategy or a purely emergent one and that 'deliberate and emergent strategy form the end points of a continuum along which the strategies which are crafted in the real world may be found' (1987: 69). Thompson and Strickland (1996: 20) noted that 'a company's actual strategy is partly planned and partly reactive to changing circumstances'.

Three types of strategy can be identified: 1) broad statements of intent under various headings; 2) overall HR strategies concerned with high-performance working, high-commitment management or high-involvement management; and 3) specific strategies relating to the different aspects of HRM such as talent management, learning and development, and reward.

Broad statements of intent

HR strategy may simply consist of a broad statement of intent, which provides the framework for more specific strategic plans in individual HR areas. Mintzberg (1987) referred to this approach as 'umbrella strategy' in which senior management sets out broad guide lines, leaving the specifics to people lower down in the organization.

The CIPD-sponsored research conducted by Armstrong and Baron (2002) found in the organizations they studied that the overall objectives of their HR strategy were typically to modify values, behaviours and attitudes. However, the paths taken to get there were quite different.

Research into the formulation of HRM strategy in a number of US companies by Wright, Snell and Jacobsen (2004: 43) established that 'the core components of HR strategies seem to be building a performance culture, developing leadership capability, attracting and retaining the best talent, and providing state-of-the-art HR systems, processes, and services'. Set out below are UK examples of overall HR strategic statements of intent.

STRATEGIC HRM IN ACTION

Statements of overall HRM strategy

Aegon
'The human resources integrated approach aims to ensure that from whatever angle staff now look at the elements of pay management, performance, career development and reward, they are consistent and linked.'

Boots
'The biggest challenge will be to maintain [our] competitive advantage and to do that we need to maintain and continue to attract very high-calibre people. The key differentiator on anything any company does is fundamentally the people, and I think that people tend to forget that they are the most important asset. Money is easy to get hold of, good people are not. All we do in terms of training and manpower planning is directly linked to business improvement' (Managing Director).

GlaxoSmithKline
'We want GSK to be a place where the best people do their best work.'

Lands' End
'The overall HR strategy is based on the principle that staff who are enjoying themselves, are being supported and developed, and who feel fulfilled and respected at work, will provide the best service to customers.'

Overall HR strategy approaches

The second category of HRM strategy consists of the deliberate introduction of overall approaches to human resource management such as high-performance management, high-involvement management and high-commitment management, which are described below. There is some overlap between these approaches, especially the latter two.

High-performance management

High-performance management aims to make an impact on the performance of the organization through its people in such areas as productivity, quality, levels of customer service, growth, profits and, ultimately, the delivery of increased shareholder value. The objective is to achieve this by rigorous recruitment and selection procedures, extensive and relevant training and management development activities, incentive pay systems and performance management processes. As a bundle, these practices are often called high-performance work systems (HPWSs).

High-involvement management

High-involvement management practices were described by Wood (2010) as follows:

SOURCE REVIEW   High-involvement management defined
– Wood (2010: 410)

High-involvement management includes first, practices such as teamworking, flexible job descriptions and idea-capturing schemes, which are means of ensuring greater flexibility, proactivity and collaboration; and second, practices that give workers the opportunities for the acquisition of skills and knowledge that are needed to ensure they have the capacities to work in an involved way. They include intensive training geared towards teamworking, functional flexibility and information sharing, particularly about the economics and market of the business.

The practices included in a high-involvement system have sometimes expanded beyond this original concept and included high-performance practices. For example, as defined by Benson, Young and Lawler (2006: 519): 'High-involvement work practices are a specific set of human resource practices that focus on employee decision making, power, access to information, training and incentives.'

High-commitment management

One of the characteristics of the concept of HRM is the notion of mutuality, the belief expressed by Walton (1985) that organizations consist of people with shared interests – management and employees are interdependent and both benefit from this interdependency. According to Walton, this meant that organizations had to abandon their traditional emphasis on control and replace it with a commitment strategy that involved giving employees broader responsibilities, encouraging them to contribute and helping them to achieve satisfaction from their work. This was the basis for the approach known as high-commitment management, which was described by Wood (1996: 41) as: 'A form of management which is aimed at eliciting a commitment so that behaviour is primarily self-regulated rather than controlled by sanctions and pressures external to the individual, and relations within the organization are based on high levels of trust.'

Specific HR strategies

Specific HR strategies set out what the organization intends to do in areas such as:

- *Organization design and development*: designing and modifying organization structures and planning and implementation of programmes designed to enhance the effectiveness with which an organization functions and responds to change.
- *Human capital management*: treating people as assets to be invested in through resourcing, learning and development policies. Applying HR analytics to assess the contribution of people and to measure the effectiveness of the HR practices used to manage them.
- *Knowledge management*: creating, acquiring, capturing, sharing and using knowledge to enhance learning and performance.
- *Corporate social responsibility*: a commitment to managing the business ethically in order to make a positive impact on society and the environment.
- *Diversity and inclusion*: acknowledging cultural and individual differences in the workplace, valuing the different qualities that people bring to their jobs.
- *Engagement*: the development and implementation of policies designed to increase the level of employees' engagement with their work and the organization.
- *Performance*: strategies for improving organizational and individual performance.
- *Resourcing*: attracting and retaining high-quality people.
- *Talent management*: how the organization ensures that it has the talented people it needs to achieve success.

- *Learning and development*: providing an environment in which employees are encouraged to learn and develop.
- *Reward*: defining what the organization wants to do in the longer term to develop and implement reward policies, practices and processes that will further the achievement of its business goals and meet the needs of its stakeholders.
- *Employment relationships*: defining the intentions of the organization about what needs to be done and what needs to be changed in the ways in which the organization manages its relationships with employees and trade unions.

These strategies may be developed individually or, preferably, the HR strategy includes specific and articulated plans to create 'bundles' of HR practices and develop a coherent HR system.

STRATEGIC HRM IN ACTION

The people strategy at Diageo

The three broad strands to the *Organization and People Strategy* at Diageo are:

- *Reward and recognition*: use recognition and reward programmes to stimulate outstanding team and individual performance contributions.
- *Talent management*: drive the attraction, retention and professional growth of a deep pool of diverse, talented employees.
- *Organizational effectiveness*: ensure that the business adapts its organization to maximize employee contribution and deliver performance goals.

It provides direction to the company's talent, operational effectiveness and performance and reward agendas. The company's underlying thinking is that the people strategy is not for the HR function to own but is the responsibility of the whole organization, hence the title 'Organization and People Strategy'.

SOURCE: Armstrong, M and Baron, A (2002) *Strategic HRM: The route to improved business performance*, CIPD, London

Evaluating HR strategy

HR strategy should be evaluated by comparing achievements against goals. This is not possible where strategies are emergent rather than deliberate. In this case they can only be judged by reference to the degree to which the organization is successful in achieving its objectives through people, in so far as this judgement is possible. As Boxall and Purcell (2003: 28) observed: 'strategy is best discerned in behaviour'.

Deliberate strategies, as long as they incorporate strategic goals and strategic plans, can be evaluated according to the extent to which, ideally, they:

- 'indicate something of genuine significance for the future of the firm' (Boxall and Purcell, 2003: 30);
- satisfy the needs of the business and its employees;
- are founded on detailed analysis and study, not just wishful thinking;
- can be turned into actionable programmes that anticipate implementation requirements and problems;
- are coherent and integrated, being composed of components that fit with and support each other.

KEY LEARNING POINTS

- *HRM strategies defined*
  HR strategies provide a framework within which is set out what the organization is proposing to do about people management generally or in particular areas of HRM.

  HRM strategies set out what the organization intends to do about its human resource management policies and practices and how they should be integrated with the business strategy and each other.

- *Purpose of HRM strategies*
  The purpose of HRM strategies is to articulate what an organization intends to do about its human resource management policies and practices now and in the longer term in order to ensure that they contribute to the achievement of business objectives.

- *Types of HRM strategies*
  Because all organizations are different, all HR strategies are different.

  HRM strategies can be deliberate or they can emerge in response to evolving situations, or they may be partly deliberate and partly emergent.

  HRM strategy may simply consist of a broad statement of intent that provides the framework for more specific strategic plans in individual HR areas, or it may include the deliberate introduction of overall approaches to HRM such as high-performance management, or it may include plans for specific areas of HRM such as talent management and reward.

• *Evaluating HR strategies*
Where strategies are emergent rather than deliberate their effectiveness cannot be assessed by a formal process of evaluating their achievements against their goals. They can only be judged by reference to the degree to which the organization is successful in achieving its objectives through people.

Deliberate strategies can be evaluated according to the extent to which they meet specified objectives.

References

Armstrong, M and Baron, A (2002) *Strategic HRM: The route to improved business performance*, CIPD London

Armstrong, M and Long, P (1994) *The Reality of Strategic HRM*, Institute of Personnel and Development, London

Benson, G S, Young, S M and Lawler, E E (2006) High involvement work practices and analysts' forecasts of corporate performance, *Human Resource Management*, **45** (4), pp 519–27

Boxall, P F (1996) The strategic HRM debate and the resource-based view of the firm, *Human Resource Management Journal*, **6** (3), pp 59–75

Boxall, P F and Purcell, J (2003) *Strategy and Human Resource Management*, Palgrave Macmillan, Basingstoke

Dyer, L and Reeves, T (1995) Human resource strategies and firm performance: what do we know and where do we need to go?, *The International Journal of Human Resource Management*, **6** (3), pp. 656–70

Fombrun, C J, Tichy, N M and Devanna, M A (1984) *Strategic Human Resource Management*, Wiley, New York

Grant, R M (1998) *Contemporary Strategic Analysis*, Blackwell, Malden MA

Mintzberg, H (1987) Crafting strategy, *Harvard Business Review,* July–August, pp 66–74

Mintzberg, H, Quinn, J B and James, R M (1988) *The Strategy Process: Concepts, contexts and cases*, Prentice-Hall, New York

Pettigrew, A and Whipp, R (1991) *Managing Change for Competitive Success*, Blackwell, Oxford

Purcell, J (2001) 'The meaning of strategy in human resource management', in *Human Resource Management: A critical text*, 2nd edn, ed J Storey, pp 59–77, Thompson Learning, London

Richardson, R and Thompson, M (1999) *The Impact of People Management Practices on Business Performance: A literature review*, Institute of Personnel and Development, London

Thompson, A A and Strickland, A J (1996) *Strategic Management: Concepts and cases*, 9th edn, Irwin, Ontario

Tyson, S and Witcher, M (1994) Human resource strategy emerging from the recession, *Personnel Management*, August, pp 20–23

Walton, R E (1985) Towards a strategy of eliciting employee commitment based on principles of mutuality, in *HRM Trends and Challenges*, ed R E Walton and P R Lawrence, pp 35–68, Harvard Business School Press, Boston MA

Wood, S (1996) High commitment management and organization in the UK, *International Journal of Human Resource Management*, 7 (1), pp. 41–58

Wood, S (2010) High involvement and performance, in *The Oxford Handbook of Participation in Organizations*, ed A Wilkinson, P J Gollan, M Marchington and D Lewins, pp 407–26, Oxford University Press, Oxford

Wright, P M and McMahan, G C (1999) Theoretical perspectives for human resource management, in *Strategic Human Resource Management*, ed R S Schulker and S E Jackson, pp 49–72, Blackwell, Oxford

Wright, P M, Snell, S A and Jacobsen, H H (2004) Current approaches to HR strategies: inside-out versus outside-in, *Human Resource Planning*, 27 (4), pp 36–46

Developing HR strategy

Considerations affecting the development of HR strategy

The formulation of HR strategy is not such a straightforward process, as some people believe. There are a number of considerations that affect how it takes place, as discussed below.

Limits to an entirely rationalistic approach

The limits of excessively rationalistic models of HR strategic planning were noted by Hendry and Pettigrew (1990). They observed that strategies could emerge from the actions and reactions of managers and others. As pointed out earlier by Johnson (1987: 12):

> Strategic decisions are characterized by the political hurly-burly of organizational life with a high incidence of bargaining, a trading off of costs and benefits of one internal group against another, all within a notable lack of clarity in terms of environmental influences and objectives.

Anyone who, like the writer of this book, has sat for a number of years on an executive board and played a full part in business decisions knows that this is the way in which strategic decisions are typically made at the top level in an organization.

When considering approaches to the formulation of HR strategy it is therefore necessary to emphasize the interactive (not unilinear) relationship between business strategy and HR strategy. Boxall (1993) stressed that the strategy formation process is complex, and excessively rationalistic models that advocate formalistic linkages between strategic planning and HR planning are not particularly helpful to our understanding of it.

It is advisable to treat HR strategy as a perspective rather than a rigorous procedure for mapping the future. Mintzberg (1987: 66) made it clear that strategic management is a learning process: 'Formulation and implementation merge into a fluid process of learning through which creative strategies evolve.'

On the basis of research in 30 well-known companies Tyson and Witcher (1994: 22) concluded that:

> The process of formulating HR strategy was often as important as the content of the strategy ultimately agreed. It was argued that by working through strategic issues and highlighting points of tension, new ideas emerged and a consensus over goals was found.

They also commented that: 'The different approaches to strategy formation reflect different ways to manage change and different ways to bring the people part of the business into line with business goals. In developing HR strategies, process may be as important as content' (Tyson and Witcher, 1994: 24).

Strategic options and choices

The process of developing HR strategy involves generating strategic options and then making appropriate strategic choices. It was noted by Cappelli (1999: 8) that: 'The choice of practices that an employer pursues is heavily contingent on a number of factors at the organizational level, including their own business and production strategies, support of HR policies, and co-operative labour relations.' It is necessary to adopt a contingent approach in generating strategic HRM options and then making appropriate strategic choices. There is seldom, if ever, one right way forward.

Choices should relate to but also anticipate the critical needs of the business and the people in it. They should be evidence-based – founded on detailed analysis and study, not just wishful thinking – and should incorporate the experienced and collective judgement of top management about the organizational requirements, while also taking into account the needs of line managers and employees generally. The emerging strategy should anticipate the problems of implementation, which may arise if line managers are not committed to the strategy and/or lack the skills and time to play their part, and the strategies should be capable of being turned into actionable programmes. Strategy should always be formulated with implementation in mind.

The rhetoric/reality gap

There is too often a wide gap between the rhetoric of strategic HRM and the reality of its impact. Gratton *et al* (1999) maintained that good intentions can too easily be subverted by the harsh realities of organizational life. For example, strategic objectives such as increasing commitment by providing more security and offering training to increase employability may have to be abandoned, or at least modified, because of the short-term demands made on the business as a result of financial pressures.

Approaches to the development of HR strategy

These limitations need to be taken into account when formulating HR strategy but they do not preclude it. There is everything to be said for thinking ahead about what needs to be done and for planning the changes required.

Research conducted by Wright, Snell and Jacobsen (2004) identified two approaches that can be adopted by HR to strategy formulation. The 'inside-out' approach begins with the status quo HR function (in terms of skills, processes, technologies etc) and then attempts (with varying degrees of success) to identify linkages to the business (usually through focusing on 'people issues'), making minor adjustments to HR activities along the way.

The preferred 'outside-in' starts with the customer, competitor and other issues that the business faces. The HR strategy then derives directly from these challenges to 'create real solutions and add real value' (Wright, Snell and Jacobsen, 2004: 37). They made the point that 'the most advanced linkage was the "integrative" linkage in which the senior HR executive was part of the top management team, and was able to sit at the table and contribute during development of the business strategy'. Their recommendations on adopting an outside-in approach are set out below.

SOURCE REVIEW   Adopting an outside-in approach to the formulation of HRM strategy – Wright, Snell and Jacobsen (2004: 45–46)

1   Develop a formal process for involving line executives in the development of HR strategy.

2   Have formal mechanisms for tracking developments in the external environment as part of the process.

3   Begin with the assumption that everything the current HR function is doing is either wrong or does not exist.

4   Identify the key business and people metrics that will determine or indicate the success of the business, then constantly track and communicate those metrics to the entire internal HR community.

5   Based on the business issues and metrics, develop the HR strategy that will maximally drive performance on those metrics.

Remember that the HR strategy is a process, not a document, intervention or event. Any strategy is a pattern in a stream of decisions, and as business and people issues change or obstacles appear, the pattern (strategy) will also have changed.

STRATEGIC HRM IN ACTION

Formulating HRM strategy at Boots

The Director of HR explained that:

> I start with the top line, the four or five things that are the strategic platform for the company. I get my managers together to look at the implications. We then pull it together so that it is all derived from the original strategic platforms and then work top-down and bottom-up to get the amalgam of what we can achieve. This then feeds into the final operating plan so we can agree budgets.

SOURCE: Armstrong, M and Long, P (1994) *The Reality of Strategic HRM*, IPD, London

Formulating HR strategy

The formulation of HR strategy involves the following steps:

1 Scan the internal and external environment and analyse the implications.

2 Analyse the effectiveness of existing HR strategies and the implications for HR strategy.

3 Conduct a diagnostic review drawing on the outcomes of steps 1 and 2.

4 Consider how vertical integration or fit can be achieved, ie linking the HR strategy to the business strategy.

5 Consider how horizontal integration can be achieved, ie linking different HR practices together so that they are mutually supportive and therefore complement and reinforce each other (bundling).

6 Set out the HR strategy.

Step 1: scan the internal and external environments

The analytical frameworks set out in Figures 6.1 and 6.2 can be used for this purpose.

FIGURE 6.1 Analysis of the internal environment

Question	Response	Implications for HR strategy
1 What are the key objectives of our business strategy?		
2 What are the main drivers of success in our business?		
3 What are the core values of the organization?		
4 What evidence is there that these values are used in the everyday life of the organization?		
5 What are the implications of the type of business we are in on our HR strategy?		
6 What characteristics do we look for in our people?		
7 What do the people we want, want?		
8 What is our employee value proposition and does it help to attract and retain high-quality people?		
9 What are we doing about developing the talented people we need?		
10 How engaged are our people? (as established by employee surveys)		

FIGURE 6.2   Analysis of the external environment

External factor	Impact on HR policy and practice
Competitive pressures	
Business/economic trends	
Globalization	
Employment and demographic trends	
Legislation/regulations	
Availability of key skills	
Market rates of pay	

Step 2: analyse the effectiveness of existing HR strategies (Figure 6.3)

FIGURE 6.3   Analysis of the effectiveness of existing HR strategies

To what extent does HR strategy:	Wholly	Partly	Not at all	If partly or not at all, what needs to be done about it?
1 Support the achievement of business goals?				
2 Promote the well-being of all employees?				
3 Contribute to enhancing the levels of employee engagement?				
4 Enable the organization to recruit and retain the talented people it needs?				
5 Enable the organization to develop the talented people it needs?				
6 Focus on improving organizational performance?				
7 Focus on improving individual performance?				
8 Ensure that people are rewarded according to their contribution?				
9 Contribute to the creation of a positive employee-relations climate?				

Step 3: conduct a diagnostic review

To draw together the threads of the analyses in steps 1 and 2 the diagnostic framework shown in Figure 6.4 can be used.

FIGURE 6.4 Diagnostic framework

Issues identified by analysis	Reasons for issues	Proposals to deal with issues	Actions required to implement the proposals

Step 4: integrating business and HR strategy

It is not enough to simply list a set of strategic priorities. It is also necessary to see that they are integrated with the business strategy, a key requirement of strategic HRM. In doing this, account should be taken of the fact that strategies for change have also to be integrated with changes in the external and internal environments. 'Fit' may exist at a point in time but circumstances will change and 'fit' no longer exists. An excessive pursuit of 'fit' with the status quo will inhibit the flexibility of approach, which is essential in turbulent conditions. This is the 'temporal' factor in achieving fit, identified by Gratton *et al* (1999). An additional factor that will make the achievement of good vertical fit difficult is that the business strategy may not be clearly defined – it could be in an emergent or evolutionary state. This would mean that there could be little or nothing with which to fit the HR strategy.

The process of integration should start with an analysis of the business model and continue with a more detailed analysis of the business strategy and the drivers of business success (the critical success factors).

Analysis of the business model

Business models as defined by Magretta (2002: 87) 'are at heart stories – stories that explain how enterprises work... They answer the fundamental questions every manager needs to ask: How do we make money in this business? What is the underlying economic logic that explains how we can deliver value to customers at an appropriate cost?' She explained that a business model 'focuses attention on how all the elements in a system fit into a working whole' (2002: 90). It is essential for those responsible for formulating HR strategy to understand the business model and how it affects people management.

It is also essential to remember that business models develop and change – the process of 'business model innovation'. The role of HR in dealing with business model change was spelt out by Paul Sparrow and his colleagues as follows:

SOURCE REVIEW   The role of HR in business model innovation – Sparrow *et al* (2010: 14–15)

A central task for HR directors is to identify how they as a leader – and how their function's own delivery model, structure and the people processes it manages – add value during periods of business model change. In order for organizations to make their models work, they have to understand the potentially deep implications they have for people management. People management experts have to make sure that those engineering the new business models are working on assumptions that can reasonably be executed.

Analysis of the business strategy and drivers

Within the context of the business model analysis a more detailed analysis of the business strategy can be made using a framework such as that illustrated in Figure 6.5 to identify any specific HR areas that need to be developed to support the achievement of the business strategy.

Step 5: achieving horizontal integration (bundling)

Horizontal integration or 'fit' takes place when the various HRM strategies cohere and are mutually supporting. It can be attained by the process of 'bundling', which is carried out by: 1) identifying appropriate HR approaches; 2) by assessing how the items in the bundle can be linked together so that they become mutually reinforcing; and 3) drawing up programmes for the development of these practices, paying particular attention to the links between them.

Bundling can take place in a number of ways. For example, competency frameworks could be devised that are used to specify recruitment standards, identify learning and development needs, and to play an important part in

FIGURE 6.5 HR implications of business strategy and business drivers

	Content	Possible HR supporting activities	What needs to be done about it?
Business strategy	• Growth – revenue/profit • Maximize shareholder value • Growth through acquisitions/mergers • Product development • Market development • Cost leadership	• Workforce planning	
		• Talent management	
		• Skills development	
		• Targeted recruitment	
		• Retention policies	
		• Leadership development	
		• Other	
Business drive	• Attract and retain talented people (more talented than those employed by competitors) • Innovation • Maximize added value • Productivity • Customer service • Quality • Satisfy stakeholders – investors, shareholders, employees, elected representatives	• Enhance engagement	
		• Talent management	
		• Performance management	
		• Reward management	
		• High-performance working*	
		• Smart working*	
		• Agile working*	
		• Other	
* Described in Chapter 12			

assessment and development centres. They could also be incorporated into performance management processes in which the aims are primarily developmental and competencies are used as criteria for reviewing behaviour. Job evaluation could be based on levels of competency, and competency-based pay systems could be introduced. Grade structures could define career ladders in terms of competency requirements (career family structures) and thus provide the basis for learning and development programmes. They can serve the dual purpose of defining career paths and pay progression opportunities. A high-performance work system bundles a number of HR practices together, as does talent management.

Step 6: set out the HR strategy

The outcomes of steps 1 to 5 form the basis for deciding on the strategy. How this is done will vary according to the circumstances of the organization. But the following are the typical areas that might be covered in a written strategy:

1 Analysis of the environmental and business factors affecting the strategy.
2 The business case: how the strategy will meet business needs in terms of the business model and likely changes to it (business model innovation) and the key elements of the business strategy.
3 Content: details of the proposed HR strategy.
4 Implementation plan:
   - action programme;
   - responsibility for each stage;
   - resources required;
   - proposed arrangements for communication, consultation, involvement and training;
   - project management arrangements.
5 Costs and benefits analysis: an assessment of the resource implications of the plan (costs, people and facilities) and the benefits that will accrue, for the organization as a whole, for line managers and for individual employees (so far as possible these benefits should be quantified in terms of return on investment or value added).

STRATEGIC HRM IN ACTION

Strategic review of human resource management in UNICEF

UNICEF's total staff complement is 8,594, drawn from 178 nationalities located at its headquarters (New York and Geneva) and in eight regional offices.

Purpose of the strategic review

'How well is UNICEF managing and enhancing its human resource capacity to reach its strategic objectives?'

Key questions

The review will address the following key questions:

- Does UNICEF have clear and workable HR policies relevant to the strategic goals of the organization? What impact is UNICEF HR policy and practice having on the achievement of UNICEF strategic goals?

- How well suited are UNICEF HRM policy, process, employment contracts and budgeting to the long-term maintenance of a skilled UNICEF workforce?

- Are the accountabilities for HRM clear, understood and fulfilled?

- What progress has been made in the implementation of the Brasilia strategy and what factors underlie UNICEF achievements and failings in improving HRM?

- To what extent do UNICEF staff have the appropriate competencies to meet the organization's strategic goals?

- To what extent do managers in UNICEF have the competencies to effectively manage resources (human and financial) to achieve the organization's goals and motivate their teams?

- To what extent do UNICEF management culture, management structures and HR systems encourage or constrain effective HRM?

- To what extent do UNICEF (non-financial) rewards, incentives and sanctions encourage managers to be effective in their management of human resources?

- To what extent is UNICEF HRM helped or constrained by the HR regulations and procedures of the United Nations system, and to what extent is it free to be creative in generating its own HRM solutions?

- Does UNICEF have the appropriate HR expertise to support the realization of its strategic goals, both in the HR division and across the organization?

- To what extent do UNICEF levels of investment in HR personnel and systems encourage or constrain effective HRM?

- How efficiently and cost-effectively deployed are the staff resources within the HR division, and other HR-related posts globally?

SOURCE: hrmreview@unicef.org [accessed May 2015]

KEY LEARNING POINTS

- *Considerations*
  The formulation of HR strategy is not such a straightforward process as some people believe. The considerations that affect how it takes place are:

  - the limits of an entirely rationalistic approach;
  - the existence of strategic options and choices;
  - the rhetoric/reality gap.

- *Approaches to the development of HR strategy*
  These limitations need to be taken into account when formulating HR strategy but they do not preclude it. There is everything to be said for thinking ahead about what needs to be done and for planning the changes required.

  Two approaches that can be adopted by HR to strategy formulation were identified by Wright, Snell and Jacobsen (2004): the inside-out approach and the preferred outside-in approach.

- *Formulating HR strategy*
  The formulation of HR strategy involves the following steps:

  - Scan the internal and external environment and analyse the implications.
  - Analyse the effectiveness of existing HR strategies and the implications for HR strategy.
  - Conduct a diagnostic review drawing on the outcomes of the above two steps.
  - Consider how vertical integration or 'fit' can be achieved, ie linking the HR strategy to the business strategy.
  - Consider how horizontal integration can be achieved, ie linking different HR practices together so that they are mutually supportive and therefore complement and reinforce each other (bundling).
  - Set out the HR strategy.

References

Boxall, P F (1993) The significance of human resource management: a reconsideration of the evidence, *The International Journal of Human Resource Management*, 4 (3), pp 645–65

Cappelli, P (1999) *Employment Practices and Business Strategy*, Oxford University Press, New York

Gratton, L A, Hailey, V H, Stiles, P and Truss, C (1999) *Strategic Human Resource Management*, Oxford University Press, Oxford

Hendry, C and Pettigrew, A (1990) Human resource management: an agenda for the 1990s, *International Journal of Human Resource Management*, **1** (1), pp 17–44

Johnson, G (1987) *Strategic Change and the Management Process*, Blackwell, Oxford

Magretta, J (2002) Why business models matter, *Harvard Business Review*, May, pp 86–93

Mintzberg, H (1987) Crafting strategy, *Harvard Business Review*, July–August, pp 66–74

Sparrow, P, Hesketh, A, Hird, M, Marsh, C and Balain, S (2010) Using business model change to tie HR into strategy: reversing the arrow, in *Leading HR*, ed P Sparrow, A Hesketh, M Hird and C Cooper, pp 68–89, Palgrave Macmillan, Basingstoke

Tyson, S and Witcher, M (1994) Human resource strategy emerging from the recession, *Personnel Management*, August, pp 20–23

Wright, P M, Snell, S A and Jacobsen, H H (2004) Current approaches to HR strategies: inside-out versus outside-in, *Human Resource Planning*, **27** (4), pp 36–46

07 Delivering HR strategy

KEY CONCEPTS AND TERMS

Change management
Partnership
The say–do gap
Strategy

LEARNING OUTCOMES

On completing this chapter you should be able to define these key concepts. You should also understand more about:

- the features of a good strategy;
- the problems involved in implementing strategy;
- how to tackle these problems;
- the role of line managers in implementing HR strategy;
- the partnership role of HR in implementing strategy;
- how to manage change.

Introduction

A good strategy is one that works. HR strategy can too easily become no more than an optimistic aspiration. In the words of Kanter (1984: 301), it needs to be an 'action vehicle'. There is a risk of saying, in effect: 'We need to get from here to there but we don't care how.' Getting strategy to work is hard. Intent does not always lead to action. Too often, strategists act like Mr Pecksmith who was compared by Charles Dickens (2004 [1843]: 23) to 'a direction-post which is always telling the way to a place and never goes there'.

The 'say–do' gap

Gaps can easily exist between what the strategy says will be achieved and what is actually done. Gratton *et al* (1999: 202) noted 'the disjunction between rhetoric and reality in the area of human resource management, between HRM theory and HRM practice, between what the HR function says it is doing and how that practice is perceived by employees, and between what senior management believes to be the role of the HR function, and the role it actually plays'.

The factors identified by Gratton *et al* that contribute to creating this gap are:

- the tendency of employees in diverse organizations only to accept initiatives they perceive to be relevant to their own areas;
- the tendency of long-serving employees to cling to the status quo;
- complex or ambiguous initiatives may not be understood by employees or will be perceived differently by them, especially in large, diverse organizations;
- it is more difficult to gain acceptance of non-routine initiatives;
- employees will be hostile to initiatives if they are believed to be in conflict with the organization's identity, eg downsizing in a culture of 'job-for-life';
- the initiative is seen as a threat;
- inconsistencies between corporate strategies and values;
- the extent to which senior management is trusted;
- the perceived fairness of the initiative;
- the extent to which existing processes could help to embed the initiative;
- a bureaucratic culture, which leads to inertia.

To which could be added:

- failure to understand the strategic needs of the business (which may be difficult);
- inadequate assessment of the environmental and cultural factors, including internal politics, which affect the content of the strategies;
- the development of ill-conceived, unmanageable and irrelevant initiatives, possibly because they are current fads or because there has been a poorly digested analysis of 'best practice' that does not fit the organization's requirements;
- and, importantly, failure to involve stakeholders in the formulation of strategy.

These problems are compounded when insufficient attention is paid to practical implementation problems, particularly where line managers are concerned and there is a need for supporting systems. The role of line managers is vital.

Ensuring the effective delivery of HR strategy

To provide for the effective delivery of HR strategy it is necessary to adopt the approaches described below.

Formulate practical strategies

A practical strategy is one that can be put into effect without too much difficulty. HR strategy should take into account all the barriers referred to above, which create the say–do gap. Particularly careful thought has to be given to the practical issues involved in implementing them. It is necessary to consider the role of line managers in delivering HR strategy, as well as that of HR specialists. The aims should be to: 1) keep it simple; 2) spell out *how* the strategy is to be implemented as well as *what* is to be implemented; 3) ensure that support is given to line managers in the shape of advice, guidance and training.

Involve

Involve as many line managers and other employees as possible in formulating the strategy – people support what they help to create. This can be done through formal consultation processes or through workshops and focus groups whose members are representative of the different constituencies in the organization and who can be encouraged to pass on what they have been doing to their colleagues. Involvement can make use of the analytical tools described in Chapter 6. The questions can be answered individually and then discussed by a group to gain greater understanding and as much consensus as possible. Alternatively, the questions can be considered initially by a group or groups of employees. It is also possible to involve everyone by conducting an opinion survey. The survey should be followed up by discussions with employee groups on its implications for HR strategy and practice.

Communicate

It is essential to communicate details of the strategy to line managers and employees. The communication should explain what is proposed, why it has been proposed (indicating the benefits both to the organization and employees), how it will work, who will be affected and the timetable for introduction. As far as possible it should be by word of mouth to individuals or through team briefing or briefing group arrangements involving everyone in an organization, level by level, in face-to-face meetings to present, receive and discuss information.

Build skills

New strategies may require the use of new skills or the development of existing ones. This applies to employees generally as well as line managers, who should be trained in what they have to do to implement the strategy. Skills can be built through formal off-the-job training courses but there is much to be said for coaching and the use of techniques such as e-learning.

Monitor and evaluate

The introduction of HR strategy should be monitored in order to evaluate its effectiveness. Corrective action in the shape of modifications to the strategy or training can then be taken.

Manage change

The implementation of HRM strategy involves change, which can be hard to introduce and may be resisted. The problems of implementing strategic change were summed up by Lawler and Mohrman (2003: 24) as follows:

> Most strategies, like most mergers, fail not because of poor thinking, but because of poor implementation. Implementation failures usually involve the failure to acknowledge and build the needed skills and organizational capabilities, to gain support of the workforce, and to support the organizational changes and learning required to behave in new ways. In short, execution failures are often the result of poor human capital management. This opens the door for HR to add important value if it can deliver change strategies, plans and thinking that aid in the development and execution of business strategy.

Implementing change can indeed be difficult. Research by Carnall (1991) in 93 organizations identified the following explanations for failures to implement change effectively:

- implementation took more time than originally allowed;
- major problems that had not been identified beforehand emerged during implementation;
- co-ordination of implementation activities was not effective enough;
- competing activities and other crises distracted management from implementing the change decision;
- the capabilities of the employees involved were not sufficient;
- training and instruction to lower-level employees was inadequate;
- uncontrollable factors in the external environment had an adverse effect on implementation.

The following suggestions on how to minimize such problems were put forward by Nadler and Tushman (1980):

- *Motivate* in order to achieve changes in behaviour by individuals.
- *Manage the transition* by making organizational arrangements designed to ensure that control is maintained during and after the transition and by developing and communicating a clear image of the future.
- *Shape the political dynamics of change* so that power centres develop that support the change rather than block it.
- *Build in stability* of structures and processes to serve as anchors for people to hold on to – organizations and individuals can only stand so much uncertainty and turbulence, hence the emphasis by Quinn (1980) on the need for an incremental approach.

As reported by Surowiecki (2013: 44), Professor Michael Roberto of Bryant University suggested that: 'Any time you are trying to change the ways you do things, small wins are important. Small wins help you to build support both internally and externally, and they make it easier for people to buy in.'

The role of HR in facilitating change was described by Vere and Butler (2007: 34) as follows:

- The issue needs to be on the strategic business agenda and managers must see how action will improve business results: that is, there needs to be a sound business case for the initiative. HR managers need to be able to demonstrate the return on the planned investment.
- The change needs to have the active backing of those at the top of the organization, so it is for the HR director to gain the commitment of the top team and engage them in a practical way in taking the work forward.
- HR needs to engage managers in the design of change from the outset (or, if this is a business-driven change, HR needs to be involved at the outset).
- The programme needs to be framed in the language of the business in order to have real meaning and achieve 'buy in' for all parties; if there is too much HR jargon, this will be a turn-off.
- Project and people management skills are crucial to ensure the programme is well planned and resourced and that risks are assessed and managed.
- As in all change programmes the importance of communication is paramount in order to explain, engage and commit people to the programme.
- In this respect, the crucial role that HR can play is to ensure that employees are fully engaged in the design and implementation of the change.
- HR needs to draw on others' experience and learning.

The role of line managers in implementing HR strategy

HR strategy has to be converted into policies and practices and these have to be implemented by line managers. Purcell *et al* (2003: 72) pointed out that: 'Implementing and enacting policies is the task of line managers. The way they exercise leadership in the sense of communicating, solving problems, listening to suggestions, asking people's opinions, coaching and guiding, and controlling lateness, absence and quality make the vital difference.'

Jonathon Trevor (2011) established through his research into the implementation of reward strategy that, too often, line managers compromised, even sabotaged, the implementation of HR strategies because they were not convinced that they were necessary, or lacked the skills or motivation to put them into practice. It could be said that HR may *propose* but line managers *dispose* – line managers can bring HR policies to life but they can also put them to death.

There are three ways of dealing with this problem: 1) involve line managers in the development of HR strategy – bear in mind that things done *with* line managers are much more likely to work than things done *to* line managers; 2) ensure that the HR policies they are expected to put into practice are *manageable* with the resources available; 3) provide them with the training and on-the-spot guidance they need.

The partnership role of HR in implementing strategy

HR has to adopt a partnership approach with line managers when implementing the strategy. This is a necessary component of the role besides the more obvious activities of communicating the strategy, setting up and managing involvement programmes, coaching and training, monitoring implementation, evaluating the effectiveness of the strategy and proposing any remedial action required.

Partnership means working with line managers using a joint approach to dealing with issues, solving problems and, importantly, introducing new HR policies and practices. Traditionally, many HR specialists have tended to lay down the law to their line manager clients: 'This is the policy, this is what you have to do about it, this is how I am going to help you.' In a partnership mode, they will still explain what the policy is and what the responsibilities of the manager are in implementing it, and they will still provide guidance and advice. But in adopting a partnership approach the HR professional will be more concerned with understanding the particular preoccupations and concerns of individual managers, and working alongside them to produce a joint agreement on how to proceed based on that understanding. It will be a matter of agreeing rather than prescribing.

When acting as partners HR specialists need to demonstrate to line managers that they understand the situation in which the latter operate and the pressures they face. HR people need to be appreciated as colleagues who understand the business and will listen to managers when they make suggestions or express doubts about a new policy. They will discuss possible approaches and even agree modifications to fit particular circumstances, as long as these do not fundamentally affect the policy. They will work alongside line managers when the new policy is being introduced – not as prescriptive trainer but as, in effect, a coach.

An HR specialist interviewed by Pritchard (2010: 182) gave the following advice on partnership:

> I think the way you change their [the business clients'] behaviours in the longer term is by getting to be a trusted advisor, and the way to become a trusted advisor is to know your individual, to know your client and to know how to hook the individual, right?

STRATEGIC HRM IN ACTION

Implementing HRM strategy: change management at the Children's Trust

A few years ago the Children's Trust was facing a chronic skills shortage, high staff turnover and loss of morale. There was a culture of avoidance when it came to tackling difficult HR issues such as poor performance or sickness absence. There was also a 'can't do' attitude, because people were constantly under pressure as a result of staff shortages. Following the change programme summarized below, which was planned and managed by the new head of HR, the Children's Trust has won awards from both *Charity Times* and *Nursing Times* for being a great place to work, based on the views of its staff. The change programme consisted of a series of sensible, well-planned HR interventions, spearheaded by the head of HR and implemented gradually over 18 months with the full backing of the board.

The main features of the change programme were:

- HR issues were put on the senior team's agenda, which met more often and considered issues such as recruitment and retention.

- A development programme for senior managers was delivered by an external consultancy to help them improve their skills and confidence; it included a training needs analysis, psychometric testing and 360-degree appraisal.

- Everything was done in a low-key, non-threatening way that emphasized development opportunities rather than the need for change.

- Nurses and carers were asked what they liked about working for the Children's Trust and they said that they had time to build relationships and really care for the children, that there was high-quality training on offer – and that 'everyone smiles around here'.
- These personal testimonials were used to devise new recruitment campaigns for nurses and, as a result, the number of job applications soon increased, helped by a recruitment video filmed at the Children's Trust.
- Pay scales for carers were reviewed and the time it would take them to reach higher rates was shortened.
- The trust's NVQ course in health and social care was developed and it became an accredited centre, able to issue its own awards.
- New job descriptions were produced with five to seven headings detailing their accountabilities, plus a series of behavioural competencies.
- A new performance management system was implemented.
- Better sick pay was provided, combined with tools to help managers handle absence more effectively – with the result that sickness absence fell by 10 per cent in the first year and 12 per cent in the next year.
- A fast-track nursing training programme was developed to build a cavalry of cross-trained nurses that would allow the trust to react quickly to changing circumstances.

SOURCE: Armstrong, M (2010) *Essential Human Resource Management Practice*, Kogan Page, London

KEY LEARNING POINTS

A good strategy is one that works.

- The problem with SHRM is that too often there is a gap between what the strategy says will be achieved and what is actually done.
- To provide for the effective delivery of HRM strategy it is necessary to:
  - formulate practical strategies;
  - involve people;
  - communicate;
  - build skills;
  - monitor and evaluate.

- The implementation of HR strategy involves change, which can be hard to introduce and may be resisted.
- The role of HR in facilitating change is to:
  - produce a sound business case;
  - gain the commitment of top management;
  - engage managers in the design of change from the outset;
  - frame the programme in the language of the business;
  - deploy effective project and people management skills;
  - ensure that employees are fully engaged in the design and implementation of the change;
  - draw on others' experience and learning.
- HRM strategies have to be converted into policies and practices and these have to be implemented by line managers.
- HR has to adopt a partnership approach with line managers when implementing the strategy. Partnership involves working with line managers using a joint approach to dealing with issues, solving problems and, importantly, introducing new HR policies and practices.

References

Carnall, C (1991) *Managing Change*, Routledge, London

Dickens, C (2004 [1843]) *Martin Chuzzlewit*, Penguin, London

Gratton, L A, Hailey, V H, Stiles, P and Truss, C (1999) *Strategic Human Resource Management*, Oxford University Press, Oxford

Kanter, R M (1984) *The Change Masters*, Allen & Unwin, London

Lawler, E E and Mohrman, S A (2003) HR as a strategic partner: what does it take to make it happen?, *Human Resource Planning*, **26** (3), pp 15–29

Nadler, D A and Tushman, M L (1980) A congruence model for diagnosing organizational behaviour, in *Resource Book in Macro-organizational Behaviour*, ed R H Miles, Goodyear Publishing, Santa Monica, CA

Pritchard, K (2010) Becoming an HR strategic partner: tales of transition, *Human Resource Management Journal*, **20** (2), April, pp 175–88

Purcell, J, Kinnie, K, Hutchinson, S, Rayton, B and Swart, J (2003) *Understanding the People and Performance Link: Unlocking the black box*, CIPD, London

Quinn, J B (1980) Managing strategic change, *Sloane Management Review*, **11** (4/5), pp 3–30

Surowiecki, J (2013) The turnaround trap, *The New Yorker*, 25 March, p 44

Trevor, J (2011) *Can Pay be Strategic?*, Palgrave Macmillan, Basingstoke

Vere, D and Butler, L (2007) *Fit for Business: Transforming HR in the public service*, CIPD, London

PART THREE
HRM strategies related to organizational capability and organizational and individual performance

Organization development strategy

08

KEY CONCEPTS AND TERMS

Behavioural science   Organizational/corporate culture
Culture change   Organization development
Organization capability   Organizational transformation

LEARNING OUTCOMES

On completing this chapter you should be able to define these key concepts. You should also understand:

- the nature of organization development;
- the nature of organization development strategy;
- the process of formulating and implementing organization development strategy;
- the process of managing cultural change.

Introduction

Organization development strategy is concerned with what needs to be done to improve how well the business functions. This chapter starts with a definition of organization development and a brief description of the processes involved. It continues with an examination of the purpose and content of an organization development strategy and concludes with a discussion of an important aspect of organization development – the management of culture change.

Organization development defined

Organization development is a systematic approach to improving organizational capability, ie the capacity of an organization to function effectively in order to achieve desired results. It is concerned with process – how things get done. An early definition by Beer (1980: 10) stated that organization development operates as 'a system-wide process of data collection, diagnosis, action planning, intervention and evaluation'.

The CIPD (2010: 1) defined organization development as a 'planned and systematic approach to enabling sustained organization performance through the involvement of its people'.

The original version of organization development, or 'OD' as it was known, was based on behavioural science concepts relating to the study of human behaviour. It was practised through what were called 'interventions'. During the 1980s and 1990s a number of other approaches were developed. More attention was paid to culture-change activities and organization-wide processes such as high-performance working and total quality management (TQM). Further changes occurred in the next decade, during which a more strategic focus was adopted and business-orientated activities such as smart working came to the fore.

Organization development activities

There is a wide range of organization development activities, as shown in Table 8.1.

TABLE 8.1 Organization development activities

Organization Development Activity	Brief Description	Objective
Business model innovation	The process followed by an organization to develop a new business model or change an existing one.	To obtain insight into the business issues facing the organization, leading to plans for practical interventions that address those issues.

(Continued)

TABLE 8.1 *Continued*

Organization Development Activity	Brief Description	Objective
Change management	The process of planning and introducing change systematically, taking into account the likelihood of it being resisted.	To achieve the smooth implementation of change.
Culture change	The process of changing the organization's culture in the shape of its values, norms and beliefs.	To improve the ability of an organization to achieve its goals by making effective use of the resources available to it and to ensure that the organization's core values are put into practice.
Engagement, enhancement of	The development of improved levels of job and organizational engagement.	To ensure that people are committed to their work and the organization and motivated to achieve high levels of performance.
High-performance working*	Developing work system processes, practices and policies to enable employees to perform to their full potential.	To impact on the performance of the organization through its people in such areas as productivity, quality, levels of customer service, growth and profits.

(Continued)

TABLE 8.1 *Continued*

Organization Development Activity	Brief Description	Objective
Knowledge management	Storing and sharing the wisdom, understanding and expertise accumulated in an organization about its processes, techniques and operations.	To get knowledge from those who have it to those who need it in order to improve organizational effectiveness.
Lean*	A process improvement methodology, which focuses on continuous improvement, reducing waste and ensuring the flow of production.	To deliver value to customers.
Organizational learning	The acquisition and development of knowledge, understanding, insights, techniques and practices.	To facilitate performance improvement and major changes in strategic direction.
Organization design	The process of deciding how organizations should be structured in terms of the ways in which the responsibility for carrying out the overall task is allocated to individuals and groups of people and how the relationships between them function.	To ensure that people work effectively together to achieve the overall purpose of the organization.

(Continued)

TABLE 8.1 *Continued*

Organization Development Activity	Brief Description	Objective
Performance management	A systematic process involving the agreement of performance expectations and the review of how those expectations have been met.	To improve organizational performance by developing the performance of individuals and teams.
Smart working*	An approach to organizing work that through a combination of flexibility, autonomy and collaboration, in parallel with optimizing tools and working environments for employees.	To drive greater efficiency and effectiveness in achieving job outcomes.
Team building	Using interactive skills training techniques to improve the ways in which people in teams work together.	To increase group cohesion, mutual support and co-operation.
Total rewards	The combination of financial and non-financial rewards available to employees. It involves integrating the various aspects of reward.	To blend the financial and non-financial elements of reward into a cohesive whole so that together they make a more powerful and longer-lasting impact on job satisfaction and performance.

* Covered in more detail in Chapter 12

Organization development strategy defined

The strategic nature of organization development is based on the role it can play in the implementation of business strategy. For example, business model innovation as a strategy could result in the need for new organization processes. This would involve organization development and change management activities.

Organization development strategy sets out intentions on how the organization is going to cope with new demands arising from system-wide change, the management of culture change and the need to improve organizational processes involving people such as teamwork and communications. These intentions will be converted into actions on structure design, systems development and, possibly, organization development-type interventions.

Formulating and implementing organization development strategy

The formulation and implementation of organization development strategy can take place through the process of integrated strategic change as conceived by Worley, Hitchin and Ross (1996). The steps required are:

1 Carry out strategic analysis, a review of the organization's strategic orientation (its strategic intentions within its competitive environment) and a diagnosis of the organization's readiness for change.

2 Develop strategic capability – the ability to implement the strategic plan quickly and effectively.

3 Integrate individuals and groups throughout the organization into the processes of analysis, planning and implementation in order to maintain the firm's strategic focus, direct attention and resources to the organization's key competencies, improve co-ordination and integration within the organization and create higher levels of shared ownership and commitment.

4 Create the strategy, gain commitment and support for it and plan its implementation.

5 Implement the strategic change plan, drawing on knowledge of motivation, group dynamics and change processes, dealing with issues such as alignment, adaptability, teamwork and organizational and individual learning.

6 Allocate resources, provide feedback and solve problems as they arise.

Culture change

The implementation of organization development strategy can involve a cultural change programme. The aim of such a programme is to ensure that people are aware of what the change involves for them and that they will act accordingly. The change programme may be wide-ranging, aimed at the development of a strong and pervasive culture that will keep organization members pulling in the same direction. This could take the form of transformational change involving fundamental and comprehensive alterations in structures, processes and behaviours that have a dramatic effect on the ways in which the organization functions. Or it may focus on a specific issue, for example in a bank, ensuring that all its operations, especially those in its foreign exchange trading function, conform to the values of integrity and fair dealing that have been espoused by top management. However, because cultural values and norms are often deeply embedded, a change programme can present considerable difficulties. To mitigate these problems the following steps need to be taken:

1 *Analysis*: an analysis of the existing culture. This could make use of a diagnostic tool such as the *Organizational Culture Inventory* devised by Cooke and Lafferty (1989).

2 *Diagnosis*: a review of the analysis to identify any cultural issues or problems.

3 *Definition of the desired culture*: this might take the form of a statement of core values, as produced by Johnson & Johnson (see box).

STRATEGIC HRM IN ACTION

Statement of core values by Johnson & Johnson

We believe our first responsibility is to the doctors, nurses and patients, to mothers and all others who use our products and services.

- Our suppliers and distributors must have an opportunity to make a fair profit.
- We must respect the dignity of our employees and recognize their merit.
- We must maintain in good order the property we are privileged to use, protecting the environment and natural resources.

SOURCE: Aguilar, E and Bhambri, A (1983) *Johnson & Johnson*, HBS Case Services, Boston

4 *Plan the action required*: this could include communicating the details of the change covering how people will be affected and the part they are expected to play in implementing it, and briefing and educational programmes.

5 *Implement*: this is where HR can play a major part.

6 *Monitor*: review how well the change has been or is being implemented and take corrective action if it is not going according to plan.

A successful change programme is more likely to be achieved if top management demonstrates its commitment to the change, plays a major part in implementing it and is seen to be acting in accordance with the values associated with the change. Involving managers and other employees in each of the six steps set out above is very desirable.

HR specialists help by acting as change agents to facilitate the change. A change agent was defined by Caldwell (2001: 139–40) as 'an individual or team responsible for initiating, sponsoring, managing and implementing a specific change initiative or complete change programme'. Alfes *et al* (2010) noted that change agents establish what is required, involve people in planning and managing change, advise on how change should be implemented and communicate to people the implications of change.

Ulrich (1997: 7) observed that HR professionals should be 'as explicit about culture change as they are today about the requirements for a successful training programme or hiring strategy.' He later emphasized that: 'HR should become an agent of continuous transformation, shaping processes and a culture that together improve an organization's capacity for change' (Ulrich, 1998: 125).

STRATEGIC HRM IN ACTION

Managing culture change at Cisco

The management of Cisco, the global technology giant, spanning 62 countries with over 12,000 employees working in 62 countries, wanted to steer the company towards a more collaborative leadership culture, fully embracing the company's own virtual communications technology. The strategic aim was to ensure that leaders exhibited the essential behaviours for a globally connected business. This heralded a move away from autocratic leadership towards collaborative leadership, from functions and silos in isolated country branches to cross-departmental, global team working.

Leaders who once ran a small team in a single office could now find themselves leading a team of remote workers dispersed around the globe. It was necessary to ensure that leaders could still lead in this new kind of environment.

Leaders were given the freedom to translate organizational change as they saw fit within their regions, but they had to demonstrate that they were viable and in touch. HR's role in this development was to guide and support business leaders, but the process is continually evolving.

SOURCE: *People Management* (2011), April, pp 30–32

KEY LEARNING POINTS

Organization development is a systematic approach to improving organizational capability, ie the capacity of an organization to function effectively in order to achieve its objectives.

- The strategic nature of organization development is based on the role it can play in the implementation.
- Organization development strategy is concerned with mapping out intentions on how the organization is going to cope with new demands; on system-wide change in fields such as reward and performance management; on how change should be managed; on what needs to be done to improve organizational processes involving people such as teamwork, communications and participation, and how the organization can acquire and retain the right people.
- The implementation of an organization development strategy may involve a culture change management programme.

References

Alfes, K, Truss, C, Soane, E C, Rees, C and Gatenby, M (2010) *Creating an Engaged Workforce*, CIPD, London

Beer, M (1980) *Organization Change and Development: A systems view*, Goodyear, Santa Monica CA

Caldwell, R (2001) Champions, adapters, consultants and synergists: the new change agents in HRM, *Human Resource Management Journal*, **11** (3), pp 39–52

Chartered Institute of Personnel and Development (2010) *Organization Development Fact Sheet*, CIPD, London

Cooke, R and Lafferty, J (1989) *Organizational Culture Inventory*, Human Synergistic, Michigan

Ulrich, D (1997) Judge me more by my future than my past, *Human Resource Management*, **36** (1), pp 5–8

Ulrich, D (1998) A new mandate for human resources, *Harvard Business Review,* January–February, pp 124–34

Worley, C, Hitchin, D and Ross, W (1996) *Integrated Strategic Change: How organization development builds competitive advantage*, Addison-Wesley, Reading, MA

Human capital management strategy

09

KEY CONCEPTS AND TERMS

Evidence-based human resource management
Human capital
Human capital management

LEARNING OUTCOMES

On completing this chapter you should be able to define these key concepts. You should also understand:

- the meaning and significance of human capital management (HCM);
- the aims of HCM;
- the role of HCM strategy;
- the link between HCM and business strategy;
- developing an HCM strategy.

Introduction

Human capital management (HCM) is concerned with obtaining, analysing and reporting on data that informs the direction of people management strategy. An HCM strategy is therefore closely associated with strategic HRM. Manocha (2005: 29) suggested that it can also provide 'evidence of a robust people strategy mapped to the business strategy'.

HCM involves the use of metrics or HR analytics to guide an approach to managing people who are regarded as assets rather than costs. It emphasizes that competitive advantage is achieved by strategic investments in those assets through employee engagement and retention, talent management, and learning and development programmes. HCM is a bridge between HR and business strategy. It provides the basis for 'evidence-based human resource management', ie the process of ensuring that decisions and proposals on the development and application of HR strategies and practices are backed up with hard data derived from research, benchmarking and the analysis and evaluation of the organizational context and management activities.

The Accounting for People Task Force Report (2003: 3) stated that HCM involves 'the systematic analysis, measurement and evaluation of how people policies and practices create value'. In this report HCM was defined as 'an approach to people management that treats it as a high-level strategic issue rather than an operational matter 'to be left to the HR people' (2003: 7). The task force expressed the view that HCM had been underexploited as a way of gaining competitive edge.

Scarborough and Elias (2002: 3) defined human capital as 'something that employees bring to the organization but is also developed through training and experience within the organization'. Nalbantian *et al* (2004: 75) described human capital as: 'the accumulated stock of skills, experience and knowledge that resides in an organization's workforce and drives productive labour' and suggest that HCM involves 'putting into place the metrics to measure the value of these attributes and using that knowledge to effectively manage the organization'.

HCM is sometimes defined more broadly without the emphasis on measurement, and this approach makes it almost indistinguishable from strategic HRM. Chatzkel (2004: 139) claimed that: 'Human capital management is an integrated effort to manage and develop human capabilities to achieve significantly higher levels of performance.' Kearns (2004: 14) asserted that 'everything done in the name of HRM is done in the name of value'. He described HCM as: 'The total development of human potential expressed as organizational value.' He further emphasized that it is about creating value through people and that it is 'a people development philosophy, but the only development that means anything is that which is translated into value' (Kearns, 2004: 205).

Aims of HCM

The four fundamental objectives of HCM are:

1 To determine the impact of people on the business and their contribution to value.

2 To demonstrate that HR practices produce value for money in terms, for example, of return on investment.

3 To provide guidance on future HR and business strategies.

4 To provide data that will inform strategies and practices designed to improve the effectiveness of people management in the organization.

As Manocha (2005: 28) observed: 'Essentially, it [HCM] is a discipline that enables organizations to identify how their people contribute to and drive business performance.'

The role of HCM strategy

Human capital strategy was defined by Nalbantian *et al* (2004: 79) as 'a blueprint for securing, managing and motivating the workforce needed to support the organization's strategic goals. To be effective, the management practices that influence the workforce should be consistent with one another and mutually reinforcing.' The whole area of HCM presents both an opportunity and a challenge – an opportunity to recognize people as assets that contribute directly to organizational performance, and a challenge to develop the skills needed to identify, analyse and communicate that contribution and ensure it is recognized in business decision making. By developing strategies to generate better and more accurate information on human capital, and communicating this information both internally and externally, organizations not only will improve their business decision making but also enable stakeholders to make more accurate assessments about the long-term future performance of the organization. There is evidence of a growing demand, from the investment community in particular, for better information to explain intangible value. Many organizations are beginning to understand that, in an increasingly knowledge-intensive environment, the key to good management lies in understanding the levers that can be manipulated to change employee behaviour and develop commitment and engagement. This, in turn, encourages individuals to deliver discretionary behaviour or willingly share their knowledge and skills to achieve organizational goals.

An HCM strategy that includes the systematic collection and analysis of human capital data can help managers to begin to understand factors that will have a direct impact on the people they manage. It can also help executives to understand and identify areas in which there are issues regarding the effective management of staff, and to design management development programmes to address these.

The link between HCM and business strategy

HCM and business strategy are closely linked and an HCM approach provides guidance on both HR and business strategy. For example:

- 'By linking good HR practice and strategic management to human capital measurement firms are able to make a number of better informed decisions that will help to ensure long-term business success' (Scarborough and Elias, 2002: 17).
- 'If HR people can demonstrate they can articulate the worth and contribution of the organization's people by linking the human capital strategy to the overall business strategy, they will not only prove invaluable but play a part in improving management practices' (Manocha, 2005: 28).
- The HCM proposition 'emphasizes the connections and value flows between strategy, statistical analysis and the key stakeholders – employees, customers and investors' (Donkin, 2005: 3).

The issue is to determine what this link is and how to make it work. A proposition that HCM informs HR strategy, which in turn informs business strategy, tells us nothing about what is involved in practice. If we are not careful we are saying no more than that all business strategic plans for innovation, growth and price/cost leadership depend on people for their implementation. This is not a particularly profound or revealing statement and is in the same category as the discredited cliché 'Our people are our greatest asset.' We must try to be more specific, otherwise we are only doing things – such as more training, succession planning, performance management, performance-related pay and so on – in the hope rather than the expectation that they will improve business results.

One way of being more specific is to use HCM assessments of the impact of HR practices on performance in order to justify these practices and improve the likelihood that they will work. The future of HCM as a strategic management process largely depends on getting this done.

A second way to specify the link is to explore in more detail the people implications of business strategy and, conversely, the business implications of HR strategy. This can be done by analysing the elements of the business strategy and the business drivers, and deciding on the HR supporting activities and HCM data required, as illustrated in Table 9.1.

A third, and potentially the most productive, way to link HR and business strategy is to relate business results to HR practices in order to determine how they can best contribute to improving performance.

TABLE 9.1 Analysis of business strategy and business drivers

	Content of Business Strategy	HR Supporting Activities	Supporting Data Required
Business Strategy	• Growth – revenue/profit • Maximize shareholder value • Growth through acquisitions/mergers • Growth in production/servicing facilities • Product development • Market development • Price/cost leadership	• Human resource planning • Talent management • Skills development • Targeted recruitment • Retention policies • Leadership development	• Workforce composition • Attrition rates • Skills audit • Outcome of recruitment campaigns • Learning and development activity levels • Outcome of leadership surveys
Business Drivers	• Innovation • Maximize added value • Productivity	• Talent management • Skills development • Total reward management	• Balanced scorecard data • Added value ratios (eg added value per employee, added value per £ of employment cost) • Productivity ratios (eg sales revenue per employee, units produced or serviced per employee)

TABLE 9.1 *Continued*

Content of Business Strategy	HR Supporting Activities	Supporting Data Required
• Customer service • Quality • Satisfy stakeholders – investors, shareholders, employees, elected representatives	• Performance management • Develop high-performance /smart/agile working • Enhance motivation, engagement and commitment • Leadership development	• Outcomes of general employee opinion survey and other surveys covering engagement and commitment, leadership, reward management and performance management • Analysis of competence level assessments • Analysis of performance management assessments • Analysis of customer surveys • Analysis of outcomes of total quality programmes • Return on investment from training activities • Internal promotion rate • Succession planning coverage

Developing an HCM strategy

The programme for introducing HCM is illustrated in Figure 9.1.

FIGURE 9.1 Developing an HCM strategy

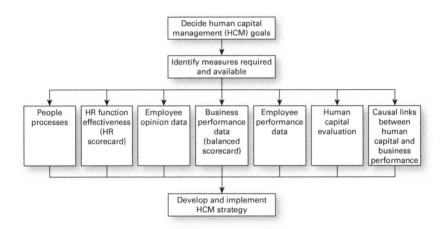

The development programme starts with a definition of the aims of the HCM strategy, for example, to:

- inform the development of business strategy;
- use HR analytics to prove that superior HRM strategies and processes deliver superior results;
- reinforce the belief that HRM strategies and processes create value through people;
- determine the impact of people on business results;
- assess the value of the organization's human capital to improve the effectiveness of HR;
- obtain, analyse and report on data that informs the direction of HR strategies and processes;
- provide data on the performance of the organization's human capital for the Operating and Financial Report;
- demonstrate that HR processes provide value for money.

The programme continues with the identification of possible measures and how they can be used, as set out in Table 9.2. The analysis of possible measures leads to the development of a strategy for introducing and using them. It is often best to start with information that is readily available and extend the range of data as experience is gained. And it is important to remember that it is the quality of the information that counts – not the quantity.

TABLE 9.2 Possible HCM measures and their use

Possible Measures	Possible Use – Analysis Leading to Action
Workforce composition – gender, race, age, full-time, part-time	• Analyse the extent of diversity • Assess the implications of a preponderance of employees in different age groups, eg extent of losses through retirement • Assess the extent to which the organization is relaying on part-time staff
Length of service distribution	• Indicate level of success in retaining employees • Indicate preponderance of long- or short-serving employees • Enable analyses of performance of more experienced employees to be assessed
Skills analysis/assessment – graduates, professionally/technically qualified, skilled workers	• Assess skill levels against requirements • Indicate where steps have to be taken to deal with shortfalls
Attrition – employee turnover rates for different categories of management and employees	• Indicate areas where steps have to be taken to increase retention rates • Provide a basis for assessing levels of commitment
Attrition – cost of	• Support business case for taking steps to reduce attrition
Absenteeism/sickness rates	• Identify problems and need for more effective attendance management policies
Average number of vacancies as a percentage of total workforce	• Identify potential shortfall problem areas

TABLE 9.2 *Continued*

Possible Measures	Possible Use – Analysis Leading to Action
Total payroll costs (pay and benefits)	• Provide data for productivity analysis
Compa-ratio – actual rates of pay as a percentage of policy rates	• Enable control to be exercised over management of pay structure
Percentage of employees in different categories of contingent pay or payment-by-result schemes	• Demonstrate the extent to which the organization believes that pay should be related to contribution
Total pay review increases for different categories of employees as a percentage of pay	• Compare actual with budgeted payroll increase costs • Benchmark pay increases
Average bonuses or contingent pay awards as a percentage of base pay for different categories of managers and employees	• Analyse cost of contingent pay • Compare actual and budgeted increases • Benchmark increases
Outcome of equal pay reviews	• Reveal pay gap between male and female employees
Personal development plans completed as a percentage of employees	• Indicate level of learning and development activity
Training hours per employee	• Indicate actual amount of training activity (note that this does not reveal the quality of training achieved or its impact)
Percentage of managers taking part in formal management development programmes	• Indicate level of learning and development activity
Internal promotion rate (percentage of promotions filled from within)	• Indicate extent to which talent management programmes are successful

(Continued)

TABLE 9.2 *Continued*

Possible Measures	Possible Use – Analysis Leading to Action
Succession planning coverage (percentage of managerial jobs for which successors have been identified)	• Indicate extent to which talent management programmes are successful
Percentage of employees taking part in formal performance reviews	• Indicate level of performance management activity
Distribution of performance ratings by category of staff and department	• Indicate inconsistencies, questionable distributions and trends in assessments
Accident severity and frequency rates	• Assess health and safety programmes
Cost savings/revenue increases resulting from employee suggestion schemes	• Measure the value created by employees
Measures of impact of HR practices	• Evaluation of effectiveness

STRATEGIC HRM IN ACTION

Use of HCM measures in Standard Chartered Bank

Standard Chartered Bank began at the strategic level when it came to designing HCM measures. Their starting point for the development of metrics was the identification of people levers for the achievement of business strategy. Next, the bank set out a series of questions designed to inform progress against these people levers. The bank has avoided reporting on data that is readily available but does not address the strategic business questions that had been identified.

SOURCE: Baron, A and Armstrong, M (2007) *Human Capital Management: Achieving added value through people*, Kogan Page, London

KEY LEARNING POINTS

- *Human capital management defined*
  Human capital management (HCM) is concerned with obtaining, analysing and reporting on data that informs the direction of value-adding people management.

  HCM involves the systematic analysis, measurement and evaluation of how people policies and practices create value.

- *Objectives of HCM*
  The four fundamental objectives of HCM are:

  - To determine the impact of people on the business and their contribution to value.
  - To demonstrate that HR practices produce value for money in terms, for example, of return on investment.
  - To provide guidance on future HR and business strategies.
  - To provide data that will inform strategies and practices designed to improve the effectiveness of people management in the organization.

By developing strategies to generate better and more accurate information on human capital, and communicating this information both internally and externally, organizations not only will improve their business decision making but also enable stakeholders to make more accurate assessments about the long-term future performance of the organization.

- *HCM strategy*
  An HCM strategy that includes the systematic collection and analysis of human capital data can help managers to begin to understand factors that will have a direct impact on the people they manage. HCM assessments of the impact of HR practices on performance can be used to justify these practices and improve the likelihood that they will work.

- *Developing an HCM strategy*
  The development programme starts with a definition of the aims of the HCM strategy, for example, to:

  - obtain, analyse and report on data that informs the direction of HR strategies and processes;
  - inform the development of business strategy;
  - use measurements to prove that superior HRM strategies and processes deliver superior results;

- reinforce the belief that HRM strategies and processes create value through people;
- determine the impact of people on business results;
- assess the value of the organization's human capital;
- improve the effectiveness of HR;
- provide data on the performance of the organization's human capital for the Operating and Financial Report;
- demonstrate that HR processes provide value for money.

The programme continues with the identification of possible measures and how they can be used. The analysis of possible measures leads to the development of a strategy for introducing and using them. It is often best to start with information that is readily available and extend the range of data as experience is gained.

References

Accounting for People Task Force (2003) *Accounting for People*, DTI, London

Chatzkel, J L (2004) 'Human capital: the rules of engagement are changing', *Lifelong Learning in Europe*, **9** (3), pp 139–45

Donkin, R (2005) *Human Capital Management: A management report*, Croner, London

Kearns, P (2004) *Human Capital Management*, Personnel Today, London

Manocha, R (2005) Grand totals, *People Management*, 7 April, pp 27–31

Nalbantian, R, Guzzo, R A, Kieffer, D and Doherty, J (2004), *Play to Your Strengths: Managing your internal labour markets for lasting competitive advantage*, McGraw-Hill, New York

Scarborough, H and Elias, J (2002) *Evaluating Human Capital*, CIPD, London

Knowledge management strategy

10

KEY CONCEPTS AND TERMS

Communities of practice
Explicit knowledge
Knowledge management
Tacit knowledge

LEARNING OUTCOMES

On completing this chapter you should be able to define these key concepts. You should also understand about:

- the process of knowledge management;
- the sources and types of knowledge;
- the approaches to the development of knowledge management strategies;
- strategic knowledge management issues;
- the components of a knowledge management strategy.

Introduction

Knowledge management strategy plans how to capture an organization's collective expertise and distribute it to where it can be best used. It ensures that knowledge is shared, by linking people with people and by linking them to information so that they learn from experiences. This is in accordance with the resource-based view of the firm, which, as argued by Grant (1991), suggests that the source of competitive advantage lies within the firm (ie in its people and their knowledge), not in how it positions itself in the market. A successful company is a knowledge-creating company.

The process of knowledge management

Knowledge management was defined by Scarborough, Swan and Preston (1999: 1) as 'any process or practice of creating, acquiring, capturing, sharing and using knowledge, wherever it resides, to enhance learning and performance in organizations'. They suggested that it focuses on the development of firm-specific knowledge and skills that are the result of organizational learning processes. Knowledge management is concerned with both stocks and flows of knowledge. Stocks include expertise and encoded knowledge in computer systems. Flows represent the ways in which knowledge is transferred from people to people or from people to a knowledge database.

The purpose of knowledge management is to transfer knowledge from those who have it to those who need it in order to improve organizational effectiveness. It is concerned with storing and sharing the wisdom and understanding accumulated in an organization about its processes, techniques and operations. It treats knowledge as a key resource. It can be argued that, in the information age, knowledge rather than physical assets or financial resources is the key to competitiveness.

Knowledge management is as much if not more concerned with people and how they acquire, exchange and disseminate knowledge as it is about information technology. That is why it has become an important strategic HRM area. Scarborough, Swan and Preston (1999: 59) believe that HR specialists should have 'the ability to analyse the different types of knowledge deployed by the organization... (and) to relate such knowledge to issues of organizational design, career patterns and employment security'.

The concept of knowledge management is closely associated with intellectual capital theory in that it refers to the notions of human, social and organizational or structural capital. It is also linked to the concepts of organizational learning and the learning organization.

Sources and types of knowledge

Strategies for knowledge management should be founded on an understanding of the sources and types of knowledge to be found in organizations.

Knowledge can be stored in databanks and found in presentations, reports, libraries, policy documents and manuals. It can be moved around the organization through information systems and by traditional methods such as meetings, workshops, courses, 'master classes', written publications, disks, e-mails and social media. An intranet provides an effective medium for communicating knowledge.

As argued by Nonaka (1991) and Nonaka and Takeuchi (1995), knowledge is either explicit or tacit. Explicit knowledge can be codified – it is recorded and available and is held in databases, in corporate intranets and intellectual property portfolios. Tacit knowledge exists in people's minds. It is difficult to articulate in writing and is acquired through personal experience. Hansen, Nohria and Tierney (1999) suggested that it includes scientific or technological expertise, operational know-how, insights about an industry and business judgement. The main challenge in knowledge management is how to turn tacit knowledge into explicit knowledge.

Approaches to the development of knowledge management strategies

Two approaches to knowledge management have been identified by Hansen, Nohria and Tierney (1999):

- *The codification strategy*: knowledge is carefully codified and stored in databases where it can be accessed and used easily by anyone in the organization. Knowledge is explicit and a 'people-to-document' approach is used. This strategy is therefore document-driven. Knowledge is extracted from the person who developed it, made independent of that person and reused for various purposes. It will be stored in some form of electronic repository for people to use and allows many people to search for and retrieve codified knowledge without having to contact the person who originally developed it. This strategy relies largely on information technology to manage databases, and also on the use of the intranet.

- *The personalization strategy*: knowledge is closely tied to the person who has developed it and is shared mainly through direct person-to-person contacts. This is a 'person-to-person' approach that is concerned with tacit knowledge. The exchange is achieved by creating networks and encouraging face-to-face communication between individuals and teams by means of informal conferences, 'communities of practice' (groups of people bound together by shared expertise who meet together to share knowledge), workshops, brainstorming and one-to-one sessions.

The research conducted by Hansen, Nohria and Tierney established that companies that use knowledge effectively pursue one strategy predominantly and use the second strategy to support the first. Those who try to excel at both strategies risk failing at both.

Strategic knowledge management issues

The issues below need to be addressed in developing knowledge management processes:

The pace of change

How can the strategy ensure that knowledge management processes keep up with the pace of change and identify what knowledge needs to be captured and shared?

Relating knowledge management strategy to business strategy

Hansen, Nohria and Tierney (1999: 109) contended that it is not knowledge per se but the way it is applied to strategic objectives that is the critical ingredient in competitiveness: 'A company's knowledge management strategy should reflect its competitive strategy: how it creates value for customers, how that value supports an economic model, and how the company's people deliver on the value and the economics.'

Technology and people

Technology is central to organizations adopting a codification strategy. But for those following a broader and potentially more productive personalization strategy, IT assumes more of a supportive role. As Hansen, Nohria and Tierney (1999: 113) commented: 'In the codification model, managers need to implement a system that is much like a traditional library – it must contain a large cache of documents and include search engines that allow people to find and use the documents they need. In the personalization model, it's more important to have a system that allows people to find other people.'

Scarborough, Swan and Preston (1999: 35) suggested that 'technology should be viewed more as a means of communication and less as a means of storing knowledge'. Knowledge management is more about people than technology. As research by Davenport (1996) established, managers get two-thirds of their information from face-to-face or telephone conversations. There is a limit to how much tacit knowledge can be codified. In organizations relying more on tacit than explicit knowledge, a person-to-person approach works best, and IT can only support this process; it cannot replace it.

The significance of process and social capital and culture

A preoccupation with technology may mean that too little attention is paid to the processes (social, technological and organizational) through which knowledge combines and interacts in different ways (Blackler, 1995) The key process is the interactions between people. This is the social capital of an organization, ie the 'network of relationships [that] constitute a valuable resource for the conduct of social affairs' (Nahpiet and Ghoshal, 1998). Social networks can be particularly important to ensure that knowledge is shared. What is also required is another aspect of social capital, ie trust. People will not be willing to share knowledge with those whom they do not trust.

The culture of the company may inhibit knowledge sharing. The norm may be for people to keep knowledge to themselves as much as they can because 'knowledge is power'. An open culture will encourage people to share their ideas and knowledge.

Components of a knowledge management strategy

A knowledge management strategy could be concerned with organizational people management processes that help to develop an open culture. This will be one in which the values and norms emphasize the importance of sharing knowledge and that facilitates knowledge sharing through networks. It might aim to encourage the development of communities of practice, defined by Wenger and Snyder (2000: 139) as 'groups of people informally bound together by shared expertise and a passion for joint enterprise'. The strategy could refer to methods of motivating people to share knowledge – and rewarding those who do so. The development of processes of organizational and individual learning, including the use of seminars and symposia that will generate and assist in disseminating knowledge, could also be part of the strategy.

STRATEGIC HRM IN ACTION

Knowledge management
The 'communities of practice' approach at ABB
Engineering company ABB has made a considerable commitment to developing face-to-face communities among its service engineers.

The engineers always had an informal network whereby they telephoned each other for advice on technical problems, which was generally on a one-to-one basis. However, the company's senior management wanted to share knowledge more systematically and use it to add value.

Accordingly, they divided the engineers into three regional groups, each of which met for a day every month. Half of the time at these meetings was spent listening to ideas and updates about the company from their manager, and the other half involved running through reports prepared by the engineers. But after 12 months it was established that most participants were not completing their reports and that the meeting had become a top-down process.

The engineers then made a number of proposals, which were accepted. They minimized the reporting requirements so that a one-line e-mail would be acceptable; they elected the co-ordinator of each community from their own number; the agenda of meetings was driven much more by the needs of the engineers themselves; and the co-ordinators of the three groups met regularly to share experiences and ideas.

SOURCE: Easterby-Smith, M and Mikhailava, I (2012) Knowledge management in perspective, *People Management*, June, pp 34–37

KEY LEARNING POINTS

- *Knowledge management defined*
  Knowledge management involves transforming knowledge resources within organizations by identifying relevant information and then disseminating it so that learning can take place.

  Knowledge management is 'any process or practice of creating, acquiring, capturing, sharing and using knowledge, wherever it resides, to enhance learning and performance in organizations' (Scarborough, Swan and Preston, 1999).

- *Purpose of knowledge management*
  The purpose of knowledge management is to transfer knowledge from those who have it to those who need it in order to improve organizational effectiveness. Knowledge can be stored in databanks and found in presentations, reports, libraries, policy documents and manuals. Knowledge is either explicit or tacit.

- *Knowledge management strategy defined*
  Knowledge management strategy aims to capture an organization's collective expertise and distribute it to where it can be best used. It ensures that knowledge is shared, by linking people with people and by linking them to information so that they learn from documented experiences.

- *Approaches to knowledge management strategy*
  Two approaches can be taken to knowledge management: the codification strategy and the personalization strategy.

- *Strategic knowledge management issues*
  These are: the pace of change; relating knowledge management strategy to business strategy; technology and people; the significance of process and social capital and culture.

- *Components of a knowledge management strategy*
  A knowledge management strategy could be concerned with organizational people management processes that help to develop an open culture. It might aim to encourage the development of communities of practice.

References

Blackler, F (1995) Knowledge, knowledge work and experience, *Organization Studies*, **16** (6), pp 16–36

Davenport, T H (1996) Why re-engineering failed: the fad that forgot people, *Fast Company*, Premier Issue, pp 70–74

Grant, R M (1991) The resource-based theory of competitive advantage: implications for strategy formation, *California Management Review*, **33** (3), pp 14–35

Hansen, M T, Nohria, N and Tierney, T (1999) What's your strategy for managing knowledge?', *Harvard Business Review*, March–April, pp 106–16

Nahpiet, J and Ghoshal, S (1998) Social capital, intellectual capital and the organizational advantage, *Academy of Management Review*, **23** (2), pp 242–66

Nonaka, I (1991) The knowledge-creating company, *Harvard Business Review*, Nov–Dec, pp 96–104

Nonaka, I and Takeuchi, H (1995) *The Knowledge-Creating Company*, Oxford University Press, New York

Scarborough, H, Swan, J and Preston, J (1999) *Knowledge Management: A literature review*, Institute of Personnel and Development, London

Wenger, E and Snyder, W M (2000) Communities of practice: the organizational frontier, *Harvard Business Review*, January–February, pp 139–45

Corporate social responsibility strategy

Introduction

Corporate social responsibility (CSR) strategy is concerned with planning how to ensure that the organization conducts its business in an ethical way, taking account of the social, environmental and economic impact of its operations and going beyond compliance. As Windsor (2006: 99) commented: 'Ethical managers engage in impartial moral reflection beyond the law.'

Wood (1991: 695) reflected that: 'The basic idea of corporate social responsibility is that business and society are interwoven rather than distinct entities; therefore, society has certain expectations for appropriate business behaviour and outcomes.' CSR, as explained in this chapter, is largely a strategic matter, which impinges strongly on the behaviour of organizations as it affects their stakeholders. Strategic HRM has an important contribution to make.

CSR defined

As defined by McWilliams, Siegel and Wright (2006: 1) CSR refers to the actions taken by businesses 'that further some social good beyond the interests of the firm and that which is required by law'. CSR was described by Husted and Salazar (2006) as being concerned with 'the impact of business behaviour on society'. Porter and Kramer (2006: 83) argued that to advance CSR: 'we must root it in a broad understanding of the interrelationship between a corporation and society while at the same time anchoring it in the strategies and activities of specific companies'. They see CSR as a process of integrating business and society.

The rationale for CSR

The philosophy of CSR is largely based on stakeholder theory, which was originated by Freeman (1984). This proposes that managers should tailor their policies to satisfy a number of constituents, not just shareholders. Stakeholding is based on the idea that a company is responsible not just to its shareholders but to a plurality of groups. The inclusion of such groups assumes that they all have an interest in the operation of the company. Investors, employees, suppliers and customers come into this category.

The rationale for CSR as defined by Hillman and Keim (2001) is based on two propositions: first, there is a moral imperative for businesses to 'do the right thing' without regard to how such decisions affect firm performance (the social issues argument); and second, firms can achieve competitive advantage (achieving and sustaining better results than business rivals thus placing the firm in a competitive position) by tying CSR activities to primary stakeholders (the stakeholders argument). Their research in 500 firms implied that investing in stakeholder management may be complementary to shareholder value creation and could indeed provide a basis for competitive advantage, as important resources and capabilities are created that differentiate a firm from its competitors (the resource-based view). The arguments identified by Porter and Kramer (2006) that support CSR are:

- *The moral appeal*: companies have a duty to be good citizens.
- *Sustainability*: an emphasis on environmental and community stewardship. As expressed by the World Business Council for Sustainable Social Development (2006: 1), this involves 'meeting the needs of the present without compromising the ability of future generations to meet their own needs'.
- *Licence to operate*: every company needs tacit or explicit permission from government, communities and other stakeholders in order to do business.
- *Reputation*: CSR initiatives can be justified because they improve a company's image, strengthen its brand, enliven morale and even raise the value of its stock.

Much research has been conducted on the relationship between CSR and firm performance. Russo and Fouts (1997) found that there was a positive relationship between environmental performance, and Waddock and Graves (1997) established that CSR results in an improvement in firm performance. But McWilliams and Siegel (2001) discovered only a neutral relationship between CSR and profitability.

An opposing view was expressed forcibly by Theodore Levitt, marketing expert. In a *Harvard Business Review* article 'The dangers of social responsibility', Levitt (1958: 44) emphasized that: 'The essence of free market enterprise is to go after profit in any way that is consistent with its own survival as an economic system.' Milton Friedman (1970), the Chicago monetarist, expressed the same sentiment. His view was that the social responsibility of business is to maximize profits within the bounds of the law. He argued that the mere existence of CSR was an agency problem within the firm in that it was a misuse of the resources entrusted to managers by owners, which could be better used on value-added internal projects or returned to the shareholders.

But it can be argued, as do Moran and Ghoshal (1996), that what is good for society does not necessarily have to be bad for the firm, and what is good for the firm does not necessarily have to come at a cost to society. This notion may support a slightly cynical view that there is room for enlightened self-interest – doing well by doing good.

Strategic CSR defined

CSR can be an integral element of a firm's business and corporate-level differentiation strategies. Therefore, it should be considered as a form of strategic investment. Even when it is not directly tied to a product feature or production process, CSR can be viewed as a form of reputation building or maintenance. Baron (2001) pointed out that CSR is what a firm does when its business and marketing strategy is concerned with the public good. And Husted and Salazar (2006: 83) commented that: 'There are additional benefits that the firm extracts from a given level of social output… precisely because the firm has designed a strategy so as to appropriate such benefits.'

Strategic CSR is about deciding initially whether or not the firm should be involved in social issues and then creating a corporate social agenda – deciding what social issues to focus on and to what extent. Porter and Kramer (2006: 85) believe that: 'It is through strategic CSR that the company will make the greatest social impact and reap the greatest business benefits.' They also stress that: 'Strategy is always about making choices, and success in corporate social responsibility is no different. It is about choosing which social issues to focus on… organizations that make the right choices and build focused, proactive and integrated social initiatives in concert with their core strategies will increasingly distance themselves from the pack' (2006: 91). McWilliams and Siegel (2001) suggested that CSR activities should be included in strategy formulation and that the level of resources devoted to CSR be determined through cost/benefit analysis.

CSR strategy needs to be integrated with the business strategy but it is also closely associated with HR strategy. This is because it is concerned with ethical behaviour both outside and within the firm – with society generally and with the internal community. In the latter case this means creating a working environment where personal and employment rights are upheld and HR policies and practices provide for the fair and ethical treatment of employees.

CSR activities

CSR activities as listed by McWilliams, Siegel and Wright (2006) include incorporating social characteristics or features into products and manufacturing processes, adopting progressive HRM practices, achieving higher levels of environmental performance through recycling and pollution abatement and advancing the goals of community organizations.

Business in the Community (2007) surveyed the CSR activities of 120 leading British companies and summarized them under four headings:

- *Community*: skills and education, employability and social exclusion were frequently identified as key risks and opportunities. Other major activities were support for local community initiatives and being a responsible and safe neighbour.
- *Environment*: most companies reported climate change and resource-use as key issues for their business; 85 per cent of them managed their impacts through an environmental management system.

- *Marketplace*: the issues most frequently mentioned by companies were research and development, procurement and supply chain, responsible selling, responsible marketing and product safety. There was a rising focus on fair treatment of customers, providing appropriate product information and labelling, and on the impacts of products on customer health.

- *Workplace*: this was the strongest management performing area as most companies have established employment management frameworks that can cater for workplace issues as they emerge. Companies recognized the crucial role of employees to achieve responsible business practices. Increasing emphasis was placed on internal communications and training in order to raise awareness and understanding of why it is relevant to them and valuable for the business. Attention was being paid to health and well-being issues as well as the traditional safety agenda. More work was being done on diversity, both to ensure the business attracts a diverse workforce and to communicate the business care for diversity internally.

Business in the Community (2007) also reported a growing emphasis on responsible business as a source of competitive advantage when firms move beyond minimizing risk to creating opportunities.

STRATEGIC HRM IN ACTION

First Choice Homes Oldham – the 'live well' programme

By involving colleagues in setting up a health and well-being programme, First Choice Oldham created an action plan that has led to healthier, happier and better-motivated staff with improved physical and mental well-being. Priorities were set using sickness statistics, health and well-being information from a colleague survey and general health information from the borough of Oldham.

Staff can now access health and lifestyle assessments, a health kiosk, and help to stop smoking and, as a result, awareness of cancer risk and mental health has been raised.

Employee engagement has increased as healthier employees demonstrate higher levels of commitment, and sickness absence has been reduced.

SOURCE: *Business in the Community* [Online] www.bitc.org.uk/our-resources/case-studies [accessed 29 May 2015]

Role of HR

The CIPD (2003: 5) stated that: 'The way a company treats its employees will contribute directly to the picture of a company that is willing to accept its wider responsibilities.' The CIPD (2009: 2) also expressed the view that: 'HR has a key role in making CSR work. CSR without HR runs the risk of being dismissed as PR or shallow "window-dressing".' And CSR is an opportunity for HR to demonstrate a strategic focus and act as a business partner.

The arguments for HR people taking the CSR agenda seriously were summarized by the CIPD (2003, 2009) as follows:

- Companies are increasingly required to take account of the impact of their activities on society.
- The credibility of CSR is dependent on delivery, not on rhetoric, and HR is responsible for many of the key systems and processes (eg recruitment, training, communications) on which effective delivery depends.
- HR people have relevant knowledge and skills in relation to CSR, eg organizational learning and culture change.
- Managing trust and risk raises fundamental issues about how people are managed.
- CSR offers the HR community opportunities to demonstrate its strategic focus.
- HR policy and practice on the way an organization treats its employees – including what it does about diversity, employee representation and development – will contribute to the picture of a company that is willing to accept its wider responsibilities.
- HR already works at communicating and implementing ideas, policies, cultural and behavioural change across organizations. Its role in influencing attitudes and links with line managers and the top team mean it is ideally placed to do the same with CSR.

Developing a CSR strategy

The basis for developing a CSR strategy is provided by the Competency Framework of the CSR Academy (2006), which is made up of six characteristics:

- *Understanding society*: understanding how business operates in the broader context and knowing the social and environmental impact that the business has on society.

- *Building capacity*: building the capacity of others to help manage the business effectively. For example, suppliers understand the business's approach to the environment and employees can apply social and environmental concerns in their day-to-day roles.
- *Questioning business as usual*: individuals continually questioning the business in relation to a more sustainable future and being open to improving the quality of life and the environment.
- *Stakeholder relations*: understanding who the key stakeholders are, and the risks and opportunities they present. Working with them through consultation and taking their views into account.
- *Strategic view*: ensuring that social and environmental views are included in the business strategy such as that they are integral to the way in which the business operates.
- *Harnessing diversity*: respecting that people are different, which is reflected in fair and transparent business practices.

To develop and implement a CSR strategy based on these principles it is necessary to:

- Understand the business and social environment in which the firm operates.
- Understand the business and HR strategies and how the CSR strategy should be aligned to them.
- Know who the stakeholders are (including top management) and find out their views and expectations on CSR.
- Identify the areas in which CSR activities might take place by reference to their relevance in the business context of the organization and an evaluation of their significance to stakeholders.
- Prioritize as necessary on the basis of an assessment of the relevance and significance of CSR to the organization and its stakeholders and the practicalities of introducing the activity or practice.
- Draw up the strategy and make the case for it to top management and the stakeholders.
- Obtain approval for the CSR strategy from top management and key stakeholders.
- Communicate information on the whys and wherefores of the strategy, both comprehensively and regularly.
- Provide training to employees on the skills they need to use in implementing the CSR strategy.
- Measure and evaluate the effectiveness of CSR.

KEY LEARNING POINTS

- *CSR strategy defined*
  Corporate social responsibility (CSR) strategy is concerned with planning how to ensure that the organization conducts its business in an ethical way, taking account of the social, environmental and economic impact of how it operates and going beyond compliance.

- *Rationale for CSR*
  The philosophy of CSR is largely based on stakeholder theory, which was originated by Freeman (1984). This states that managers should tailor their policies to satisfy a number of constituents, not just shareholders.

  The rationale for CSR as defined by Hillman and Keim (2001) is based on two propositions: first, there is a moral imperative for businesses to 'do the right thing' without regard to how such decisions affect firm performance (the social issues argument); second, firms can achieve competitive advantage by tying CSR activities to primary stakeholders (the stakeholders argument).

- *Strategic CSR*
  CSR can be an integral element of a firm's business and corporate-level differentiation strategies. Therefore, it should be considered as a form of strategic investment.

  McWilliams and Siegel (2001) suggest that CSR activities be included in strategy formulation and that the level of resources devoted to CSR be determined through cost/benefit analysis.

- *CSR activities*
  CSR activities as listed by McWilliams, Siegel and Wright (2006) include incorporating social characteristics or features into products and manufacturing processes, adopting progressive HRM practices, achieving higher levels of environmental performance through recycling and pollution abatement, and advancing the goals of community organizations.

- *The role of HR*
  'The way a company treats its employees will contribute directly to the picture of a company that is willing to accept its wider responsibilities'; 'HR has a key role in making CSR work' (CIPD, 2003: 5; 2009: 2).

References

Baron, D (2001) Private policies, corporate policies and integrated strategy, *Journal of Economics and Management Strategy*, **10** (1), pp 7–45

Business in the Community (2007) [accessed 29 May 2015] *Benchmarking Responsible Business Practice* [Online] www.bitc.org.uk/our-resources/case-studies

Chartered Institute of Personnel and Development (2003) *Corporate Social Responsibility and HR's Role*, CIPD, London

Chartered Institute of Personnel and Development (2009) *Corporate Social Responsibility*, CIPD, London

CSR Academy (2006) *The CSR Competency Framework*, Stationery Office, Norwich

Freeman, R E (1984) *Strategic Management: A stakeholder perspective*, Prentice Hall, Englewood Cliffs, New Jersey

Friedman, M (1970) The social responsibility of business is to increase its profits, *New York Times Magazine*, September, p 13

Hillman, A and Keim, G (2001) Shareholder value, stakeholder management and social issues: what's the bottom line?, *Strategic Management Journal*, **22** (2), pp 125–39

Husted, B W and Salazar, J (2006) Taking Friedman seriously: maximizing profits and social performance, *Journal of Management Studies*, **43** (1), pp 75–91

Levitt, T (1958) The dangers of social responsibility, *Harvard Business Review*, September–October, pp 41–50

McWilliams, A and Siegel, D (2001) Corporate social responsibility: a theory of the firm perspective, *Academy of Management Review*, **26** (1), pp 117–27

McWilliams, A, Siegel, D S and Wright, P M (2006) Corporate social responsibility: strategic implications, *Journal of Management Studies*, **43** (1), pp 1–12

Moran, P and Ghoshal, S (1996) Value creation by firms, *Best Paper Proceedings*, Academy of Management Annual Meeting, Cincinnati, Ohio

Porter, M E and Kramer, M R (2006) Strategy and society: the link between competitive advantage and corporate social responsibility, *Harvard Business Review*, December, pp 78–92

Russo, M V and Fouts, P A (1997) A resource-based perspective on corporate environmental performance and profitability, *Academy of Management Review*, **40** (3), pp 534–59

Waddock, S A and Graves, S B (1997) The corporate social performance – financial performance link, *Strategic Management Journal*, **18** (4), pp 303–19

Windsor, D (2006) Corporate social responsibility: three key approaches, *Journal of Management Studies*, **43** (1), pp 93–114

Wood, D J (1991) Corporate social performance revisited, *Academy of Management Review*, **16** (4) 691–718

World Business Council for Sustainable Social Development (2006) *From Challenge to Opportunity: The role of business in tomorrow's society*, WBCSSD, Geneva

Organizational performance strategy

LEARNING OUTCOMES

On completing this chapter you should be able to define these key concepts. You should also understand more about:

- the process of managing performance;
- the strategic approach to managing organizational performance;
- the development of organizational capability;
- developing a high-performance culture;
- how HR strategies support the business performance strategy.

Introduction

Developing and implementing a strategy for the management of organizational performance is the continuing responsibility of top management who plan, organize, monitor and control activities and provide leadership to achieve strategic goals and satisfy the needs and requirements of stakeholders. Individual performance management systems (as covered in Chapter 10) play an important part. But they function within the context of what is done to manage organizational performance.

Top management will devise and implement the corporate strategy for improving organizational performance. But HR in its strategic role has an important part to play by being involved in both the formulation and implementation of the strategy. It is people who implement the corporate plan. To carry out this role it is necessary for members of the HR function, especially the more senior ones, to understand what is involved. This is strategic human resource management (SHRM) in action – HR strategies affecting performance (and they all do) must be integrated with the business strategy.

The process of managing organizational performance

As Gheorghe and Hack (2007: 17) observed: 'Actively managing performance is simply running a business – running the entire business as one entity. It is a continuous cycle of planning, executing, measuring results and planning the next actions. In the context of a larger strategic initiative, that means continuous improvement.' They noted that:

> The management of organizational performance is a strategic approach that takes place on a number of dimensions. It has to take account of the needs of multiple stakeholders, and makes use of business performance management systems. (Gheorghe and Hack, 2007: 18)

The dimensions of managing organizational performance

Sink and Tuttle (1990) stated that managing organizational performance includes five dimensions:

1 Creating visions for the future.
2 Planning – determining the present organizational state and developing strategies to improve that state.
3 Designing, developing and implementing improvement interventions.
4 Designing, redesigning, developing and implementing measurement and evaluation systems.
5 Putting support systems in place to reinforce progress.

The overall approach to managing organizational performance

The overall approach to managing organizational performance, as described in the rest of this chapter, is based on processes of strategic performance management supported by the use of a business performance management system. In general it is concerned with developing organizational capability through such processes as high-performance work systems; lean working; quality management; increasing agility; and the supporting HRM processes of talent management, learning and development, and the enhancement of engagement and motivation.

The strategic approach to managing organizational performance

A strategic approach to managing organizational performance means taking a broad and longer-term view of where the business is going and then managing performance in ways that ensure this strategic thrust is maintained. The objective is to provide a sense of direction in an often turbulent environment so that the business needs of the organization, and the individual and collective needs of its employees, can be met by the development and implementation of integrated systems for managing and developing performance.

Organizational performance management systems are strategic in the sense that they are aligned to the business strategy of the organization and support the achievement of its strategic goals. They focus on developing work systems and the working environment as well as developing individuals. To create the systems and make them function effectively it is necessary to ensure that the strategy is understood, including, as Kaplan and Norton (2000) put it: 'The crucial but perplexing processes through which intangible assets will be converted into tangible outcomes.' Kaplan and Norton originated the concept of the balanced score card to ensure that all aspects of the performance of a business could be understood and measured from four related perspectives: the customer, internal processes, innovation and learning, and finance. The notion of mapping strategy was also created by them.

Strategy maps show the cause-and-effect links by which specific improvements create desired outcomes. They describe the elements of the organization's systems and their interrelationships, and therefore provide a route map for systems improvement leading to performance improvement. They also give employees a clear line of sight into how their jobs are linked to the overall objectives of the organization, and provide a visual representation of a company's critical goals and the relationships between them that drive organizational performance. Bourne, Franco and Wilkes (2003) call them 'success maps' that act as diagrams showing the logic of how the goals of the organization interact to deliver overall performance. An example of a strategy map is given in Figure 12.1.

The strategy map in Figure 12.1 shows an overall objective to improve profitability as measured by return on capital employed. Directly below this

FIGURE 12.1 A strategy map

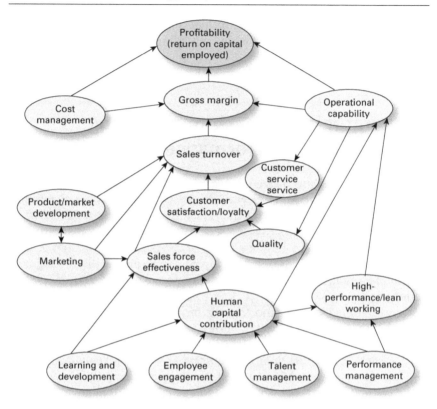

objective the map indicates that the main contributors to increased profitability are increases to the gross margin (the difference between the value of sales and the cost of sales), improvements to operational capability and better cost management. At the next level down the objective is to increase sales turnover in order to increase the gross margin. How this is to be achieved is set out in the next group of goals and their interconnections comprising increases in customer satisfaction and sales force effectiveness, innovations in product/market development and marketing, and improvements in customer service and quality levels. The key objective of improving operational capability is underpinned by developments in high-performance working and the contribution of the organization's human capital. The latter is supported by human resource management goals in the fields of performance management, talent management, employee engagement and learning and development.

The overall objective of increasing profitability in this example addresses the concerns of only one section of the stakeholders of an organization – the investors. This need would probably be given precedence by many quoted companies. But there are other goals, which relate to their other stakeholders, for example those related to corporate social responsibility (CSR). These could be catered for in separate strategy maps. Better still, they could be linked to their commercial goals. Public and voluntary sector organizations will certainly have goals, which relate to all their stakeholders as well as their overall purpose. A stakeholder approach to the strategic management of performance is required.

Organizational performance strategy is based on the resource-based view that it is the strategic development of the organization's rare, hard-to-imitate and hard-to-substitute human resources that produces its unique character and creates competitive advantage. The strategic goal will be to 'create firms that are more intelligent and flexible than their competitors' (Boxall, 1996) by developing more talented staff and by extending their skills base.

STRATEGIC HRM IN ACTION

A strategic approach to the management of organizational performance, as described by Johnson & Johnson

As we embarked on developing an integrated performance and development process into the organization, we knew that driving change and an enhanced process requires a cultural shift within an organization. The best performance management becomes a continuous process and is not a one-time event; it takes time and effort and a dedication to developing people. We also knew that from a business standpoint it was critical to build and develop the talent pipeline of the organization to meet the aggressive business goals and dynamically changing marketplace.

SOURCE: Wortzel-Hoffman, N and Boltizar, S (2007) Performance and development planning: a culture shift perspective, *Organization Development Journal*, **25** (2), pp 195–200

Implementing strategic organizational performance management

Strategic organizational performance management starts with a definition of the areas of activity and achievement that are most important to the organization. These could be called organizational key result areas. They might include all or a selection of the following:

- financial (profitability, shareholder value, cost control etc);
- market share;
- sales;
- productivity;
- quality;
- customer service;
- innovation;

- people management;
- CSR.

In each of these areas strategic goals are set to which individual goals can be aligned (as described in Chapter 13). Alignment is a key aspect of a performance management system for individuals.

Organizational capability

Organizational capability is the capacity of an organization to function effectively. It is about the ability of an organization to identify its critical success factors, guarantee high levels of performance for each of these factors, achieve its purpose, deliver results and meet the needs of its stakeholders. The development of organizational capability is concerned with the organization as a system, in line with the belief expressed by Coens and Jenkins (2002) that to 'focus on the overall "system" of the organization yields better results than [simply] trying to get individual employees to improve their performance'.

The aim is to increase organizational capability by improving organizational processes such as the formulation and implementation of strategy and the achievement of high quality and levels of customer service, facilitating the management of change and obtaining better performance from people, getting them to work well together.

This has to take place in a context in which organizations are increasingly embracing a new management culture based on inclusion, involvement and participation, rather than on the traditional command, control and compliance paradigm that Flaherty (1999) claimed 'cannot bring about the conditions and competence necessary to successfully meet the challenges of endless innovation, relentless downsizing, re-engineering and multicultural working holistically'. This new management paradigm requires the development of a high-performance work environment through management practices that value and support achievement, growth and learning. It also calls for facilitative behaviours that focus on employee empowerment, learning and development. In other words, it needs performance management.

Developing a high-performance culture

High-performance cultures are ones in which the improvement of performance levels is a way of life. The characteristics of such cultures are:

- Management defines what it requires in the shape of performance improvements, sets goals for success and monitors performance to ensure that the goals are achieved.

- People know what is expected of them – they understand their goals and accountabilities.
- People feel that their job is worth doing, and there is a strong fit between the job and their capabilities.
- There is strong leadership from the top, which engenders a shared belief in the importance of continuing improvement.
- There is a focus on promoting positive attitudes that result in an engaged, committed and motivated workforce.
- Work practices such as 'lean' are adopted and there is an emphasis on agility and flexibility.
- There is a climate of trust and teamwork, aimed at delivering a distinctive service to the customer.
- A clear line of sight exists between the strategic aims of the organization and those of its departments and its staff at all levels.

Organizations develop high-performance cultures through the systems of work they adopt, but these systems are managed and operated by people. Ultimately, therefore, high-performance working is about improving performance through people. But this process can be facilitated through such methods as high-performance work systems, smart working, agile working, lean manufacturing and organization restructuring, as described below.

High-performance work systems

A high-performance work system (HPWS) has been defined by Becker and Huselid (1998: 55) as: 'An internally consistent and coherent HRM system that is focused on solving operational problems and implementing the firm's competitive strategy.' They suggested that such a system 'is the key to the acquisition, motivation and development of the underlying intellectual assets that can be a source of sustained competitive advantage'.

The basic features of a HPWS were described by Shih, Chiang and Hsu (2005) as follows:

- *Job infrastructure*: workplace arrangements that equip workers with the proper abilities to do their jobs, provide them with the means to do their jobs and give them the motivation to do their jobs. These practices must be combined to produce their proper effects.
- *Training programmes to enhance employee skills*: investment in increasing employee skills, knowledge and ability.
- *Information sharing and worker involvement mechanisms*: to understand the available alternatives and make correct decisions.
- *Compensation and promotion opportunities that provide motivation*: to encourage skilled employees to engage in effective discretionary decision making in a variety of environmental contingencies.

STRATEGIC HRM IN ACTION

High-performance work systems

TABLE 12.1 High-performance work systems

Organization	High-performance working ingredients
Halo Foods	• A strategy that maintains competitiveness by increasing added value through the efforts and enhanced capability of all staff. • The integration of technical advance with people development. • Continuing reliance on teamworking and effective leadership, with innovation and self and team management skills.
Land Registry	• Organizational changes to streamline processes, raise skill levels and release talents. • Managers who could see that the problems were as much cultural as organizational. • Recruitment of people whose attitudes and aptitudes match the needs of high-performance work practices.
Meritor Heavy Vehicle Braking Systems	• Skill enhancement, particularly of management and self-management skills using competence frameworks. • Teamworking skills and experience used on improvement projects. • Linking learning, involvement and performance management.
Orangebox	• A strategy that relies on constant reinvention of operational capability. • Engagement and development of existing talent and initiative in productivity improvement. • Increasing use of cross-departmental projects to tackle wider opportunities.

TABLE 12.1 *Continued*

Organization	High-performance working ingredients
Perkinelmer	• A vision, and values, worked through by managers and supervisors. • Engagement of everyone in the organization and establishment of a continuous improvement culture. • Learning as a basis for change.
United Welsh Housing Association	• Linking of better employment relations with better performance. • Using staff experience to improve customer service. • Focusing management development on the cascading of a partnership culture.

SOURCE: Stevens, J (2005) *High Performance Wales: Real experiences, real success*, Wales Management Council, Cardiff

Developing a high-performance work system

The steps required are described below; the more that line managers and other employees can be involved at every stage the better:

1 *Analyse the business strategy*:
   - What is the business model?
   - Where is the business going? (What innovations to the model are planned?)
   - What are the strengths and weaknesses of the business?
   - What threats and opportunities face the business?
   - What are the implications of the above on the type of people required by the business, now and in the future?
   - To what extent do we – can we – obtain competitive advantage through people?

2 *Define the desired performance culture of the business and the objectives of the exercise*: refer to the characteristics of an effective performance culture set out earlier and produce a list of desirable characteristics that is aligned to the culture and context of the business, and a statement of the objectives of developing a HPWS.

3 *Analyse the existing arrangements*: start from the desirable characteristics defined at step 2 and analyse against each characteristic:

- What is happening now in the form of practices, attitudes and behaviours? (What do you want people to do differently?)
- What should be happening?
- What do people feel about it? (The more involvement in this analysis from all stakeholders the better.)

4 *Identify the gaps between what is and what should be*: clarify specific practices where there is considerable room for improvement.

5 *Draw up a list of practices that need to be introduced or improved*: at this stage only a broad definition should be produced of what ideally needs to be done.

6 *Establish links*: identify the practices that can be linked together in 'bundles' in order to complement and support one another.

7 *Assess practicality*: the ideal list of practices or, preferably, bundles of practices, should be subjected to a reality check:

- Is it worth doing? What is the business case in terms of added value? What contribution will it make to supporting the achievement of the organization's strategic goals?
- Can it be done?
- Who does it?
- Have we the resources to do it?
- How do we manage the change?

8 *Prioritize*: in the light of the assessment of practicalities, decide on the priorities that should be given to introducing new or improved practices. Adopt a realistic approach. There will be a limit on how much can be done at once or at any future time. Priorities should be established by assessing:

- the added value that the practice will create;
- the availability of the resources required;
- anticipated problems in introducing the practice, including resistance to change by stakeholders (too much should not be made of this, change can be managed, but there is much to be said for achieving some quick wins);
- the extent to which they can form bundles of mutually supporting practices.

9 *Define project objectives*: develop the broad statement of objectives produced at stage 2 and define *what* is to be achieved, why and how.

10 *Get buy in*: this should start at the top with the chief executive and members of the senior management team, but so far as possible it should extend to all the other stakeholders (best to involve them at earlier stages and communicate intentions in full).

11 *Plan the implementation*: this is where things become difficult. Deciding what needs to be done is fairly easy; getting it done is the hard part. The implementation plan needs to cover:
   – who takes the lead: this must come from the top of the organization as nothing will work without it;
   – who manages the project and who else is involved;
   – the timetable for development and introduction;
   – the resources (people and money required);
   – how the change programme will be managed, including communication and further consultation;
   – the success criteria for the project.

12 *Implement*: too often, 80 per cent of the time spent on introducing a HPWS is spent on planning and only 20 per cent on implementation. It should be the other way around. Whoever is responsible for implementation must have considerable project and change management skills.

Smart working

As defined by the CIPD (2008: 4), smart working is: 'An approach to organizing work that aims to drive greater efficiency and effectiveness in achieving job outcomes through a combination of flexibility, autonomy and collaboration, in parallel with optimizing tools and working environments for employees.' The characteristics of smart working are:

- self-management: a high degree of autonomy and a philosophy of empowerment;
- the use of virtual teams or work groups;
- focus on outcome-based indicators of performance;
- high-performance working;
- flexibility in work locations and hours;
- use of more advanced communications technology;
- hot-desking and working from home;
- ways of working that are underpinned by or drive high-trust working relationships;
- alignment of smart working with business objectives.

Typical smart-working arrangements identified by CIPD research include flexible working, high-performance working, 'lean manufacturing' and designing jobs in which there is a higher degree of freedom to act.

Agile working

Agile working is an approach to running a business that enables it to respond rapidly to change, new demands and increasing complexity. A report by the Economist Intelligence Unit (2009) stated that the characteristics of an 'agile' business were a high-performance culture; flexibility of management practices and resources; and organizational structures that support collaboration, rapid decision making and execution. Nearly 90 per cent of senior executives surveyed across the world by the Economist Intelligence Unit believe that organizational agility (ability to anticipate and address the forces affecting the business) is critical for business success.

STRATEGIC HRM IN ACTION

Agile working in Deloitte

Agile working in Deloitte, the professional services firm, is based on three principles:

1 *Outcomes, not inputs, matter*: the focus had to be shifted from the visibility of an individual in the office to the actual outputs of their work.
2 *Mutual trust*: an underlying assumption that the majority of employees are motivated, ambitious and are there to do a good job.
3 *Two-way open communication*: between the manager, other team members and the individual.

SOURCE: CIPD (2014) *HR: Getting smart about agile working*, CIPD, London

Research conducted by the CIPD (2014) found that the main methods that organizations use to achieve agility are:

- flexible working;
- providing the skills required to meet new demands through the use of multiskilling and rapid retraining;
- workforce planning to ensure that the supply of people matches requirements; improving leadership and management capability;
- organization restructuring.

Lean manufacturing

Lean manufacturing or lean production, often known simply as 'lean', is a process improvement methodology developed by Toyota in Japan. Lean focuses on reducing waste and ensuring the flow of production in order to deliver value to customers. It concentrates initially on the design of the process so that waste can be minimized during manufacture. It then examines operations to identify opportunities to improve the flow of production, remove wasteful practices and engage in continuous improvement. Various tools are available such as 'FiveS', a workplace methodology involving sorting, straightening, systematic cleaning, standardizing and sustaining. Reference to these enables a dialogue to take place with employees on how work should be done.

But as noted by the CIPD (2008: 11), the success of lean depends not so much on the tools but on its approach to work. Lean is implemented by communities of people who carry out and supervise the work and may include stakeholders such as customers. Lean team members are encouraged to think flexibly and be adaptable to change. They have a sense of ownership of what they do and achieve.

Organization restructuring

Organization restructuring is about enabling people to work effectively together. It means deciding how organizations should be structured in terms of the ways in which the responsibility for carrying out the overall task is allocated to individuals and groups of people, how the relationships between them function, and job design. There is no ideal structure, but in any organization that depends on innovation and the ability to cope with change and turbulence the best outcomes are likely to be achieved when the structure is informal with flat, lean and flexible horizontal processes. Roles should be flexible and enriched with more autonomy and teams should be self-managed.

How HR strategies enhance organizational performance

HR strategies enhance organizational performance first by making a significant contribution to the development of a high-performance culture through such methods as high-performance, smart or agile working. They may be involved in organization restructuring exercises and the operation of organization development programmes. Marsh, Sparrow and Hird (2010) suggested that organization design and organization development need to be merged into one HR capability, with organization design taking precedence.

Specifically, HR strategies help to ensure that the skilled, motivated and engaged people are available to implement corporate plans for improving organizational performance. These strategies (as considered elsewhere in this book) include those for individual performance management, resourcing (workforce planning), talent management, learning and development, and developing a positive employment relationship.

KEY LEARNING POINTS

- The management of organizational performance is the continuing responsibility of top management.

- But HR in its strategic role has an important part to play by being involved in both the formulation and implementation of the strategy.

- Actively managing performance is simply running a business.

- A strategic approach to managing organizational performance means taking a broad and longer-term view of where the business is going and then managing performance in ways that ensure that this strategic thrust is maintained.

- Strategic organizational performance management starts with a definition of the areas of activity and achievement that are most important to the organization.

- Organizational capability is the capacity of an organization to function effectively. The aim is to increase organizational capability by obtaining better performance from people, getting them to work well together, improving organizational processes such as the formulation and implementation of strategy and the achievement of high quality and levels of customer service, and facilitating the management of change.

- High-performance working is about improving performance through people. This can be done by the development and implementation of a high-performance culture through such methods as high-performance work systems and lean working, and by increasing the agility with which the organization responds to challenges and manages change.

- HR strategies enhance organizational performance by making a significant contribution to the development of a high-performance culture through such methods as high-performance, smart or agile working.

References

Becker, B E and Huselid, M A (1998) High performance work systems and firm performance: a synthesis of research and managerial implications, *Research on Personnel and Human Resource Management*, **16**, pp 53–101

Bourne, M, Franco, M and Wilkes, J (2003) Corporate performance management, *Measuring Business Excellence*, **7** (3), pp 15–21

Boxall, P F (1996) The strategic HRM debate and the resource-based view of the firm, *Human Resource Management Journal*, **6** (3), pp 59–75

CIPD (2008) *Smart Working: The impact of work organisation and job design*, CIPD, London

CIPD (2014) *HR: Getting smart about agile working*, CIPD, London

Coens, T and Jenkins, M (2002) *Abolishing Performance Appraisals: Why they backfire and what to do instead*, Berrett-Koehler, San Francisco

Economist Intelligence Unit (2009) [accessed 13 October 2014] Organisational Agility: How Business Can Survive and Thrive in Turbulent Times, *Economist Intelligence Unit* [Online] http://www. emc.com/collateral/leadership/ organisa-tional-agility-230309.pdf

Flaherty, J (1999) *Coaching: Evoking excellence in others*, Butterworth-Heinemann, Burlington MA

Gheorghe, C and Hack, J (2007) Unified performance management: how one company can tame its many processes, *Business Performance Management*, November, pp 17–19

Kaplan, R S and Norton, D P (2000) Having trouble with your strategy? Then map it, *Harvard Business Review*, September–October, pp 167–76

Marsh, C, Sparrow, P and Hird, M (2010) Improving organization design: the new priority for HR directors, in *Leading HR*, ed P Sparrow, A Hesketh, M Hird and C Cooper, pp 136–61, Palgrave Macmillan, Basingstoke

Shih, H-A, Chiang, Y-H and Hsu, C-C (2005) Can high-performance work systems really lead to better performance?, *Academy of Management Conference Paper*, pp 1–6

Sink, D S and Tuttle, T C (1990) The performance management question in the organization of the future, *Industrial Management*, **32** (1), pp 4–12

Individual performance management strategy

Introduction

Performance management for individuals is defined as a process of agreeing goals, aligning those goals with the strategic goals of the organization, planning performance to achieve the goals, reviewing and assessing progress, and developing the capabilities of individuals.

Individual performance management strategy is concerned with planning how a performance management system should be designed and operated. It operates as a strategic process because it enables individual and corporate goals to be aligned. Performance management is a powerful means of ensuring that the organization's strategic goals are achieved. It contributes to the achievement of culture change and it is integrated with other key HR activities, especially human capital management, talent management, learning and development, and reward management. Thus performance management helps to achieve horizontal integration and the 'bundling' of HR practices so that they are interrelated and therefore complement and reinforce each other. It can also play an important part in increasing levels of employee engagement.

The nature of a performance management system

The defining features of an effective performance management system are that it operates in accordance with a set of principles and is a continuous process.

Principles of performance management

The overarching principles governing effective performance management were defined as follows by Egan (1995):

> Most employees want direction, freedom to get their work done, and
> encouragement not control. The performance management system should be
> a control system only by exception. The solution is to make it a collaborative
> development system, in two ways. First, the entire performance management
> process – coaching, counselling, feedback, tracking, recognition, and so forth –
> should encourage development. Ideally, team members grow and develop
> through these interactions. Second, when managers and team members ask what
> they need to be able to do to do bigger and better things, they move to strategic
> development.

Strebler, Bevan and Robertson (2001) suggested that the principles set out below were required for performance management to work effectively:

- Have clear aims and measurable success criteria.
- Be designed and implemented with appropriate employee involvement.

- Be simple to understand and operate.
- Have its effective use core to all management goals.
- Allow employees a clear 'line of sight' between their performance goals and those of the organization.
- Focus on role clarity and performance improvement.
- Be closely allied to a clear and adequately resourced training and development infrastructure.
- Make crystal clear the purpose of any direct link to reward, and build in proper equity and transparency safeguards.
- Be regularly and openly reviewed against its success criteria.

Performance management as a continuous process

A performance management system, as modelled in Figure 13.1, flows from the organization's goals and then operates as a continuous and self-renewing cycle.

FIGURE 13.1 The performance management cycle

Performance management activities

The activities involved in operating the performance management cycle are described below.

Plan performance

The planning part of the performance management sequence starts by reaching agreement on a role profile. This involves two activities: first, the agreement of expectations in the form of the results, competencies and actions required, defined as performance and learning goals; second, the agreement of action plans to improve performance and to develop abilities. Together these constitute the performance agreement, which provides the basis for managing performance throughout the year and for guiding improvement and development activities. It is used as a reference point when reviewing performance.

Definition of role profiles

An important part of performance planning is the agreement or updating of a role profile for the role holder. A role profile defines key result areas; behavioural expectations described as competencies; and knowledge, skill and ability requirements.

Setting performance goals

Performance goals set out how individuals are expected to perform in terms of results. These goals are cascaded down from the goals of the organization to achieve strategic alignment. The expected results in the form of outputs (quantified results) or outcomes (a result that cannot necessarily be measured in quantified terms) will be defined within the framework of the role profile.

Development planning

Action planning involves the manager and the individual reaching agreement on a development plan. This includes the actions required to achieve goals and improve performance as necessary and plans for developing abilities and skills, which may be recorded in a personal development plan. First, they decide jointly on any actions required by the individual *and* the manager to achieve the overall objectives of the job. Second, and importantly, they agree a development plan:

- *Performance improvement plans*: plans to improve performance. These will spell out what employees, in conjunction as necessary with their managers, need to do better in specified areas of their jobs such as reaching sales or productivity targets, working more accurately, providing better services to internal customers, reducing waste, meeting deadlines. In any improvement area, goals will be set on what has to be done and agreement reached on how the expected results will be achieved. If there are any behavioural issues, such as being uncooperative, plans would be agreed on how the problems could be overcome.

- *Personal development plans*: learning action plans to achieve learning objectives for which individuals are responsible with the support of their managers and the organization.

Act

Action by individuals means that they manage their own performance, with guidance as required from their manager or team leader. They are there to meet the demands of their roles as defined at the planning stage in the form of key result areas, goals and development plans.

Monitor

Monitoring involves reviewing outcomes against plans and ensuring that corrective action is taken when necessary. This process can be described as 'managing performance throughout the year'. Feedback and recognition of good work is provided by the manager when appropriate, which means at the time or immediately after an event has occurred rather than being saved up for a later formal performance review session. Objectives are updated and continuous learning occurs on the job or through coaching. Attention is given to underperformers in good time so that improvements can take place.

Review

Although performance management is a continuous process it is still useful to have a formal review once or twice yearly. This provides a focal point for the consideration of key performance and development issues, and leads to the completion of the performance management cycle by providing the basis for updating performance agreements. The performance review meeting is an important means of ensuring that the five primary performance management elements – agreement, feedback, assessment, positive reinforcement and dialogue – can be put to good use.

The outcome of a review will be expressed in a performance appraisal, which may be either in the form of a narrative or a rating. If there is a performance pay scheme, these ratings will inform decisions on the amount payable.

STRATEGIC HRM IN ACTION

Guidance notes issued by Hitachi Europe on the purpose of performance review meetings

The purpose of a meeting is to ensure that an open, two-way discussion takes place between an employee and their manager. The discussion should review both past performance and development; identify whether past objectives have been met; and agree future objectives. The objectives set should align to both group and team objectives. During the meeting, managers are encouraged to use examples to illustrate to employees where they have performed adequately, exceptionally and below expectations.

SOURCE: Armstrong, M (2015) *Handbook of Performance Management*, Kogan Page, London

Limitations of the model

Like all models, the performance management cycle as described above has its limitations. It is normative in that it seems to prescribe a norm or standard pattern as best practice, by presenting an ideal picture of what a performance management system should look like and how it should work. But how it works will be related to the context in which it operates. Fletcher (1998) noted the evolution in many organizations of a number of separate but linked processes applied in different ways according to the needs of local circumstances and staff levels. Some organizations reject the concept of a bureaucratic, centrally controlled and uniform system of performance management, which is implied by the model, and instead accept that, within an overall policy framework, different approaches may be appropriate in different parts of the organization and for different people.

One problem with the model as presented here is that it can encourage an over-elaborate approach. Systems designers may be tempted to cover every aspect of the model in detail and turn what should be a natural and straightforward management process into a bureaucratic nightmare with complex procedures and intricate paper- or computer-based forms. Managers don't like this and will not do it properly, if at all. Employees generally regard it as yet another control mechanism imposed from above.

When developing a performance management system the watchwords are 'keep it simple'. Terms such as role profile, key result areas or key performance indicators make perfect sense as explanations of how the system works. But to the managers and employees who have to run the system they can appear to be impenetrable jargon – prime examples of 'managerese' or

HR speak. Such terms should be avoided, or at least minimized, in communications about the scheme or during training.

Another problem with the model is the suggestion that there is a smooth transition from the organization's strategic goals to individual goals. But this is much more difficult than it sounds. Strategic goals at organizational level may not always translate easily into individual goals because organizational goals are not defined well enough or are too remote from the work of individual employees. Many commentators have extolled the virtue of alignment; few have made practical suggestions about how it can be achieved. It can also be argued that strategic goals will inevitably be determined by top management without consulting employees, and that simply 'cascading' goals downwards contradicts the performance management principle that people should be involved in agreeing their own goals. The answer to this objection is that, although at individual level account should be taken of overarching goals, individuals can usefully take part in discussions on how they can further the achievement of those goals.

Thereafter, the model indicates a steady progression through the stages of performance management, each of them linked together. This is both logical and desirable but in reality it may be difficult to achieve. The natural tendency of managers is to compartmentalize these activities, if they carry them out at all. Managers do not always appreciate how they are connected and what they should do to ensure that the cycle works smoothly.

Performance management is applied in many different ways according to the context in which it is used. These ways will not necessarily conform to those prescribed by the model. The contextual factors include the type of operation and the organization's structure. Importantly, they also include the organization's culture as expressed in its philosophy or norms (explicit or implicit) on how people should be managed and the prevailing management style, for example, the degree to which it is controlling or participative. As Stoskopf (2002) put it: 'A [performance management] system with the most academically correct competencies or performance measures may fail if it does not fit with the company's culture or workforce.' Pulakos (2009: 3) noted that: 'Performance management is known as the "Achilles heel" of human capital management, and is the most difficult system to implement in organizations.'

STRATEGIC HRM IN ACTION

The performance management system at DHL

DHL is a global market leader in the international express and logistics industry with 45,000 staff in Europe.

DHL's annual performance management process begins in August when the core elements of the scheme are designed at the top level.

Following this, in mid-November, based on the aims decided upon in August, targets are set for the year by a panel of senior staff. Once devised, these targets are cascaded down the organization into individual personal objectives following discussions between line managers and HR.

The cascading process is designed to ensure that targets are refined and altered to align with each individual's actual job. Further discussions then take place to decide what each target means for employees in practice and their implications for competencies. Around the same time, attainment levels and scoring based on the previous year's performance take place to determine bonus levels and salary rises. Following this, with targets already set, around the middle of January an outline for recording performance targets for personal and financial performance for the coming year is designed and, in mid-February, the company's financial results become known. This makes it possible to determine the pot available for bonus payments and salary increases relating to the previous year. Bonuses are paid in either March or April, while salary reviews takes place in April.

The initial stage of establishing overall objectives and the target-setting framework sets the tone for the year. From year to year, conditions change, with the priorities of senior management reflecting the current state of affairs. As a result, each year there are a number of overarching themes such as serving customers, for example, or health and safety. These core individual key objectives (IKOs) are strictly adhered to, although local managers can determine themselves how to manage their attainment. In contrast, more flexibility exists for other objectives, with managers at lower levels able to alter them to align with their particular needs. There is further flexibility in the system with regard to its timing.

SOURCE: Armstrong, M (2015) *Handbook of Performance Management*, Kogan Page, London

Implementation problems

Performance management systems are quite easy to conceive but very hard to deliver. Duncan Brown (2010: 1) remarked that:

> The problems [of performance management] are... not of ambition or intent, but rather practice and delivery. Low rates of coverage and, even more frequently, low-quality conversations and non-existent follow-up are commonplace in the wake of uncommitted directors, incompetent line managers, uncomprehending employees and hectoring HR with their still complex and bureaucratic HR processes.

The many-faceted nature of performance was commented on as follows by Cascio (2010: 34): 'It is an exercise in observation and judgement, it is a feedback process, it is an organizational intervention. It is a measurement process as well as an intensely emotional process. Above all, it is an inexact, human process.'

As a human process, performance management can promise more than it achieves. Coens and Jenkins (2002: 1) delivered the following judgement:

> Throughout our work lives, most of us have struggled with performance appraisal. No matter how many times we redesign it, retrain the supervisors, or give it a new name, it never comes out right. Again and again, we see supervisors procrastinate or just go through the motions, with little taken to heart. And the supervisors who do take it to heart and give it their best mostly meet disappointment.

Shields (2007: 6) argued that: 'Ill-chosen, badly designed or poorly implemented performance management schemes can communicate entirely the wrong messages as to what the organization expects from its employees.'

The belief that staff were more demotivated than motivated by performance management was expressed by 23 per cent of the respondents to the e-reward (2014) performance management survey – a disturbingly high proportion.

The problem may be the result of an inappropriate or over-engineered system, but the most typical reason is that line managers do not have the skills or the inclination to manage the system properly. The skills required are considerable and it is all too easy for managers to go through the motions without really believing that what they are doing is worthwhile. This is why attention must be given to involving them in developing the scheme; briefing them thoroughly on the nature and importance of performance management; emphasizing that managing performance is an important part of their job and that they will be judged on how well they do it; providing them with training and individual coaching; and monitoring how well they carry out their performance management duties.

The nature of performance management strategy

Performance management strategy defines the intentions of the organization on what it wants to do about performance management. It may decide that it does not want to do anything, but if it is believed that a performance management system of some kind is required then the strategy may cover:

- the extent to which the organization wants the system to be formalized;
- the design of the system, including the use of performance agreements and performance reviews;

- the importance attached to the system as a means of developing people;
- whether or not the system should be used to inform performance-related pay decisions;
- if it is decided to include performance rating, the scale that should be adopted and how the distribution of ratings should be controlled;
- how managers and other employees will be involved in designing the system;
- how the system's aims and processes should be communicated;
- how the system should be introduced, including the provision of training in the skills required for managers and other employees;
- the methods to be used to monitor the operation of the system and evaluate its effectiveness.

KEY LEARNING POINTS

- Performance management is defined as a process of agreeing goals for individuals, aligning those goals with the strategic goals of the organization, planning performance to achieve the goals, reviewing and assessing progress, and developing the capabilities of individuals.
- Performance management operates as a strategic process because it enables individual and corporate goals to be aligned.
- The defining features of an effective performance management system are that it operates in accordance with a set of principles and is a continuous process that can be expressed as a cycle of activities.
- The activities involved in operating the performance management cycle are: 1) plan performance; 2) act; 3) monitor; and 4) review.
- Performance management is applied in many different ways according to the context in which it is used. These ways will not necessarily conform to those prescribed by the model.
- Performance management strategy defines the intentions of the organization on what it wants to do about performance management.

References

Brown, D (2010) [accessed 6 December 2010] Practice What We Preach?, *CIPD*, posted by Reward Blogger, 6 December [Online] @duncanbrown

Cascio, W F (2010) *Managing Human Resources: Productivity, quality of work life, profits*, 8th edn, McGraw-Hill/Irwin, New York

Coens, T and Jenkins, M (2002) *Abolishing Performance Appraisals: Why they backfire and what to do instead*, Berrett-Koehler, San Francisco

Egan, G (1995) A clear path to peak performance, *People Management*, 18 May, pp 34–37

e-reward (2014) *Survey of Performance Management Practice*, e-reward, Stockport

Fletcher, C (1998) Circular argument, *People Management*, 1 October, pp 46–49

Pulakos, E D (2009) *Performance Management: A new approach for driving business results*, Wiley-Blackwell, Malden MA

Shields, J (2007) *Managing Employee Performance and Reward*, Cambridge University Press, Port Melbourne

Stoskopf, G A (2002) Taking performance management to the next level, *Workspan*, **45** (2), pp 28–30

Strebler, M T, Bevan, S and Robertson D (2001) *Performance Review: Balancing objectives and content*, Institute for Employment Studies, Brighton

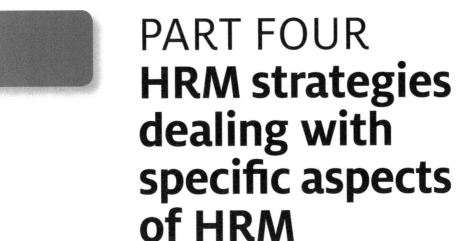

PART FOUR
HRM strategies dealing with specific aspects of HRM

Employee engagement strategy

Introduction

Employee engagement takes place when people are committed to their work and the organization and are motivated to achieve high levels of performance. According to the CIPD (2012: 13): 'Engagement has become for practitioners an umbrella concept for capturing the various means by which employers can elicit additional or discretionary effort from employees – a willingness on the part of staff to work beyond contract. It has become a new management mantra.' As David Guest (2014: 231) remarked: 'One of the attractions of engagement is that it is clearly a good thing. Managers are attracted to the concept because they like the idea of having engaged employees and dislike the prospect of having disengaged employees.'

A strategic approach to enhancing employee engagement is required as organizations need to be clear about what they are proposing to do about this important factor affecting the behaviour of their employees, taking account of information about their engagement levels and trends.

Before examining the nature and content of an engagement strategy it is necessary to answer three questions: 1) What is engagement? 2) Why is engagement important? 3) What are the factors affecting engagement?

What is engagement?

Kahn (1990: 894) originated the notion of employee engagement, defining it as 'the harnessing of organization members' selves to their work roles; in engagement, people employ and express themselves physically, cognitively, and emotionally during role performances'. There have been dozens of definitions since the explosion of interest in the concept during the 2000s. Harter, Schmidt and Hayes (2002: 269) stated that engagement was 'the individual's involvement and satisfaction with as well as enthusiasm for work'. A later definition was produced by Macey et al (2009: 7) who defined engagement as 'an individual's purpose and focused energy, evident to others in the display of personal initiative, adaptability, effort and persistence directed towards organizational goals'.

The term 'engagement' can be used in a specific job-related way. It describes what takes place when people are interested in and positive (even excited) about their jobs, exercise discretionary behaviour in choosing to do more than is expected of them – 'going the extra mile' – and are motivated to achieve high levels of performance. It is sometimes described as job or work engagement. Truss et al (2006: ix) stated that: 'Put simply, engagement means feeling positive about your job.' They went on to explain that: 'The engaged employee is the passionate employee, the employee who is totally immersed in his or her work, energetic, committed and completely dedicated' (Truss et al, 2006: 1).

Engagement can also be described as attachment to or identification with the organization. The Conference Board (2006) defined employee engagement as the heightened connection that employees feel for their organization. Robinson, Perryman and Hayday (2004: 9) emphasized the organizational aspect of engagement when they referred to it as 'a positive attitude held by the employee towards the organization and its values'. This concept of organizational engagement resembles the traditional notion of commitment.

Perhaps the most illuminating approach to the definition of engagement is to recognize that it involves both job and organizational engagement, as suggested by Saks (2006) and Balain and Sparrow (2009).

Why is engagement important?

Truss *et al* (2014: 1) noted: 'the potential for employee engagement to raise levels of corporate performance and profitability'. Evidence for this had been provided by Gallup (2006) who examined over 23,000 business units and compared top quartile and bottom quartile financial performance with engagement scores. They found that:

- Those with engagement scores in the bottom quartile averaged 31–51 per cent more employee turnover, 51 per cent more inventory shrinkage and 62 per cent more accidents.
- Those with engagement scores in the top quartile averaged 12 per cent higher customer advocacy, 18 per cent higher productivity and 12 per cent higher profitability.

Other studies have also indicated that higher levels of engagement produce a range of organizational benefits, for example:

- Higher productivity/performance: engaged employees perform 20 per cent better than the average (Conference Board, 2006).
- Lower staff turnover: engaged employees are 87 per cent less likely to leave (Corporate Leadership Council, 2004).
- Better attendance: engaged employees have lower sick leave (CIPD, 2007).

What are the factors that influence employee engagement?

Research cited by IDS (2007) identified two key elements that have to be present if genuine engagement is to exist. The first is the rational aspect that relates to an employee's understanding of their role, where it fits in the wider organization and how it aligns with business objectives. The second is the emotional aspect, which has to do with how the person feels about the organization, whether their work gives them a sense of personal accomplishment and how they relate to their manager.

Crawford *et al* (2014: 59–62) listed the following drivers of employee engagement:

- *Job challenge*: this takes place when the scope of jobs is broad and job responsibility is high. It enhances engagement because it creates potential for accomplishment and personal growth.

- *Autonomy*: the freedom, independence and discretion allowed to employees in scheduling their work and determining the procedures for carrying it out. It provides a sense of ownership and control over work outcomes.
- *Variety*: jobs that allow individuals to perform many different activities or use many different skills.
- *Feedback*: providing employees with direct and clear information about the effectiveness of their performance.
- *Fit*: the existence of compatibility between an individual and a work environment (eg job, organization, manager, co-workers) that allows individuals to behave in a manner consistent with how they see – or want to see – themselves.
- *Opportunities for development*: these make work meaningful because they provide pathways for employee growth and fulfilment.
- *Rewards and recognition*: these represent both direct and indirect returns on the personal investment of the time of employees in carrying out their work.

By exercising leadership, line managers can make an important contribution in all of the above areas.

The nature and content of employee engagement strategy

Employee engagement strategy is concerned with what needs to be done about enhancing engagement, bearing in mind the factors affecting levels of engagement. When developing the strategy the first step is to establish what is happening now and, in the light of that, determine what should happen in each of those areas. Levels of engagement should be measured in order to identify trends, successes and failures and analyse any gaps between what is wanted and what is actually happening. This can be done through published surveys such as those operated by Gallop, which enable benchmarking to take place with the levels of engagement achieved in other organizations. Alternatively, organizations can create their own surveys to suit their circumstances. The strategy can be developed in the light of this information. It will be concerned with what needs to done to provide for a better work environment, improve job design, offer opportunities for personal growth and ensure that performance management is effective. In each of these areas, strategies, policies and practices can be developed for the organization by HR but, ultimately, the most important ingredient for enhanced engagement is the leadership provided by line managers.

Leadership

A leadership strategy is required that focuses on how line managers can take the lead in increasing levels of engagement. The competencies they need to do so are set out in Table 14.1.

The competencies set out in Table 14.1 need to be developed through learning programmes that enable managers to understand how they are expected to act and develop the skills they need to use. The programmes

TABLE 14.1 Employee engagement management competency framework

Competency	Description
Autonomy and empowerment	Trusts and involves employees
Development	Helps to develop employee's career
Feedback, praise and recognition	Gives positive feedback and praise and rewards good work
Individual interest	Shows concern for employees
Availability	There when needed
Personal manner	Positive approach, leads by example
Ethics	Treats employees fairly
Reviewing and guiding	Helps and advises employees
Clarifying expectations	Sets clear goals and defines what is expected
Managing time and resources	Ensures resources are available to meet workload
Following processes and procedures	Understands and explains processes and procedures

SOURCE: Adapted from Lewis, Donaldson-Feilder and Tharani (2012: 9)

can include formal training (especially for potential managers or those in their first leadership role) but more impact will be made by blending various learning methods such as coaching, mentoring and e-learning. A blended approach ensures that managers are helped to learn for themselves within a framework and with guidance. This is the best form of learning. The performance of managers in applying these competencies should be reviewed and assessed.

The work environment

The work environment impacts on engagement by influencing how people regard their roles and carry them out. The strategy should aim to create a work environment that is enabling, supportive and inspirational. An enabling environment will establish the conditions that encourage high performance and effective discretionary behaviour. These include work processes, equipment and facilities, and the physical conditions in which people work. A supportive environment will be one in which proper attention is paid to achieving a satisfactory work–life balance, emotional demands are not excessive, care is taken to provide healthy and safe working conditions, job security is a major consideration and personal needs are taken into consideration. An inspirational environment is one in which effective leadership is provided by managers, the work is challenging, feedback to employees ensures that their contribution is recognized and rewarded, and there is plenty of scope for career development.

Job design

The strategy should be to encourage, guide and, as necessary, train line managers on how to increase job engagement by designing or modifying jobs that, as far as possible, meet the requirement to provide challenge, autonomy and variety.

Opportunities for personal growth

The engagement strategy should consider what steps are required to ensure that people have the opportunity and are given the encouragement to learn and grow in their roles and develop their future careers.

Performance management

Performance management activities – ie role definition, performance and personal development planning, joint involvement in monitoring performance, and feedback – can all enhance engagement.

STRATEGIC HRM IN ACTION

Enhancing engagement at Telefónica O2 UK

The seven-point People Promise outlines O2's commitment to creating the best possible employee experience:

- It promises its people *a warm welcome*, providing a full induction programme and welcome day for all new starters.

- People are given *the opportunity to get on*. Everyone forms a personal development plan with their manager and talks through their career goals at least twice per year. People can learn new skills by applying for a matched contribution Learning Scheme or by using the online academies, which offer training on a broad range of subjects.

- O2 wants to create a workplace where people trust their senior managers and their line manager. It invests heavily in the leadership skills of its managers, affirming that *your manager will be there for you*.

- O2 people are *trusted to do a great job*. They are encouraged to suggest new ways of doing things in advisor forums, manager forums, skip level meetings and Ignite, an online system enabling advisors to capture customer insights and share their own.

- O2 wants to be *a great place to work*. In the current economic climate, it is focusing even harder on looking after its people, improving its total reward offering by introducing new flexible benefits and a broad range of discounts with high-street retailers. Vielife, an online health and well-being programme, helps people to manage their sleep, nutrition, stress and physical activity. And O2 Confidential offers free 24-hour advice on issues including benefits, debt, housing and other financial matters.

- O2 people should feel *part of something special*. For example, people are encouraged to volunteer for charities and may be afforded time out for their chosen projects. And they can apply for awards or refer friends and family under the 'It's Your Community' programme, which gives grants of up to £1,000 to community projects all over the UK.

- O2 says *thanks for a job well done*, praising its people and giving them recognition for their work. A new scheme launching in 2015 will highlight outstanding individual and team contributions to strategic goals, offering people high-street vouchers and the chance to attend a glittering annual ceremony.

SOURCE: MacLeod, D and Clarke, N (2009) *Engaging for Success: Enhancing performance through employee engagement*, Department for Business Innovation and Skills, London

KEY LEARNING POINTS

- *Engagement defined*
Engagement happens when people are committed to their work and the organization, and are motivated to achieve high levels of performance.
    Engaged people at work are positive, interested in – even excited about – their jobs and are prepared to put discretionary effort into their work, beyond the minimum, in order to get it done. Job engagement can be distinguished from organizational engagement.

- *Importance of engagement*
A considerable amount of research has indicated that higher levels of engagement produce a range of organizational benefits.

- *Discretionary behaviour*
There is a close link between high levels of engagement and positive discretionary behaviour.

- *Factors affecting engagement*
The factors affecting engagement are the quality of leadership, the work environment, the work itself, opportunities for personal growth, opportunities to contribute and commitment to the organization.

- *Developing engagement strategies*
When developing engagement strategies the first step is to establish what is happening now and, in the light of that, determine what strategies are required.

References

Balain, S and Sparrow, P (2009) *Engaged to Perform: A new perspective on employee engagement*, Lancaster University Management School, Lancaster

Chartered Institute of Personnel and Development (2007) *Working Life: Employee attitudes and engagement*, CIPD, London

Chartered Institute of Personnel and Development (2012) [accessed June 2015] Employee Engagement Factsheet, available [Online] www.cipd.co.uk/hr-resources/factsheets/employee-engagement.aspx

Conference Board (2006) *Employee Engagement: A review of current research and its implications*, Conference Board, New York

Corporate Leadership Council (2004) Driving performance and retention through employee engagement, Corporate Executive Board, Washington DC

Crawford, E R, Rich, B L, Buckman, B and Bergeron, J (2014) The antecedents and drivers of employee engagement in *Employee Engagement in Theory and Practice*, ed C Truss, R Deldridge, K Alfes, A Shantz and E Soane, pp 57–81, Routledge, London

Gallup (2006) *Feeling Good Matters in the Workplace*, Gallup Inc, Washington DC

Guest, D E (2014) Employee engagement: fashionable fad or long-term fixture?, in *Employee Engagement in Theory and Practice*, ed C Truss, R Deldridge, K Alfes, A Shantz and E Soane, pp 221–35, Routledge, London

Harter, J K, Schmidt, F L and Hayes, T L (2002) Business-unit level relationship between employee satisfaction, employee engagement, and business outcomes: a meta-analysis, *Journal of Applied Psychology*, 87, pp 268–79

IDS (2007) Building an engaged workforce, *HR Studies Update*, IDS London

Kahn, W A (1990) Psychological conditions of personal engagement and disengagement at work, *Academy of Management Journal*, **33** (4), pp 692–724

Lewis, R, Donaldson-Feilder, E and Tharani, T (2012) *Management Competencies for Enhancing Employee Engagement*, CIPD, London

Macey, W H, Schneider, B, Barbera, K M and Young, S A (2009) *Employee Engagement*, Wiley-Blackwell, Malden MA

Robinson, D, Perryman, S and Hayday, S (2004) *The Drivers of Employee Engagement*, Institute for Employment Studies, Brighton

Saks, A M (2006) Antecedents and consequences of employee engagement, *Journal of Managerial Psychology*, **21** (6), pp 600–19

Truss, C, Deldridge, R, Alfes, K, Shantz, A and Soane, E (2014) Introduction, *Employee Engagement in Theory and Practice*, Routledge, London

Truss, C, Soane, E, Edwards, C, Wisdom, K, Croll, A, and Burnett, J (2006) *Working Life: Employee attitudes and engagement*, CIPD, London

Resourcing strategy

KEY CONCEPTS AND TERMS

Demand forecasting
Employee value proposition
Employer brand
Employer of choice
Realistic preview
Recruitment process outsourcing (RPO)
Resource capability
Resourcing
Resourcing strategy
Supply forecasting
Workforce planning

LEARNING OUTCOMES

On completing this chapter you should be able to define the key concepts above. You should also understand:

- the rationale for strategic resourcing;
- the strategic HRM approach to resourcing;
- the process of integrating business and resourcing strategies;
- the process of bundling resourcing strategies and activities;
- the components of employee resourcing strategy;
- what an employee value proposition does;
- how resource planning works;
- how to plan a retention strategy;
- strategy for managing diversity.

Introduction

Resourcing is what organizations do to ensure they have the people they need. Resourcing strategy is concerned with identifying how many and what sort of employees are required, and making plans to obtain and retain them and to employ them efficiently. It is also about managing diversity. Strategic resourcing is a key part of the SHRM process, which is fundamentally about matching human resources to the strategic and operational needs of the organization and ensuring the full utilization of those resources. It is concerned not only with obtaining and keeping the number and quality of staff required but also with selecting and promoting people who 'fit' the culture and the strategic requirements of the organization.

The rationale for strategic resourcing

A rationale for developing a resourcing strategy flows from the suggestion by Keep (1989: 122) that HRM should make a significant effort towards: 'obtaining the right basic material in the form of a workforce endowed with the appropriate qualities, skills, knowledge and potential for future training. The selection and recruitment of workers best suited to meeting the needs of the organization ought to form a core activity upon which most other HRM policies geared towards development and motivation could be built.'

The concept that the strategic capability of a firm depends on its resource capability in the shape of people (the resource-based view) provides the rationale for resourcing strategy. The aim of this strategy is therefore to ensure that a firm achieves competitive advantage by employing more capable people than its rivals. These people will have a wider and deeper range of skills and will behave in ways that will maximize their contribution. The organization attracts such people by being 'the employer of choice'. It retains them by providing better opportunities and rewards than others and by developing a positive employment relationship (see Chapter 19) that increases commitment and creates mutual trust. Furthermore, the organization deploys its people in ways that maximize the added value they supply.

The strategic HRM approach to resourcing

HRM places emphasis on finding people whose attitudes and behaviour are likely to be congruent with what management believes to be appropriate and conducive to success. In the words of Townley (1989: 92), organizations are concentrating more on 'the attitudinal and behavioural characteristics of employees'. This tendency has its dangers. Innovative and adaptive organizations need non-conformists, even mavericks, who can 'buck the system'.

If managers recruit people 'in their own image' there is the risk of staffing the organization with conformist clones and of perpetuating a dysfunctional culture – one that may have been successful in the past but is no longer appropriate in the face of new challenges (as Pascale, 1990, put it: 'nothing fails like success').

The HRM approach to resourcing therefore emphasizes that matching resources to organizational requirements does not simply mean maintaining the status quo and perpetuating a moribund culture. It can and often does mean radical changes in thinking about the skills and behaviours required in the future in order to achieve sustainable growth and cultural change.

Integrating business and resourcing strategies

The philosophy behind the strategic HRM approach to resourcing is that it is people who implement the strategic plan. As Quinn Mills (1985) expressed it, the process is one of 'planning with people in mind'.

The integration of business and resourcing strategies is based on an understanding of the direction in which the organization is going and the determination of:

- the numbers of people required to meet business needs;
- the skills and behaviour required to support the achievement of business strategies;
- the impact of organizational restructuring as a result of rationalization, decentralization, delayering, acquisitions, mergers, product or market development, or the introduction of new technology – for example, cellular manufacturing;
- plans for changing the culture of the organization in such areas as ability to deliver, performance standards, quality, customer service, teamworking and flexibility, which indicate the need for people with different attitudes, beliefs and personal characteristics;
- plans for introducing a high-performance work system or for creating a leaner or more agile organization;
- plans for increasing flexibility in the use of people.

These factors will be strongly influenced by the type of business strategies adopted by the organization and the sort of business it is in. These may be expressed in such terms as Miles and Snow's (1978) typology of defender, prospector and analyser organizations.

Resourcing strategies exist to provide the people and skills required to support the business strategy, but they should also contribute to the formulation of that strategy. HR directors have an obligation to point out to their colleagues the human resource opportunities and constraints that will affect the achievement of strategic plans. In mergers or acquisitions, for example, the ability of management within the company to handle the new situation and the quality of management in the new business will be important considerations.

Bundling resourcing strategies and activities

Employee resourcing is not just about recruitment and selection. It is concerned with any means available to meet the needs of the firm for certain skills and behaviours. A strategy to enlarge the skill base may start with recruitment and selection but would also extend into learning and development in order to enhance skills and modify behaviours, and methods of rewarding people for the acquisition of extra skills. Performance management processes can be used to identify development needs (skill and behavioural) and motivate people to make the most effective use of their skills. Competency frameworks and profiles can be prepared to define the skills and behaviours required, and be used in selection, employee development and employee reward processes. The aim should be to develop a reinforcing bundle of strategies along these lines. Talent management is a 'bundling' process, which is an aspect of resourcing.

The components of employee resourcing strategy

The components of employee resourcing strategy as considered in this chapter are:

- Workforce planning: assessing future business needs and deciding on the numbers and types of people required.
- Developing the organization's employee value proposition and its employer brand.
- Resourcing plans: preparing plans for finding people from within the organization and/or for learning and development programmes to help people learn new skills. If needs cannot be satisfied from within the organization, it involves preparing longer-term plans for ensuring that recruitment and selection procedures will satisfy them.
- Retention strategy: preparing plans for retaining the people the organization needs.
- Flexibility strategy: planning for increased flexibility in the use of human resources in order to enable the organization to make the best use of people and adapt swiftly to changing circumstances.
- Talent management strategy: ensuring that the organization has the talented people it requires in order to provide for management succession and meet present and future business needs (see Chapter 16).

Workforce planning

Workforce planning determines the human resources required by the organization to achieve its strategic goals and prepares and implements programmes for satisfying those requirements. It was defined by the CIPD (2010: 4) as: 'A core process of human resource management that is shaped by the organizational strategy and ensures the right number of people, with the right skills, in the right place and at the right time to deliver short- and long-term organizational objectives.'

Workforce planning (often called human resource planning) is based on the belief that people are an organization's most important strategic resource. It is generally concerned with matching resources to business needs in the longer term, although it will also deal with shorter-term requirements. It addresses people needs both in quantitative and qualitative terms. This means answering two basic questions: 1) How many people? 2) What sort of people? Workforce planning also looks at broader issues relating to the ways in which people are employed and developed in order to improve organizational effectiveness. It can therefore play an important part in strategic HRM.

Link to business planning

Workforce planning should be an integral part of business planning. The strategic planning process defines projected changes in the types of activities carried out by the organization and the scale of those activities. It identifies the core competences that the organization needs to achieve its goals and, therefore, its skill and behavioural requirements.

Workforce planning interprets these plans in terms of people requirements. But it may influence the business strategy by drawing attention to ways in which people could be developed and deployed more effectively to further the achievement of business goals. It may also focus on any problems that might have to be resolved in order to ensure that the people required will be available and will be capable of making the necessary contribution. As Quinn Mills (1985: 105) indicated, human resource planning is 'a decision-making process that combines three important activities: 1) identifying and acquiring the right number of people with the proper skills; 2) motivating them to achieve high performance; and 3) creating interactive links between business objectives and people-planning activities'.

Hard and soft workforce planning

A distinction can be made between 'hard' and 'soft' workforce planning. The former is based on quantitative analysis in order to ensure that the right number of the right sort of people is available when needed. Soft planning is more concerned with broader issues about the employment of people than is the traditional quantitative approach. But it also addresses those aspects of HRM that are primarily about the organization's requirements for people – from the viewpoint of numbers, skills and how they are deployed.

Limitations

Although the notion of workforce planning is well established in the HRM vocabulary, it does not seem to be embedded as a key HR activity. As Rothwell (1995: 175) commented about human resource planning: 'Apart from isolated examples, there has been little research evidence of increased use or of its success.' She explains the gap between theory and practice as arising from:

- the impact of change and the difficulty of predicting the future – 'the need for planning may be in inverse proportion to its feasibility';
- the 'shifting kaleidoscope' of policy priorities and strategies within organizations;
- the distrust displayed by many managers of theory or planning – they often prefer pragmatic adaptation to conceptualization;
- the lack of evidence that human resource planning works.

Research conducted by Cowling and Walters (1990) indicated that the only formal and regular activities carried out by respondents were the identification of future training needs, analysis of training costs and analysis of productivity. Fewer than half produced formal labour supply-and-demand forecasts, and less than 20 per cent formally monitored HR planning practices.

Summarizing the problem, Taylor (1998: 64–65) commented that: 'It would seem that employers, quite simply, prefer to wait until their view of the future environment clears sufficiently for them to see the whole picture before committing resources in preparation for its arrival. The perception is that the more complex and turbulent the environment, the more important it is to wait and see before acting.'

Be that as it may, it is difficult to reject out of hand the belief that some attempt should be made to determine broadly the future human resource requirements as a basis for strategic planning and action. And research conducted by the CIPD (2010) confirmed that some large organizations are taking a serious interest in it.

Approaches to workforce planning

Resourcing strategies show the way forward through the analysis of business strategies and demographic trends. They are converted into action plans based on the outcome of the following interrelated planning activities:

- Demand forecasting: estimate future needs for people and competences by reference to corporate and functional plans and forecasts of future activity levels.

- Supply forecasting: estimate the supply of people by reference to analyses of current resources and future availability, after allowing for wastage. The forecast will also take account of labour market trends relating to the availability of skills and to demographics.
- Forecasting requirements: analyse the demand and supply forecasts to identify future deficits or surpluses, with the help of models where appropriate.
- Action planning: prepare plans to deal with forecast deficits and to match supply and demand through internal promotion, training or external recruitment. If necessary, plan for unavoidable downsizing so as to avoid any compulsory redundancies, if that is possible.
- Develop retention and flexibility strategies.

FIGURE 15.1 Workforce planning flow chart

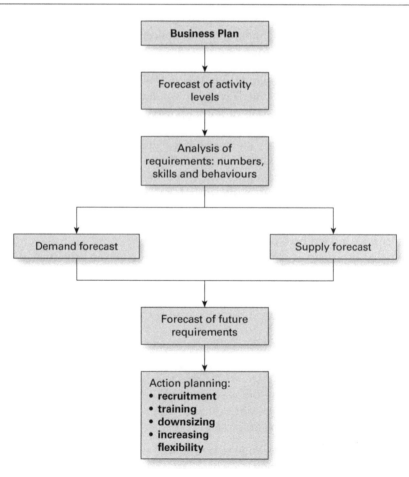

Although these are described as separate areas they are closely interrelated and often overlap. For example, demand forecasts are estimates of future requirements, and these may be prepared on the basis of assumptions about the productivity of employees. But the supply forecast will also have to consider productivity trends and how they might affect the supply of people.

A flow chart of the process of workforce planning is shown in Figure 15.1, which represents an ideal deterministic model of how it should happen. It is useful to have such a model and the activities involved in mind, but, in practice, organizations tend to do their workforce planning on the hoof, for the reasons given earlier. Some or all of the activities represented on the model may take place, but not in a neat sequential way. Mabey, Salaman and Storey (1998: 520) observed that: 'Much SHRM literature assumes a naive, over-rationalist view of organizational decision making.' This comment applies as much if not more to workforce planning as to any other SHRM activity. The model ignores both the political realities and the inability of senior managers to make SHRM decisions.

Employee value proposition

An important aspect of resourcing strategy is the development and actioning of plans, which shape what the organization has to offer to people who join and stay. This can be done by establishing an employee value proposition – a statement of what an organization will provide that people will value. It will include pay, which is important but can be overemphasized as compared with other elements. These non-financial factors may be crucial in attracting and retaining people, and include:

- the attractiveness of the organization;
- responsibility – corporate conduct and ethics;
- respect – diversity and inclusion;
- work – life balance;
- opportunities for personal and professional growth.

Employer brand

The employee value proposition can be expressed as an employer brand that defines what is special, even unique, about an organization that will attract people to join it and encourage those already there to stay. Employer branding is the creation of a brand image of the organization for prospective employees. It will be influenced by the reputation of the organization as a business or provider of services, as well as by its reputation as an employer. To create an employer brand it is necessary to:

- analyse what ideal candidates need and want and take this into account in deciding what should be offered and how it should be offered;
- establish how far the core values of the organization support the creation of an attractive brand and ensure that these are incorporated in the presentation of the brand as long as they are 'values in use' (lived by members of the organization) rather than simply espoused;
- define the features of the brand on the basis of an examination and review of each of the areas that affect perceptions of people about the organization as 'a great place to work' – the way people are treated, the provision of a fair deal, opportunities for growth, work–life balance, leadership, the quality of management, involvement with colleagues, and how and why the organization is successful;
- benchmark the approaches of other organizations (the *Sunday Times* list of the 100 best companies to work for is useful) to obtain ideas about what can be done to enhance the brand;
- be honest and realistic.

Resourcing plans

The analysis of future requirements should indicate what steps need to be taken to appoint people from within the organization and what learning and development programmes should be planned. The analysis will also establish how many people will need to be recruited in the absence of qualified employees within the organization and if it is impossible to train people in the new skills in time.

Internal resourcing

Ideally, internal resourcing should be based on data already available about skills and potential. This should have been provided by regular skills audits and the analysis of the outcomes of performance management reviews. A 'trawl' can then be made to locate available talent, which can be accompanied by an internal advertising campaign.

External resourcing

External resourcing requirements can be met by developing a recruitment strategy. The aims of this strategy would be first to make the organization 'the employer of choice' in its particular field or for the people it wants to recruit (eg graduates). Second, the strategy should plan the best methods of defining precisely what is needed in terms of skills and competencies. Finally, the strategy should be concerned with planning to use the most effective methods of obtaining the number and type of people required. This could include the use of social media and 'recruitment process outsourcing' (RPO), the term used when an organization commissions a provider to take responsibility for the end-to-end delivery of the recruitment process, covering all vacancies or a selection of them. The strategy should be developed as follows:

1 Define skill and competency (behavioural) requirements: ideally this should be carried out by the use of systematic skill and competency analysis techniques. These can form the material upon which focused and structured interviews can take place and be used as criteria for selection. They may also indicate where and how psychometric tests could be helpful.

2 Analyse the factors affecting decisions to join the organization. These include:
   - the pay and total benefits package: this may have a considerable effect on decisions to join the organization but it is by no means the only factor; those set out below can be just as important and even more significant for some people;
   - career opportunities;
   - the opportunity to use existing skills or to acquire new skills;
   - the opportunity to use the latest technology and equipment with which the organization is well supplied (of particular interest to research scientists and engineers);
   - access to high-level training;
   - a responsible and intrinsically rewarding job;
   - a belief that what the organization is doing is worthwhile;
   - the reputation of the organization as an employer;
   - the opportunity the job will provide to further the individual's career: for example, the scope to achieve and have achievements recognized, increase in employability, or a respected company name to put on a CV.

3 Competitive resourcing: this will start from an analysis of the basis upon which the organization competes with other firms for employees. The factors mentioned above should be covered and the aim would be to seek competitive advantage by exploiting those that are superior to those of rivals. One of the factors will be pay. This may not be the only one but it can be important. It is necessary to track market rates and make a policy decision on where the organization wants to be in relation to the market.

4 Alternative strategies for satisfying people requirements: these consist of outsourcing, re-engineering, increasing flexibility skills training, multiskilling and downsizing.

5 Recruitment and selection techniques: the strategy should explore methods not only of recruiting the number of people required, but also of finding staff who have the necessary skills and experience, who are likely to deliver the right sort of behaviour and who will fit into the organization's culture readily. These processes and techniques could include the use of:

- skills analysis;
- competency mapping;
- the internet and social media for recruitment;
- biodata;
- structured interviews;
- psychometric testing;
- assessment centres.

The aim of the strategy is to develop the best mix of recruitment and selection tools. It has been demonstrated that a 'bundle' of selection techniques is likely to be more effective as a method of predicting the likely success of candidates than relying on a single method such as an interview.

Retention strategy

Retention strategy aims to ensure that key people stay with the organization and that wasteful and expensive levels of employee turnover are reduced. It will be based on an analysis of why people stay and why they leave.

The reasons why people remain with the organization can be established through attitude surveys. These could segment respondents according to their length of service and analyse the answers of longer-serving employees to establish if there are any common patterns. The survey results could be supplemented by focus groups that would discuss why people stay and identify any problems.

An analysis of why people leave, as undertaken by exit interviews, may provide some information but they are unreliable – people rarely give the full reasons why they are going. A better method is to conduct attitude surveys at regular intervals. The retention plan should address each of the areas in which lack of commitment and dissatisfaction can arise. The actions to be considered under each heading are listed below.

Pay

Problems arise because of uncompetitive, inequitable or unfair pay systems. Possible actions include:

- reviewing pay levels on the basis of market surveys;
- introducing job evaluation or improving an existing scheme to provide for equitable grading decisions;

- ensuring that employees understand the link between performance and reward;
- reviewing performance-related pay schemes to ensure that they operate fairly;
- adapting payment-by-results systems to ensure that employees are not penalized when they are engaged only on short runs;
- tailoring benefits to individual requirements and preference;
- involving employees in developing and operating job evaluation and contingent pay systems.

Job design

Dissatisfaction results if jobs are unrewarding in themselves. Jobs should be designed to maximize skill variety, task significance, autonomy and feedback, and they should provide opportunities for learning and growth.

Performance

Employees can be demotivated if they are unclear about their responsibilities or performance standards, are not given feedback on how well they are doing, or feel that their performance assessments are unfair. The following actions can be taken:

- express performance requirements in terms of hard but attainable goals;
- get employees and managers to agree on those goals and the steps required to achieve them;
- encourage managers to praise employees for good performance but also get them to provide regular, informative and easily interpreted feedback – performance problems should be discussed as they happen, in order that immediate corrective action can be taken;
- train managers in performance review techniques such as counselling;
- brief employees on how the performance management system works and obtain feedback from them on how it has been applied.

Learning and development

Resignations and turnover can increase if people are not given opportunities for learning and development, or feel that demands are being made upon them that they cannot reasonably be expected to fulfil without proper training. New employees can go through an 'induction crisis' if they are not given adequate training when they join the organization. Learning and development programmes should be developed and introduced, which:

- give employees the competence and confidence to achieve expected performance standards;
- enhance existing skills and competencies;

- help people to acquire new skills and competencies so that they can make better use of their abilities, take on greater responsibilities, undertake a greater variety of tasks and earn more under skill- and competency-based pay schemes;
- ensure that new employees quickly acquire and learn the basic skills and knowledge needed to make a good start in their jobs;
- increase employability, inside and outside the organization.

Career development

Dissatisfaction with career prospects is a major cause of turnover. To a certain extent, this has to be accepted. More and more people recognize that to develop their careers they need to move on, and there is little that their employers can do about it, especially in today's flatter organizations where promotion prospects may be limited. These are the individuals who acquire a 'portfolio' of skills and may consciously change direction several times during their careers. To a certain degree, employers should welcome this tendency. The idea of providing 'cradle to grave' careers is no longer as relevant in the more changeable job markets of today, and this self-planned, multiskilling process provides for the availability of a greater number of qualified people. But there is still everything to be said in most organizations for maintaining a stable core workforce and in this situation employers should still plan to create career opportunities by:

- providing employees with wider experience;
- introducing more systematic procedures for identifying potential, such as assessment or development centres;
- encouraging promotion from within;
- developing more equitable promotion procedures;
- providing advice and guidance on career paths.

Commitment

This can be increased by:

- explaining the organization's mission, values and strategies and encouraging employees to discuss and comment on them;
- communicating with employees in a timely and candid way, with the emphasis on face-to-face communications through such means as briefing groups;
- constantly seeking and taking into account the views of people at work;
- providing opportunities for employees to contribute their ideas on improving work systems;
- introducing organization and job changes only after consultation and discussion.

Lack of group cohesion

Employees can feel isolated and unhappy if they are not part of a cohesive team or if they are bedevilled by disruptive power politics. Steps can be taken to tackle this problem through:

● teamwork: setting up self-managing or autonomous work groups or project teams;

● teambuilding: emphasizing the importance of teamwork as a key value, rewarding people for working effectively as members of teams and developing teamwork skills.

Dissatisfaction and conflict with managers and team leaders

A common reason for resignations is the feeling that management in general, or individual managers and team leaders in particular, are not providing the leadership they should, or are treating people unfairly or bullying their staff (not an uncommon situation). As the saying goes, people tend to leave their managers, not the organization. This problem should be remedied by:

● selecting managers and team leaders with well-developed leadership qualities and people management skills, or with the potential to acquire those skills;

● training them in leadership and people management and in methods of resolving conflict and dealing with grievances;

● establishing a corporate set of values and a competency framework that include requirements on how people should be treated;

● ensuring that the performance management system as applied to managers and team leaders defines on an individual basis the values to be upheld and people management competencies required, reviews the extent to which behaviour is in accordance with the values and competencies and initiates action to develop leadership and people management skills;

● introducing better procedures for handling grievances and disciplinary problems, and training everyone in how to use them.

Recruitment, selection and promotion

Rapid turnover can result simply from poor selection or promotion decisions. It is essential to ensure that selection and promotion procedures match the capacities of individuals to the demands of the work they have to do.

Over-marketing

Creating unrealistic expectations about career development opportunities, tailored training programmes, increasing employability and varied and interesting work can, if not matched with reality, lead directly to dissatisfaction and early resignation. Care should be taken not to oversell the firm's employee development policies. This can be achieved by using realistic previews (telling people as it is) as part of the selection process.

Flexibility strategy

The aims of the flexibility strategy should be to provide for greater operational and role flexibility. The steps to be considered are:

- take a radical look at traditional employment patterns to find alternatives to full-time, permanent staff: this may take the form of segregating the workforce into a 'core group' and one or more peripheral groups;
- outsourcing: getting work done by external firms or individuals;
- multiskilling to increase the ability of people to switch jobs or carry out any of the tasks that have to be undertaken by their team.

Diversity and inclusion strategy

A diversity and inclusion strategy ensures that:

- cultural and individual differences in the workplace are acknowledged;
- the different qualities that people bring to their jobs are valued;
- people with different backgrounds are included as part of the organization on the same terms as everyone else.

The strategy will:

- Focus on fairness to ensure that merit, competence and potential are the basis for recruitment, promotion and development decisions, as well as for reviews and assessments of performance.
- Ensure that everyone is alert to the influence of conscious and unconscious biases when dealing with people.
- Pursue steps to achieve inclusion so that people with different backgrounds and characteristics feel part of the same organization and are not treated differently because of their background or characteristics.
- Generally promote to everyone the organization's commitment to managing diversity and inclusion and how it is proposed to put that commitment into effect.
- Provide guidance, advice and, as necessary, training to managers and team leaders on how to achieve inclusion and avoid bias.

STRATEGIC HRM IN ACTION

Recruitment and retention strategy at Buckingham County Council

Attracting and retaining high-quality staff is considered key to the corporate strategy of Buckingham County Council, which employs around 14,000 people. Resourcing is one of the most important things that the council does to improve performance.

Resourcing and people strategy

The resourcing strategy complements and reinforces the people strategy, which has five targets:

- being the best employer;
- bringing in additional talent;
- developing existing talent;
- championing diversity;
- transforming the organization.

The people dashboard

A people strategy dashboard has been created to ensure that human resources are managed more effectively. This extends the people strategy targets and is used to monitor progress in achieving them.

Improving recruitment and selection

This involved:

- strengthening the employer brand;
- developing a better recruitment website;
- developing a talent bank to ensure that vacancies were filled quickly;
- streamlining processes to reduce the time to fill vacancies;
- the development of a competency framework used for competency-based selection.

Retaining talent

A holistic approach is adopted to retaining talent. This involves paying attention to every aspect of the employment relationship and setting a best-employer target. A staff survey is used to measure employee engagement.

Total reward strategy

A total reward approach is adopted, including the use of total reward statements.

Talent management

A talent management toolkit is used to identify and develop potential high performers at every level in the organization.

SOURCE: CIPD (2010) *People Resourcing Practice Survey*, CIPD, London

KEY LEARNING POINTS

- *Resourcing defined*
  Resourcing is what organizations do to ensure that they have the people they need.

- *Resourcing strategy defined*
  Resourcing strategy is concerned with identifying how many and what sort of people are required, and making plans to obtain and retain them and to employ them efficiently.

- *The rationale for strategic resourcing*
  The concept that the strategic capability of a firm depends on its resource capability in the shape of people (the resource-based view) provides the rationale for resourcing strategy. Resourcing strategies exist to provide the people and skills required to support the business strategy, but they should also contribute to the formulation of that strategy.

- *Workforce planning*
  Workforce planning determines the human resources required by the organization to achieve its strategic goals, and prepares and implements programmes for satisfying those requirements. Although the notion of workforce planning is well established in the HRM vocabulary, it does not seem to be embedded as a key HR activity.

- *Resourcing strategy*
  Resourcing strategies show the way forward through the analysis of business strategies and demographic trends. This is converted into action plans based on the outcome of a number of interrelated planning activities.

Resourcing strategy is concerned with shaping what the organization has to offer to people who join and stay with the organization. This can be done by developing and articulating an employee value proposition. The employee value proposition can be expressed as an employer brand that defines what is special, even unique, about an organization – what will attract people to join it and encourage those already there to stay.

- *Resourcing plans*
  The analysis of future requirements should indicate what steps need to be taken to appoint people from within the organization and what learning and development programmes should be planned.

- *Retention strategy*
  Retention strategy aims to ensure that key people stay with the organization and that wasteful and expensive levels of employee turnover are reduced. They will be based on an analysis of why people stay and why they leave.

- *Flexibility strategy*
  Flexibility strategy aims to provide for greater operational and role flexibility.

- *Diversity and inclusion strategy*
  A diversity and inclusion strategy ensures that cultural and individual differences in the workplace are acknowledged, that the different qualities that people bring to their jobs are valued, and that people with different backgrounds are included as part of the organization on the same terms as everyone else.

References

CIPD (2010) *Workforce Planning*, Chartered Institute of Personnel and Development, London

Cowling, A and Walters, M (1990) Manpower planning: where are we today?, *Personnel Review*, March, pp 9–15

Keep, E (1989) Corporate training strategies: the vital component?, in *New Perspectives on Human Resource Management*, ed J Storey, pp 109–25, Routledge, London

Mabey, C, Salaman, G and Storey, J (1998) *Human Resource Management: A strategic introduction*, Blackwell, Oxford

Miles, R E and Snow, C C (1978) *Organizational Strategy: Structure and process*, McGraw Hill, New York

Pascale, R (1990) *Managing on the Edge*, Viking, London

Quinn Mills, D (1985) Planning with people in mind, *Harvard Business Review*, July/August, pp 139–45

Rothwell, S (1995) Human resource planning, in *Human Resource Management: A critical text*, ed J Storey, pp 167–202, Routledge, London

Taylor, S (1998) *Employee Resourcing*, IPD, London

Townley, B (1989) Selection and appraisal: reconstructing social relations?, in *New Perspectives on Human Resource Management*, ed J Storey, pp 92–108, Routledge, London

Talent management strategy

Talent management defined

Talent management is a comprehensive and integrated set of activities to ensure that the organization attracts, retains, motivates and develops the talented people it needs now and in the future.

The term talent management may refer simply to management succession planning and management development activities, although this notion does not really add anything to these familiar processes except a new (but admittedly quite evocative) name. It is better to regard talent management as a more comprehensive and integrated bundle of activities, the aim of which is to secure the flow of talent in an organization, bearing in mind that talent is a major corporate resource.

Strategic talent management

Talent management is a strategic management process because, in the words of Johnson, Scholes and Whittington (2005: 6), it involves 'understanding the strategic position of an organization, making strategic choices for the future, and turning strategy into action'. Talent management concentrates on understanding and satisfying the requirements of the business to achieve organizational capability, growth and competitive advantage. It aligns its policies with the organization's strategic intent – its competitive strategy and operational goals.

The following (somewhat elitist) view of talent management was expressed by Collings and Mellahi (2009: 304):

> Activities and processes that involve the systematic identification of key positions which differentially contribute to the organization's sustainable competitive advantage, the development of a talent pool of high potential and high-performing incumbents to fill these roles, and the development of a differentiated human resource architecture to facilitate filling these positions with competent incumbents and to ensure their continued commitment to the organization.

As suggested below, however, a more comprehensive definition based on an understanding of how talent is defined might be more appropriate.

What is talent?

If you are going to manage talent you have to understand what is meant by talent, ie who the talented people are that you are going to manage. In general, talented people could be described as those who have the skills and ability to do something well. But it is necessary to be more specific about which talented people will be the concern of talent management. An elitist definition states that talent is a quality possessed by people with exceptional ability and who are going to go far.

A less elitist and more embracing definition would be that talent is what any able person has who does well in their role and has growth potential. This is broadly in line with the view expressed by the CIPD (2007: 8): 'Talent consists of those individuals who can make a difference to organizational performance, either through their immediate contribution or in the longer term by demonstrating the highest levels of potential.'

These two approaches could be described as exclusive or inclusive. The CIPD (2007: 8) established from their research that: 'On the one hand there was an exclusive approach, in which talent is viewed on the basis of those destined for the top positions. On the other hand there was an inclusive approach, in which talent is defined as all the employees who work for the organization. The reality is that most organizations had a hybrid approach to talent, in which both exclusivity and inclusivity are accommodated and indeed driven by the changing needs of the workforce' (and, they could have added, the organization).

The concept of talent management was based on an initiative by McKinsey & Company, who coined the phrase 'the war for talent' in 1997. A book on this subject by Michaels, Handfield-Jones and Axelrod (2001) identified five imperatives that companies need to act on if they are going to win the war for managerial talent. These are:

1 Creating a winning employee value proposition that will make your company uniquely attractive to talent.

2 Moving beyond recruiting hype to build a long-term recruiting strategy.

3 Using job experience, coaching and mentoring to cultivate the potential in managers.

4 Strengthening your talent pool by investing in A players, developing B players and acting decisively on C players.

5 Central to this approach is a pervasive mindset – a deep conviction shared by leaders throughout the company that competitive advantage comes from having better talent at all levels.

The McKinsey prescription has often been misinterpreted to mean that talent management is only about obtaining, identifying and nurturing high flyers, ignoring the point they made that competitive advantage comes from having better talent at all levels.

Jeffrey Pfeffer has the following doubts about the notion of the war for talent, which he thinks is the wrong metaphor for organizational success:

SOURCE REVIEW Problems with the notion of 'the war for talent' – Pfeffer (2001: 252)

Fighting the war for talent itself can cause problems. Companies that adopt a talent war mindset often wind up venerating outsiders and downplaying the talent already in the company. They frequently set up competitive zero-sum dynamics that make internal learning and knowledge transfer difficult, activate the self-fulfilling prophesy in the wrong direction (those labelled as less able become less able), and create an attitude of arrogance instead of an attitude of wisdom. For all these reasons, fighting the war for talent may be hazardous to an organization's health and detrimental to doing the things that will make it successful.

In the light of this, three views about talent management strategy have emerged. The first is based on the belief that everyone has talent and it is not just about the favoured few. It is necessary to maximize the performance of the workforce as a whole in order to maximize the performance of the organization. Thorne and Pellant (2007: 9) wrote that: 'No organization should focus all its attention on development of only part of its human capital. What is important is recognizing the needs of different individuals within its community.'

The second view is that organizations should focus on the best. The argument is that it is not helpful to confuse talent management with overall employee development – both are important but talent management should be concerned with those who are particularly talented and have considerable potential.

The third view is that while talent management may concentrate on obtaining, identifying and developing people with high potential, this should not be at the expense of the development needs of people generally. This pragmatic approach has much to commend it.

Talent management strategy

Talent management strategy is in effect a declaration of intent on how the objective of acquiring and nurturing talent wherever it is and wherever it is needed should be achieved. It is governed by the views of the organization on what is meant by talent and therefore with whom the strategy should be concerned. Talent management strategy is expressed in the form of a 'bundle' of interrelated talent management processes that constitute the talent pipeline.

The development and implementation of a talent management strategy requires high-quality management and leadership from the top and the HR function. In many organizations a senior position of head or director of talent management has been established to ensure the delivery of the strategy.

As suggested by Younger, Smallwood and Ulrich (2007), the approaches required involve emphasizing 'growth from within'; regarding talent development as a key element of the business strategy; being clear about the competencies and qualities that matter; maintaining well-defined career paths; taking management development, coaching and mentoring very seriously; and demanding high performance.

Talent management strategy deals with each aspect of a 'talent pipeline' as shown in Figure 16.1.

FIGURE 16.1 The talent management pipeline

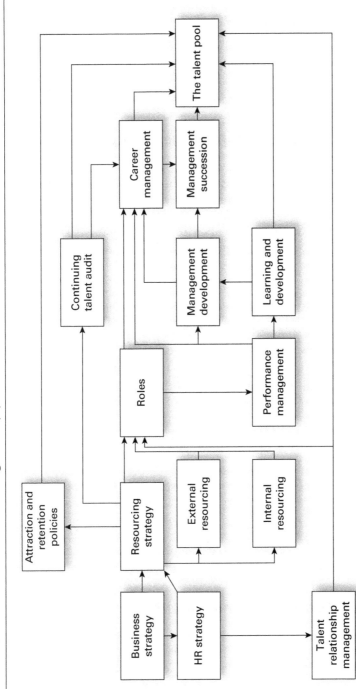

The key elements of the pipeline are described below.

The resourcing strategy

The business plan provides the basis for workforce resource planning, which defines human capital requirements and leads to attraction and retention policies and programmes for internal resourcing (identifying talented people within the organization and developing and promoting them).

Attraction and retention policies and programmes

These policies and programmes describe the approach to ensuring that the organization both gets and keeps the talent it needs. Attraction policies lead to programmes for external resourcing (recruitment and selection of people from outside the organization). Retention policies are designed to ensure that people remain as committed members of the organization. The outcome of these policies is a talent flow that creates and maintains the talent pool.

Talent audit

A talent audit identifies those with potential and provides the basis for career planning and development – ensuring that talented people have the sequence of experience supplemented by coaching and learning programmes that will fit them to carry out more demanding roles in the future. Talent audits can also be used to indicate the possible danger of talented people leaving (risk analysis) and what action may need to be taken to retain them.

Roles

Talent management is concerned with the roles people carry out. This involves job design – ensuring that roles provide the responsibility, challenge and autonomy required to create role engagement and motivation. It also means taking steps to ensure that people have the opportunity and are given encouragement to learn and develop in their roles. Talent management policies focus on role flexibility – giving people the chance to develop their roles by making better and extended use of their talents.

Talent relationship management

Talent relationship management is the process of building effective relationships with people in their roles. It is concerned generally with creating a great place to work, but in particular it is about treating individual employees fairly, recognizing their value, giving them a voice and providing opportunities for growth. The aim is to achieve 'talent engagement', ensuring that people are committed to their work and the organization. It is always best to build on an existing relationship rather than try to create a new one when someone leaves.

Performance management

Performance management processes provide a means of building relationships with people, identifying talent and potential, planning learning and development activities, and making the most of the talent possessed by the organization. Line managers can be asked to carry out separate 'risk analyses' for any key staff in order to assess the likelihood of their leaving. Properly carried out, performance management is a means of increasing the engagement and motivation of people by providing positive feedback and recognition. This is part of a total reward system.

Learning and development

Learning and development policies and programmes are essential components in the process of talent management – ensuring that people acquire and enhance the skills and competencies they need. Policies should be formulated by reference to 'employee success profiles', which are described in terms of competencies and define the qualities that need to be developed. Employee success profiles can be incorporated into role profiles.

Career management

Career management consists of the processes of career planning and management succession. Career planning shapes the progression of individuals within an organization in accordance with assessments of organizational needs; defined employee success profiles; and the performance, potential and preferences of individual members of the enterprise. 'Destination jobs' can be identified for people with high potential, which are attainable only if they continue to perform, impress and demonstrate growth potential.

Management succession planning

Management succession planning takes place to ensure that, as far as possible, the organization has the managers it requires to meet future business needs.

The talent pool

The talent pool consists of all those employees who have been identified as talented and who have undergone or are undergoing the various processes of performance management, learning and development, management development, career management, and talent relationship management that constitute the talent management pipeline.

STRATEGIC HRM IN ACTION

Talent management strategy at BAE Systems

At BAE Systems there are five mandated core business management processes to support the delivery of corporate strategy and foster high performance. Talent management is seen within a business performance context. An annual integrated business review planning process is used by individual businesses to establish and plan for the delivery of objectives in line with corporate strategy, supported by quarterly business reviews, customer reviews and data from employee surveys. Project performance is assessed by contract reviews. Performance is reviewed throughout the year by the performance management system. A performance-centred leadership framework is used to integrate management, resourcing and people development, focusing on the traditional outcomes of performance (financial, project and behavioural), reward and development. There is behavioural performance feedback and a performance potential rating (called Spectrum). Line leaders and functional directors ensure that the framework is implemented. HR's role is one of assisting in development interventions and providing some oversight and governance of the processes.

SOURCE: Sparrow, P, Hird, M and Cooper C L (2015) *Do We Need HR?*, Palgrave Macmillan, Basingstoke, reproduced with permission

KEY LEARNING POINTS

- *Talent management defined*

  Talent management is the process of identifying, developing, recruiting, retaining and deploying talented people.

  Talent management is a strategic management process; in the words of Johnson, Scholes and Whittington (2005: 6) it involves 'understanding the strategic position of an organization, making strategic choices for the future, and turning strategy into action'.

- *Talent defined*

  Talented people are those who have the skills and ability to do something well.

- *The talent pipeline*

  Talent management takes the form of a 'bundle' of interrelated talent management processes that constitute the talent pipeline.

- *Talent management strategy*
  A talent management strategy consists of a declaration of intent on how the processes in the talent pipeline should mesh together with an overall objective – to acquire and nurture talent wherever it is and wherever it is needed.

References

Chartered Institute of Personnel and Development (2007) *Talent: Strategy, management, measurement*, CIPD, London

Collings, D G and Mellahi, K (2009) Strategic talent management: a review and research agenda, *Human Resource Management Review*, **19**, pp 304–13

Johnson, G, Scholes, K and Whittington, R (2005) *Explaining Corporate Strategy*, 7th edn, FTPrentice Hall, Harlow

Michaels, E G, Handfield-Jones, H and Axelrod, B (2001) *The War for Talent*, Harvard Business School Press, Boston MA

Pfeffer, J (2001) Fighting the war for talent is hazardous to your organization's health, *Organizational Dynamics*, **29** (4), pp 248–59

Thorne, K and Pellant, A (2007) *The Essential Guide to Managing Talent*, Kogan Page, London

Younger, J, Smallwood, N and Ulrich, D (2007) Developing your organization's brand as a talent developer, *Human Resource Planning*, **30** (2), pp 21–29

17 Learning and development strategy

KEY CONCEPTS AND TERMS

Development
e-learning
Learning
Organizational learning
Strategic learning and development
Training
Workplace learning

LEARNING OUTCOMES

On completing this chapter you should be able to define the key concepts above. You should also understand:

- the meaning, aims and philosophy of strategic learning and development;
- the elements of learning and development;
- how to develop a learning culture;
- the nature of organizational learning strategies;
- the nature of individual learning strategies.

Introduction

Strategic learning and development takes a broad and long-term view about how to ensure that the organization has the knowledgeable, skilled and engaged workforce it needs. Learning and development strategy is business-led and supports the achievement of the business strategy. It does this by creating a learning culture and through strategies for organizational and individual learning, as described later in this chapter. But it also defines how the organization intends to provide employees with the opportunity to grow and develop, thus enhancing their engagement with their jobs and the organization.

The aims of strategic learning and development

The aim of strategic learning and development is to produce a coherent and comprehensive framework for developing people through the creation of a learning culture and the formulation of organizational and individual learning strategies. This is in accordance with the belief that a firm's human resources are a major source of competitive advantage. It is therefore about developing the intellectual capital required by the organization, as well as ensuring that the right quality of people are available to meet present and future needs. The main thrust of strategic HR development (SHRD) is to provide an environment in which people are encouraged to learn and develop. Although strategic learning and development is business-led, its specific strategies have to take into account individual aspirations and needs.

Strategic learning and development is associated with strategic HRM. Both are concerned with investing in people and developing the organization's human capital. As Keep (1989: 112) observed:

> One of the primary objectives of HRM is the creation of conditions whereby the latent potential of employees will be realized and their commitment to the causes of the organization secured. This latent potential is taken to include, not merely the capacity to acquire and utilize new skills and knowledge, but also a hitherto untapped wealth of ideas about how the organization's operations might be better ordered.

Strategic learning and development philosophy

The philosophy underpinning strategic learning and development is that:

- its plans and programmes should be integrated with and support the achievement of business and human resource strategies;
- it is performance-related – designed to achieve specified improvements in corporate, functional, team and individual performance;
- everyone in the organization should be encouraged and given the opportunity to learn – to develop their skills and knowledge to the maximum of their capacity;

- the framework for individual learning is provided by personal development plans that focus on self-managed learning and are supported by coaching, mentoring and formal training;
- the organization needs to invest in learning and development by providing appropriate learning opportunities and facilities, but the prime responsibility for learning and development rests with individuals, who will be given the guidance and support of their managers and, as necessary, members of the learning and development or HR department.

This involves creating a learning culture, the characteristics of which are self-managed learning not instruction, long-term capacity building not short-term fixes, and empowerment not supervision.

STRATEGIC HRM IN ACTION

People development strategy at Astra Zeneca

- The third strategic business objective of Astra Zeneca is:

  To ensure a well-motivated organization in which people are respected, enjoy their jobs and obtain fulfilment.

- Our people development strategy applies to all employees, not just to managers or people of high potential. It relates to the continuing development of ability and contribution in each person's current job and, if considered to have the potential to advance further, towards subsequent jobs.

- People development strategies are vital to the business but it is important that they support the key business strategies. The appropriate resources must be available to meet the key priorities for people development. Expenditure on education, training and development is regarded as a necessary and calculated investment, yielding considerable pay-off in terms of enhanced business performance. Managers have a clear responsibility to develop their subordinates. Performance management, which is the key management process that brings together the setting of personal work targets and development plans, is the preferred integrated approach by which employees' learning and development are managed continually in relation to all work activities.

- All employees must have a personal development plan jointly agreed with their manager, and this plan must be progressed and regularly reviewed and updated. It should be derived from the accountabilities of the jobholder and the personal targets for the coming period, plus any anticipated future needs. The plan should cover coaching and on-the-job and off-the job training.

- All employees are to be encouraged continually to develop their skills and experience both for their own benefit and that of the business through the improved contribution that will result, thus maintaining and extending the business's competitive advantage.

- Career planning will be a joint activity between the individual and the manager, with employees having a major responsibility for their own career management, including personal development.

- The development of individuals must take into account that Astra Zeneca is a complex, globally managed business. Particular emphasis should be placed on the need for good business understanding and teamwork across the business worldwide. The nature of the business requires special attention in the areas of organization development activities, team building, project management and cross-cultural management skills.

- People development activities will be regularly audited to ensure that appropriate, cost-effective investment is made in all parts of the organization to support current business activities.

SOURCE: Armstrong, M and Baron, A (2002) *Strategic HRM: The route to improved business performance*, CIPD, London

Elements of learning and development

The key elements of learning and development are:

- Learning: the process by which a person acquires and develops new knowledge, skills, capabilities, behaviours and attitudes.
- Training: the planned and systematic modification of behaviour through learning events, programmes and instruction that enables individuals to achieve the levels of knowledge, skill and competence needed to carry out their work effectively.
- Development: the growth or realization of a person's ability and potential through the provision of learning and educational experiences.

Learning should be distinguished from training: 'Learning is the process by which a person constructs new knowledge, skills and capabilities, whereas training is one of several responses an organization can undertake to promote learning' (Reynolds, Caley and Mason, 2002: 9).

Strategy for creating a learning culture

A fundamental objective of strategic learning and development strategy is to create a learning culture. A learning culture is one in which learning is recognized by top management, line managers and employees generally as an essential organizational process to which they are committed and in which they engage continuously. It is described by Reynolds (2004: 21) as a 'growth medium' that will 'encourage employees to commit to a range of positive discretionary behaviours, including learning' and that has the following characteristics: empowerment not supervision, self-managed learning not instruction, and long-term capacity building not short-term fixes. Discretionary learning as defined by Sloman (2003) happens when individuals actively seek to acquire the knowledge and skills that promote the organization's objectives.

The steps required to create a learning culture proposed by Reynolds (2004: 12–20) are:

- Develop and share the vision – belief in a desired and emerging future.
- Empower employees – provide 'supported autonomy'; freedom for employees to manage their work within certain boundaries (policies and expected behaviours) but with support available as required. Adopt a facilitative style of management in which responsibility for decision making is ceded as far as possible to employees.
- Provide employees with a supportive learning environment where learning capabilities can be discovered and applied, eg peer networks, supportive policies and systems, and protected time for learning.
- Use coaching techniques to draw out the talents of others by encouraging employees to identify options and seek their own solutions to problems.
- Guide employees through their work challenges and provide them with time, resources and, crucially, feedback.
- Recognize the importance of managers acting as role models.
- Encourage networks – communities of practice.
- Align systems to vision – get rid of bureaucratic systems that produce problems rather than facilitate work.

Organizational learning strategy

Organizations can be described as continuous learning systems, and organizational learning has been defined by Marsick (1994: 28) as a process of: 'Co-ordinated systems change, with mechanisms built in for individuals and groups to access, build and use organizational memory, structure and culture to develop long-term organizational capacity.'

Organizational learning strategy aims to develop a firm's resource-based capability. This is in accordance with one of the basic principles of HRM, namely that it is necessary to invest in people in order to develop the human capital required by the organization and to increase its stock of knowledge and skills. As stated by Ehrenberg and Smith (1994: 279–80), human capital theory indicates that: 'The knowledge and skills a worker has – which comes from education and training, including the training that experience brings – generate a certain stock of productive capital.'

Five principles of organizational learning have been defined by Harrison (1997):

1 The need for a powerful and cohering vision of the organization to be communicated and maintained across the workforce in order to promote awareness of the need for strategic thinking at all levels.

2 The need to develop strategy in the context of a vision that is not only powerful but also open-ended and unambiguous. This will encourage a search for a wide rather than a narrow range of strategic options, promote lateral thinking and orient the knowledge-creating activities of employees.

3 Within the framework of vision and goals, the major facilitators of organizational learning are frequent dialogue, communication and conversations.

4 It is essential to challenge people continuously to re-examine what they take for granted.

5 It is essential to develop a climate that is conducive to learning and innovation.

Individual learning strategy

The individual learning strategy of an organization is driven by its people requirements, which are expressed in terms of the sort of skills and behaviours that are required.

As Sloman (2003: 17) pointed out:

Interventions and activities, which are intended to improve knowledge and skills, will increasingly focus on the learner... And he or she will be encouraged to take more responsibility for his or her learning. Efforts will be made to develop a climate that supports effective and appropriate learning.

An individual learning strategy should take account of these points. It will be based on an understanding of how people learn. It will indicate how learning needs should be identified and set out the intentions of the organization on how those learning needs will be met through workplace learning (including coaching and mentoring), formal training courses or programmes, or a combination of the two in the shape of blended learning. The latter approach is preferable.

How people learn

Individuals learn for themselves but they also learn from other people – their managers and co-workers (social learning). They learn mainly by doing (experiential learning) and to a much lesser extent by instruction. The ways in which individuals learn will differ and what they learn will depend largely on how well they are motivated or self-motivated. Discretionary learning (self-directed or self-managed) takes place when individuals of their own volition actively seek to acquire the knowledge and skills they need to carry out their work effectively. It should be encouraged and supported.

The ways in which learning and development takes place are described by the 70/20/10 model, which is based on research conducted by Lombardo and Eichinger (1996). The model explains that people's development will be about 70 per cent from work experience, about 20 per cent from social learning (through managers by example and feedback, and through fellow workers) and 10 per cent from courses and reading. In other words, by far the majority of learning happens in the workplace. A learning and development strategy needs to take this into account.

Identifying learning needs

The learning and development strategy should be founded on an understanding of how learning needs can be identified. Skills analysis techniques can be used for craft or manual jobs. For other jobs, role profiles can define knowledge and skill requirements. Performance management, as described in Chapter 13, is an effective way to establish learning needs. This is done by reference to a role profile and analysing what individuals have to know and be able to do to perform their current jobs better and to enable them to develop in the future. The analysis provides the basis for personal development planning, which involves self-managed learning but also requires support from the organization in the form of guidance, coaching, learning resource centres, e-learning (the provision of learning opportunities and support via computer, networked and web-based technology), mentoring and formal internal or external training courses.

Workplace learning

Workplace learning is experiential learning. It is learning on-the-job by carrying out the work and by observing what other people do (social learning). It is embedded in work activities and is mainly an informal process.

A study by Eraut *et al* (1998) established that most of the learning described to the researchers was informal, neither clearly specified nor planned. It arose naturally from the challenges of work. Learning from experience and other people at work predominated.

Reynolds (2004: 3) observed that:

> The simple act of observing more experienced colleagues can accelerate learning; conversing, swapping stories, co-operating on tasks and offering mutual support deepen and solidify the process... This kind of learning – often very informal in nature – is thought to be vastly more effective in building proficiency.

Workplace learning can be enhanced by coaching, mentoring, e-learning and planned experience. It can be supplemented by training interventions, but they are there simply to extend experiential learning.

However, workplace learning should not be left entirely to chance. Line managers can facilitate it by giving new employees guidance on what they are expected to do and how they should do it. This should be a deliberate process using instruction and coaching techniques, which managers need to learn as part of their development programme. Coaching delivered by managers can give continued support to learning in the workplace. In some cases mentors can be used to provide pragmatic advice and continuing support to help people learn and develop.

But there are disadvantages. Relying on learning on-the-job can mean that employees are left to their own devices to pick up bad habits. It may be argued that formal training has its limits, but at least it can be planned and applied systematically.

A further difficulty is that workplace learning depends largely on the willingness and ability of line managers to take responsibility for it. Some will, many will not. This crucial aspect of learning may therefore be neglected unless the HR or learning and development function does something about it. The learning strategy should contain provisions for encouraging managers to take responsibility for workplace learning and for helping them to acquire the skills needed.

Formal training courses or programmes

Formal training courses or programmes use systematic and planned instruction activities to promote learning. As Reynolds (2004: 45) pointed out, training has a complementary role to play in accelerating learning: 'It should be reserved for situations that justify a more directed, expert-led approach rather than viewing it as a comprehensive and all-pervasive people development solution.' He also commented that the conventional training model has a tendency to 'emphasize subject-specific knowledge, rather than trying to build core learning abilities'.

Formal training is indeed only one of the ways of ensuring that learning takes place, but it can be justified in the following circumstances:

- the knowledge or skills cannot be acquired satisfactorily in the workplace or by self-directed learning;
- different skills are required by a number of people, which have to be developed quickly to meet new demands and cannot be gained by relying on experience;
- the tasks to be carried out are so specialized or complex that people are unlikely to master them on their own initiative at a reasonable speed;
- when a learning need common to a number of people has to be met that can readily be dealt with in a training event or programme, for example induction, essential IT skills, communication skills.

A fundamental problem with formal training is that it can be difficult for people to transfer their learning on the course to the entirely different circumstances in their workplace. Training can seem to be remote from reality, and the skills and knowledge acquired can appear to be irrelevant.

To tackle this problem it is necessary to make the training as relevant and realistic as possible, anticipating and dealing with any potential transfer difficulties. Individuals are more likely to apply learning when they do not find it too difficult; believe what they learnt is appropriate, useful and transferable; are supported by line managers; have job autonomy; believe in themselves; and are committed and engaged.

Blended learning

The choice of learning methods is not an either/or matter between formal training and workplace learning. The strategy might support the use of blended learning. This means combining different approaches to learning so that they complement and support one another. A blended learning programme might be planned for an individual using a mix of planned experience, self-directed learning activities defined in a personal development plan, e-learning facilities, coaching, mentoring, and instruction provided in an in- company or external course.

STRATEGIC HRM IN ACTION

Measuring the contribution of learning to business performance at Lyreco Ltd (UK)

Lyreco UK is part of a large family-owned office supplies group operating extensively in Europe, Canada and Asia.

Metrics are a central part of all management processes at Lyreco and these inform the learning investment and planning processes. In field sales, measures include sales turnover, margin and new business, whilst in customer service the performance and productivity metrics include costs per line, abandoned call rate, average call time, and average wait time. Monthly performance results in all areas are scrutinized to identify areas for attention, and the learning and development team run learning sessions and activities aimed at helping people to improve their performance. When sales margin was identified as an area for attention, over 150 people attended focused workshops and subsequent performance results were tracked to measure improvements. Similarly, warehouse supervisors with the highest staff turnover attended learning programmes and, as a consequence, staff turnover was at lowest-ever levels.

SOURCE: IRS Employment Review (2007) February, 2007 pp 6–9

KEY LEARNING POINTS

- *Aim of strategic learning and development*
  Strategic learning and development aims to produce a coherent and comprehensive framework for developing people through the creation of a learning culture and the formulation of organizational and individual learning strategies.

- *Organizational learning strategy*
  This aims to develop a firm's resource-based capability.

- *Individual learning strategy*
  This is driven by the organization's human resource requirements, which are expressed in terms of the sort of skills and behaviours they need. The strategy will be based on an understanding of how people learn. It will indicate how learning needs should be identified and will set out the intentions of the organization on how those learning needs will be met through workplace learning (including coaching and mentoring), formal training courses or programmes, or a combination of the two in the shape of blended learning.

References

Ehrenberg, R G and Smith, R S (1994) *Modern Labor Economics*, HarperCollins, New York

Eraut, M J, Alderton, G, Cole, G and Senker, P (1998) *Development of Knowledge and Skills in Employment*, Economic and Social Research Council, London

Harrison, R (1997) *Employee Development*, 1st edn, IPM, London

Keep, E (1989) Corporate training strategies: the vital component?, in *New Perspectives on Human Resource Management*, ed J Storey, pp 109–25, Routledge, London

Lombardo, M M and Eichinger, R W (1996) *The Course Architect Development Planner*, Lominger, Minneapolis

Marsick, V J (1994) Trends in managerial invention: creating a learning map, *Management Learning*, 25 (1), pp 11–33

Reynolds, J (2004) *Helping People Learn*, CIPD, London

Reynolds, J, Caley, L and Mason, R (2002) *How Do People Learn?*, CIPD, London

Sloman, M (2003) E-learning: stepping up the learning curve, *Impact*, January, pp 16–17

Reward strategy 18

KEY CONCEPTS AND TERMS

Gap analysis   Reward strategy
Guiding principles   Reward system
Reward philosophy   Total reward

LEARNING OUTCOMES

On completing this chapter you should be able to define the key concepts above. You should also understand:

- the meaning of reward strategy;
- the reasons for having a reward strategy;
- the characteristics of reward strategy;
- the basis of reward strategy;
- the content of reward strategy;
- the guiding principles that should govern reward strategy;
- how to develop reward strategy;
- what makes an effective reward strategy;
- the significance of line manager capability;
- the problem of the reward strategy concept.

Introduction

Reward strategy is concerned with the policies and practices required to ensure that the value of people and the contribution they make to achieving organizational, departmental and team goals are recognized and rewarded. It is about planning and executing the design and implementation of reward systems (interrelated reward processes, practices and procedures) that aim to satisfy the needs of both the organization and its stakeholders and to operate fairly, equitably and consistently. These systems will include arrangements for assessing the value of jobs through job evaluation and market pricing, the design and management of grade and pay structures, performance management processes, schemes for rewarding and recognizing people according to their individual performance or contribution and/or team or organizational performance, and the provision of employee benefits.

Reward strategy defined

Reward strategy is a declaration of intent. It defines what an organization wants to do in the longer term to address critical reward issues and to develop and implement reward policies, practices and processes that will further the achievement of its business goals and meet the needs of its stakeholders. It starts from where the reward practices of the business are now and goes on to describe what they should become.

Reward strategy provides a sense of purpose and direction, a pathway that links the needs of the business and its people with the reward policies and practices of the organization and thereby communicates and explains these practices. It constitutes a framework for developing and putting into effect reward policies, practices and processes that ensure that people are rewarded for doing the things that increase the likelihood of the organization's business goals being achieved.

Reward strategy is underpinned by a reward philosophy. It is concerned not only with what should be done but how it should be done; with implementation as well as planning. It is based on an understanding of the culture of the organization and an appreciation of its needs and those of its people within the context in which the organization operates. This provides the basis upon which cultural fit is achieved and needs are satisfied.

Why have a reward strategy?

Overall, in the words of Duncan Brown (2001: 44), 'Reward strategy is ultimately a way of thinking that you can apply to any reward issue arising in your organization, to see how you can create value from it.' More specifically, there are four arguments for developing reward strategies:

1 You must have some idea where you are going – or otherwise how do you know how to get there, and how do you know that you have arrived (if you ever do)?

2 Pay costs in most organizations are by far the largest item of expense – they can be 60 per cent (and are often much more in labour-intensive organizations) – so doesn't it make makes sense to think about how they should be managed and invested in the longer term?

3 There can be a positive relationship between rewards – in the broadest sense – and performance, so shouldn't we think about how we can strengthen that link?

4 As Cox and Purcell (1998: 65) wrote: 'The real benefit in reward strategies lies in complex linkages with other human resource management policies and practices.' This is a good reason for developing a reward-strategic framework that indicates how reward processes will be linked to HR processes so that they are coherent and mutually supportive.

Characteristics of reward strategy

Armstrong and Murlis (2004: 33) pointed out that: 'Reward strategy will be characterized by diversity and conditioned both by the legacy of the past and the realities of the future.' All reward strategies are different, just as all organizations are different. Of course, similar aspects of reward will be covered in the strategies of different organizations but they will be treated differently in accordance with variations between organizations in their contexts, strategies and cultures.

Reward strategists may have a clear idea of what needs to be done but they have to take account of the views of top management and be prepared to persuade them with convincing arguments that action needs to be taken. They have to take particular account of financial considerations – the concept of 'affordability' looms large in the minds of chief executives and financial directors, who will need to be convinced that an investment in rewards will pay off. They also have to convince employees and their representatives that the reward strategy will meet their needs as well as business needs.

The basis of reward strategy

Reward strategy should be based on a detailed analysis of the present arrangements for reward, which would include a statement of their strengths and weaknesses. This could take the form of a 'gap analysis', which compares what it is believed should be happening with what is actually happening and indicates which 'gaps' need to be filled. A format for the analysis is shown in Table 18.1.

TABLE 18.1 Reward strategy gap analysis

What Should Be Happening	What Is Happening	What Needs to Be Done
1. A total reward approach is adopted that emphasizes the significance of both financial and non-financial rewards.		
2. Reward policies and practices are developed within the framework of a well-articulated strategy that is designed to support the achievement of business objectives and meet the needs of stakeholders.		
3. A job evaluation scheme is used that properly reflects the values of the organization, is up to date with regard to the jobs it covers, and is non-discriminatory.		
4. Equal-pay issues are given serious attention. This includes the conduct of equal-pay reviews that lead to action.		
5. Market rates are tracked carefully so that a competitive pay structure exists that contributes to the attraction and retention of high-quality people.		
6. Grade and pay structures are based on job evaluation and market rate analysis, are appropriate to the characteristics and needs of the organization and its employees, facilitate the management of relativities,		

(Continued)

TABLE 18.1 *Continued*

What Should Be Happening	What Is Happening	What Needs to Be Done
provide scope for rewarding contribution, clarify reward and career opportunities, are constructed logically, operate transparently, and are easy to manage and maintain.		
7. Contingent pay schemes reward contribution fairly and consistently, support the motivation of staff and the development of a performance culture, deliver the right messages about the values of the organization, contain a clear 'line of sight' between contribution and reward, and are cost-effective.		
8. Performance management processes contribute to performance improvement, people development and the management of expectations; they operate effectively throughout the organization and are supported by line managers and staff.		
9. Employee benefits and pension schemes meet the needs of stakeholders and are cost-effective.		
10. A flexible benefits approach is adopted.		

(Continued)

TABLE 18.1 *Continued*

What Should Be Happening	What Is Happening	What Needs to Be Done
11. Reward management procedures exist that ensure that reward processes are managed effectively and that costs are controlled.		
12. Appropriate use is made of computers (software and spreadsheets) to assist in the process of reward management.		
13. Reward management aims and arrangements are transparent and communicated well to staff.		
14. Surveys are used to assess the opinions of staff about reward, and action is taken on the outcomes.		
15. An appropriate amount of responsibility for reward is devolved to line managers.		
16. Line managers are capable of carrying out their devolved responsibilities well.		
17. Steps are taken to train line managers and provide them with support and guidance as required.		
18. HR has the knowledge and skills to provide the required reward management advice and services, and to guide and support line managers.		

(Continued)

TABLE 18.1 *Continued*

What Should Be Happening	What Is Happening	What Needs to Be Done
19. Overall, reward management developments are conscious of the need to achieve affordability and to demonstrate that they are cost-effective.		
20. Steps are taken to evaluate the effectiveness of reward management processes and to ensure that they reflect changing needs.		

A diagnosis should be made of the reasons for any gaps or problems so that decisions can be made on what needs to be done to overcome them. It can then be structured under the headings set out below:

- A statement of intent: the reward initiatives that it is proposed should be taken.
- A rationale: the reasons why the proposals are being made. The rationale should make out the business case for the proposals, indicating how they will meet business needs and setting out the costs and the benefits. It should also refer to any people issues that need to be addressed and how the strategy will deal with them.
- A plan: how, when and by whom the reward initiatives will be implemented. The plan should indicate what steps will need to be taken and should take account of resource constraints and the need for communications, involvement and training. The priorities attached to each element of the strategy should be indicated and a timetable for implementation should be drawn up. The plan should state who will be responsible for the development and implementation of the strategy.
- A definition of guiding principles: the values that it is believed should be adopted in formulating and implementing the strategy.

The content of reward strategy

Reward strategy may be a broad-brush affair, simply indicating the general direction in which it is thought that reward management should go.

Additionally, or alternatively, reward strategy may set out a list of specific intentions dealing with particular aspects of reward management.

Broad-brush reward strategy

A broad-brush reward strategy may commit the organization to the pursuit of a total rewards policy. The basic aim might be to achieve an appropriate balance between financial and non-financial rewards. A further aim could be to use other approaches to the development of the employment relationship and the work environment, which will enhance commitment and engagement and provide more opportunities for the contribution of people to be valued and recognized.

Examples of other broad strategic aims include: 1) introducing a more integrated approach to reward management – encouraging continuous personal development and spelling out career opportunities; 2) developing a more flexible approach to reward that includes the reduction of artificial barriers as a result of overemphasis on grading and promotion; 3) generally rewarding people according to their contribution; 4) supporting the development of a performance culture and building levels of competence; and 5) clarifying what behaviours will be rewarded and why.

Specific reward initiatives

The selection of reward initiatives and the priorities attached to them will be based on an analysis of the present circumstances of the organization and an assessment of the needs of the business and its employees. The following are examples of possible specific reward initiatives, one or more of which might feature in a reward strategy:

- the development of a total reward approach in which each aspect of reward – namely base pay, contingent pay, employee benefits and non-financial rewards (which include intrinsic rewards from the work itself) – are linked together and treated as an integrated and coherent whole;
- the replacement of present methods of contingent pay with a pay for contribution scheme;
- the introduction of a new grade and pay structure, eg a broad-graded or career family structure;
- the replacement of an existing decayed job evaluation scheme with a scheme that more clearly reflects organizational values and is less bureaucratic;
- the improvement of performance management processes so that they provide better support for the development of a performance culture and more clearly identify development needs;

- the introduction of a formal recognition scheme;
- the development of a flexible benefits system;
- the conduct of equal pay reviews with the objective of ensuring that work of equal value is paid equally;
- communication programmes designed to inform everyone of the reward policies and practices of the organization;
- training, coaching and guidance programmes designed to increase the ability of line managers to play their part in managing reward.

Guiding principles

Guiding principles define the approach that an organization takes to dealing with reward. They are the basis for reward policies and provide guidelines for the actions contained in the reward strategy. They express the reward philosophy of the organization – its values and beliefs about how people should be rewarded.

Members of the organization should be involved in the definition of guiding principles, which can then be communicated to everyone to increase understanding of what underpins reward policies and practices. However, employees will suspend their judgement of the principles until they experience how they are applied. What matters to them are not the philosophies themselves but the pay practices emanating from them and the messages about the employment 'deal' that they get as a consequence. It is the reality that is important, not the rhetoric.

Guiding principles should incorporate or be influenced by general beliefs about fairness, equity, consistency and transparency. They may be concerned with such specific matters as:

- developing reward policies and practices that support the achievement of business goals;
- providing rewards that attract, retain and motivate staff and help to develop a high-performance culture;
- maintaining competitive rates of pay;
- rewarding people according to their contribution;
- recognizing the value of all staff who are making an effective contribution, not just the exceptional performers;
- allowing a reasonable degree of flexibility in the operation of reward processes and in the choice of benefits by employees;
- devolving more responsibility for reward decisions to line managers.

STRATEGIC HRM IN ACTION

Reward strategy at BT

Reward strategy at BT (British Telecom) is a fairly broad-brush affair simply indicating the general direction in which it is thought that reward management for the 90,000 staff at BT should go, with an emphasis on adopting a more holistic, total reward approach. It is summarized as follows:

> Use the full range of rewards (salary, bonus, benefits and recognition) to recruit and retain the best people, and to encourage and reward achievement where actions and behaviours are consistent with the BT values.

Guiding principles

BT's reward strategy is underpinned by a set of guiding principles defining the approach that the organization takes to dealing with reward. These guiding principles are the basis for reward policies and provide guidelines for the actions contained in the reward strategy. They express the reward philosophy of the organization – its values and beliefs about how people should be rewarded. The six guiding principles governing the design of the reward system at BT are as follows:

- business linkage;
- clarity and transparency;
- market competitiveness;
- performance differentiation;
- choice and flexibility;
- equal pay.

The three principal elements driving individual reward are:

- The individual's performance and contribution in the role – what does it mean to have high individual performance?
- The competitiveness of the individual's existing salary, together with the actual (and anticipated) salary movement in relevant local markets – how does salary align to the external market?
- The company's business results and ability to pay – can the company afford to invest money in terms of additional reward?

Underpinning these pillars are the principles of clarity (a 'focus on roles'), equal pay and choice.

Developing reward strategy

The formulation of reward strategy can be described as a process for developing and defining a sense of direction. There are four key development phases:

1 The diagnosis phase, when reward goals are agreed, current policies and practices assessed against them, options for improvement considered and any changes agreed.

2 The detailed design phase, when improvements and changes are detailed and any changes tested (pilot testing is important).

3 The final testing and preparation phase.

4 The implementation phase, followed by ongoing review and modification.

A logical step-by-step model for doing this is illustrated in Figure 18.1. This incorporates ample provision for consultation, involvement and

FIGURE 18.1 A model of the reward strategy development process

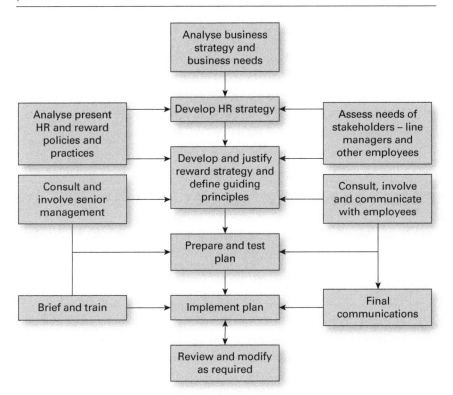

communication with stakeholders, who include senior managers as the ultimate decision makers, as well as employees and line managers.

In practice, however, the formulation of reward strategy is seldom as logical and linear a process as this. Reward strategies evolve; they have to respond to changes in organizational requirements that are happening all the time. They need to track emerging trends in reward management and may modify their views accordingly, as long as they do not leap too hastily on the latest bandwagon.

It may be helpful to record reward strategies formally as a basis for planning and communication. But this should be regarded as no more than a piece of paper that can be torn up when the needs of the organization change – as they will – rather than as a tablet of stone.

STRATEGIC HRM IN ACTION

DSG International: aligning reward with the business plan

In a difficult economic environment DSG simplified their complex mix of reward arrangements to establish a close alignment between rewards and the five components of a new business turnaround plan, primarily through the redesign of executive incentive plans. The change was designed to enhance the perception of line-of-sight between individual performance, group performance and reward. It illustrates the vital role of communications to explain the 'why' of reward change, what it means for the business and how each component of reward links to a business plan.

SOURCE: e-reward (2010) Assessing Reward Effectiveness Survey, e-reward, Stockport

Effective reward strategies

An effective reward strategy is one that provides clear guidance on development planning and implementation and achieves its objectives when implemented. Duncan Brown (2001: 14–15) has suggested that effective reward strategies have three components:

1 They have to have clearly defined goals and a well-defined link to business objectives.

2 There have to be well-designed pay and reward programmes, tailored to the needs of the organization and its people, and consistent and integrated with one another.

3 Perhaps most important and most neglected, there needs to be effective and supportive HR and reward processes in place.

Criteria for effectiveness

The questions to be answered when assessing the effectiveness of a reward strategy, as posed by Armstrong and Brown (2006), are:

- Is it aligned with the organization's business strategy (vertical alignment or integration) and its HR strategies (horizontal alignment or integration)?
- Will it support the achievement of business goals and reinforce organizational values? If so, how?
- Are the objectives of the reward strategy clearly defined, including a convincing statement of how the business needs of the organization will be met and how the needs of employees and other stakeholders will be catered for?
- Is it based on a thorough analysis and diagnosis of the internal and external environment of the organization and the reward issues that need to be addressed?
- Has a realistic assessment been made of the resources required to implement the strategy and the costs involved?
- Is it affordable in the sense that the benefits will exceed any costs?
- Have steps been taken to ensure that supporting processes such as performance management, communication and training are in place?
- Is the programme for implementation realistic?
- Have steps been taken to ensure that the strategy is supported and understood by line managers and staff?
- Will HR and line managers be capable of implementing and managing the strategy in practice?
- Has accountability and ownership for the various reward policies and practices been clarified, defining what success looks like and how it will be measured? Are effective review mechanisms in place?
- Is the reward strategy flexible in adjusting to take account of changes in the business and in the environment?

Reward strategy and line management capability

HR can initiate new reward policies and practices but it is the line manager that has the main responsibility for implementing them. The trend is, rightly, to devolve more responsibility for managing reward to line managers. Some will have the ability to respond to the challenge and opportunity; others will be incapable of carrying out this responsibility without close guidance from HR; some may not be able to cope. Managers may not always do what HR expects them to do, and if compelled to, they may be half-hearted about it.

This puts the onus on HR and reward specialists to develop line management capability; to initiate processes that can readily be implemented by line managers; to promote understanding by communicating what is happening, why it is happening and how it will affect everyone; to provide guidance and help where required; and to provide formal training as necessary.

The problem with the concept of reward strategy

To what extent can pay be strategic? This question was posed by Trevor (2009: 21), who noted that pay is seen as 'a means of aligning a company's most strategic asset – their employees – to the strategic direction of the organization' and that strategic pay theory is predicated on the notion of strategic choice. But he claimed that rationalism is limited and pointed out that pay systems tend to be selected for their legitimacy (best practice as advocated by institutions such as the CIPD and by management consultants) rather than for purely economic reasons. His research into the pay policies and practice of three large consumer goods organizations revealed a gap between intended and actual practice – intent does not necessarily lead to action: 'Irrespective of the strategic desire or the saliency of the design, ineffectual execution results in ineffectual pay practice, which then reacts negatively upon the pay outcomes experienced as a result… Attempting to use strategic pay systems, such as incentive pay, results often in unintended consequences and negative outcomes that destroy value rather than create it' (Trevor, 2009: 34). The main implications of the findings from this research were that: 'Theory is out of step with reality and may represent a largely unattainable ideal in practice… an alternative approach for the use of pay systems in support of strategy is required: one that acknowledges the relative limits on the ability of companies to manage pay strategically' (Trevor, 2009: 37). As Wright and Nishii (2006: 11) commented: 'Not all intended HR practices are actually implemented and those that are may often be implemented in ways that differ from the original intention.'

A similar point was made by Armstrong and Brown (2006) when they described 'the new reality' of strategic reward management, as follows:

SOURCE REVIEW   The reality of reward strategy – Armstrong and Brown (2006: 1–2)

When mostly North American concepts of strategic HRM and reward first entered into management thinking and practice in the UK we were both some of their most ardent advocates, writing and advising individual employers on the benefits of aligning their reward systems so as to drive business performance. We helped to articulate strategic plans and visions, and to design the pay and reward changes that would secure better alignment and performance.

Some 20 years later, we are a little older and a little wiser as a result of these experiences. We remain passionate proponents of a strategic approach to reward management. But in conducting and observing this work we have seen some of the risks as well as the opportunities in pursuing the reward strategy path: of an over-focus on planning at the expense of process and practice; on design rather than delivery; on the boardroom and the HR function rather than on front-line managers and employees; and on concept rather than communications.

At times there has been a tendency to overambition and optimism in terms of what could and could not be achieved by changing pay and reward arrangements, and how quickly real change could be delivered and business results secured. At times the focus on internal business fit led to narrow-minded reward determinism, and a lack of attention to the increasingly important external influences and constraints on reward, from the shifting tax and wider legislative, economic and social environment. And sometimes the focus on designs and desires meant that the requirements and skills of line and reward managers were insufficiently diagnosed and developed.

KEY LEARNING POINTS

- *Reward strategy defined*
  - Reward strategy is concerned with the policies and practices required to ensure that the value of people and the contribution they make to achieving organizational, departmental and team goals is recognized and rewarded.
  - It is about planning and executing the design and implementation of reward systems (interrelated reward processes, practices and procedures) that aim to satisfy the needs of both the organization and its stakeholders and to operate fairly, equitably and consistently. Reward strategy is a declaration of intent.
  - It defines what an organization wants to do in the longer term to address critical reward issues and to develop and implement reward policies, practices and processes that will further the achievement of its business goals and meet the needs of its stakeholders.
  - It starts from where the reward practices of the business are now and goes on to describe what they should become.

- *Arguments in favour of reward strategy*
  There are four arguments for developing reward strategy:
  - Reward strategy provides a sense of purpose and direction.
  - Pay costs in most organizations are by far the largest item of expense, and reward strategy can help to manage them properly.
  - The relationship between rewards and performance will be strengthened.
  - A reward strategic framework will indicate how reward processes will be linked to HR processes so that they are coherent and mutually supportive.

- *Developing reward strategy*
  Reward strategists have to:
  - Take account of the views of top management and be prepared to persuade them with convincing arguments that action needs to be taken.
  - Take particular account of financial considerations.
  - Convince employees and their representatives that the reward strategy will meet their needs as well as business needs.
  - Reward strategy should be based on a detailed analysis of the present arrangements for reward, which would include a statement of their strengths and weaknesses.
  - Reward strategy may be a broad-brush affair, simply indicating the general direction in which it is thought that reward management should go. Additionally, or alternatively, reward strategy may set out a list of specific intentions dealing with particular aspects of reward management.
  - Guiding principles define the approach that an organization takes to dealing with reward. They are the basis for reward policies and provide guidelines for the actions contained in the reward strategy. They express the reward philosophy of the organization – its values and beliefs about how people should be rewarded.
  - An effective reward strategy is one that provides clear guidance on development planning and implementation and achieves its objectives when implemented.
  - HR can initiate new reward policies and practices but it is the line manager who has the main responsibility for implementing them. The trend is, rightly, to devolve more responsibility to line managers for managing reward.
  - There are limitations to the impact of reward strategy. Intent does not necessarily lead to action.

References

Armstrong, M and Brown, D (2006) *Strategic Reward: Making it happen*, Kogan Page, London

Armstrong, M and Murlis, H (2004) *Reward Management*, 5th edn, Kogan Page, London

Brown, D (2001) *Reward Strategies: From intent to impact*, CIPD, London

Cox, A and Purcell, J (1998) Searching for leverage: pay systems, trust, motivation and commitment in SMEs, in *Trust, Motivation and Commitment: A reader*, ed S Perkins, pp 60–65, SRRC, Faringdon

Trevor, J (2009) Can pay be strategic?, in *Rethinking Reward*, ed S Corby, S Palmer and E Lindop, pp 21–46, Palgrave Macmillan, Basingstoke

Wright, P M and Nishii, L H (2006) Strategic HRM and organizational behaviour: integrating multiple levels of analysis, Working Paper 06–05, Cornell University, Ithica, NY

Employee relations strategy

Introduction

Employment relations strategy defines the intentions of the organization about what needs to be done and what needs to be changed in the ways in which the organization handles relationships with employees and, if any, their trade unions. This is an area of HRM where a strategic approach is particularly appropriate. Organizations need to have a clear idea of the route they want to follow in developing a co-operative and productive employment relations climate.

The framework for employment relations strategy is provided by the employment relationship, which describes how employers and employees work together and relate to one another. Because it is a fundamental aspect of employee relations, the nature of the employment relationship is examined in the first section of this chapter. Against this background, the next section deals with the characteristics and concerns of employment relations. The next sections cover two of the main aspects of employee relations: partnership and giving employees a voice. Finally, the chapter deals with trade union recognition strategy.

The employment relationship

As defined by Boxall (2013: 5) the employment relationship is 'the primary vehicle for "marrying" the needs of individuals and organizations'. As he points out: 'Organizations have simultaneous needs for commitment and flexibility, while individuals have enduring needs for security and community' (2013: 8).

The employment relationship can also be described as being a largely informal and constant process that happens whenever an employer has dealings with an employee, and vice versa. Underpinning the employment relationship is the psychological contract, which expresses certain assumptions and expectations about what managers and employees have to offer and are willing to deliver. The dimensions of the employment relationship as described by Kessler and Undy (1996) are shown in Figure 19.1.

FIGURE 19.1 Dimensions of the employment relationship

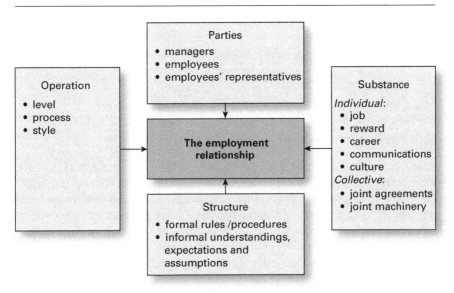

The dynamic nature of the employment relationship increases the difficulty of managing it. The problem is compounded by the multiplicity of factors that influence it – the culture of the organization, the prevailing management style, the values (espoused and practised) of top management, the existence or non-existence of a climate of trust, day-to-day interactions between employees and line managers, and the HR policies and practices of the business.

Strategies for managing the employment relationship will therefore focus on establishing overall intentions about how a constructive and co-operative employment relations climate can be developed and what approaches are adopted to achieving mutuality and trust.

A strategy for creating a constructive and positive employment relations climate

The employment relations climate of an organization consists of the perceptions of management, employees and their representatives about the ways in which employment relations are conducted and how the various parties (managers, employees and trade unions) behave when dealing with one another. An employment relations climate may be created by the management style adopted by management or by the behaviour of the trade unions or employee representatives (co-operative, hostile, militant, etc) or by the two interacting with one another. It can be good, bad or indifferent according to perceptions about the extent to which:

- management and employees trust one another;
- management treats employees fairly and with consideration;
- management is open about its actions and intentions – employment relations policies and procedures are transparent;
- harmonious relationships are generally maintained on a day-to-day basis;
- conflict, when it does arise, is resolved without resort to industrial action, and resolution is achieved by integrative processes that result in a 'win–win' solution;
- employees are generally committed to the interests of the organization and, equally, management treat them as stakeholders whose interests should be protected as far as possible.

A strategy for improving the employment relations climate may involve developing fair employment relations policies and procedures and making plans to implement them consistently. Line managers and team leaders who are largely responsible for the day-to-day conduct of employment relations need to be educated and trained on the approaches they should adopt. Transparency can be achieved by communicating policies to employees, and commitment increased by involvement and participation processes.

Importantly, as discussed below, the organization can address its obligations to the employees as stakeholders and formulate strategies for building mutuality and trust.

A strategy for achieving mutuality

The principle of mutuality was first expressed by Walton (1985: 64) as follows:

> The new HRM model is composed of policies that promote mutuality – mutual goals, mutual influence, mutual respect, mutual rewards, mutual responsibility. The theory is that policies of mutuality will elicit commitment, which in turn will yield both better economic performance and greater human development. A strategy for increasing mutuality would involve taking steps to develop a positive psychological contract (the set of reciprocal but unwritten expectations that exist between individual employees and their employers). This could be achieved by treating people as stakeholders, and relying on consensus and co-operation rather than control and coercion.

If there are recognized trade unions, plans can be made for concluding partnership agreements that emphasize unity of purpose, common approaches to working together and the importance of giving employees a voice in matters that concern them. The strategy could also emphasize the need to provide employment security and include plans for building a climate of trust, as considered below.

A strategy for building trust

Trust is a firm belief that a person may be relied on. A climate of trust is an essential ingredient in a positive employment relationship. It has been suggested by Herriot, Hirsh and Riley (1988) that trust should be regarded as social capital – the fund of goodwill in any social group that enables people within it to collaborate with one another.

A strategy for building trust must focus on how it can be created and maintained by managerial behaviour and by the development of better mutual understanding of expectations – employers of employees, and employees of employers. The sort of behaviour by managers that should be fostered by the strategy is being honest with people, keeping their word (delivering the deal) and practising what they preach. Managements that espouse values ('people are our greatest asset') and then proceed to ignore them will be low-trust organizations. More specifically, trust will be developed if management acts fairly, equitably and consistently, if a policy of transparency is implemented, if intentions and the reasons for proposals or decisions are communicated both to employees generally and to individuals, if there is full involvement in developing reward processes, and if mutual expectations are agreed through performance management.

The nature of employment relations strategy

Like all other aspects of HR strategy, employment relations strategy takes account of the business strategy and aims to support it. Support will exist if employee relations operate in a spirit of mutuality and partnership, and if this results in high levels of trust, co-operation and, ultimately, productivity.

Approaches to employment relations strategy

There are four approaches to employment relations strategy:

- Adversarial: the organization decides what it wants to do and employees are expected to fit in. Employees only exercise power by refusing to co-operate.
- Traditional: a good day-to-day working relationship, but management proposes and the workforce reacts through its elected representatives.
- Partnership: the organization involves employees in the drawing up and execution of the organization's policies, but retains the right to manage.
- Power sharing: employees are involved in both day-to-day and strategic decision making.

Adversarial approaches are much less common today in most organizations. The traditional approach is still the most typical but more interest is being expressed in partnership (as discussed later in this chapter). Power sharing is rare.

The concerns of employment relations strategy

Overall, employment relations strategy is concerned with building stable and co-operative relationships with employees that minimize conflict. More specifically, the strategy covers matters such as:

- the achievement of increased levels of commitment through involvement or participation – giving employees a voice;
- developing a 'partnership' with trade unions, recognizing that employees are stakeholders and that it is to the advantage of both parties to work together – this could be described as a unitary strategy, the aim of which is to increase mutual commitment (a unitary approach is based on the belief that management and employees share the same concerns and it is therefore in both their interests to work together);
- changing forms of recognition, including single union recognition, or de-recognition;
- changes in the form and content of procedural agreements that define the rules regulating relationships between management;

- new bargaining structures, including decentralization or single-table bargaining (negotiations are conducted simultaneously between management and more than one trade union).

Partnership agreement strategy

A partnership agreement strategy aims to get management and a trade union to collaborate to their mutual advantage and to achieve a climate of more co-operative and therefore less adversarial industrial relations. Management may offer job security linked to productivity and the union may agree to more flexible working.

The perceived benefits of partnership agreements are that management and unions will work together in a spirit of co-operation and mutuality, which is clearly preferable to an adversarial relationship. Provision is made for change to be introduced through discussion and agreement rather than by coercion or power.

Employee voice strategy

The term 'employee voice' refers to the say that employees have in matters of concern to them in their organization. It describes a forum of two-way dialogue that allows employees to influence events at work and includes the processes of involvement, participation, upward problem solving and upward communication. An employee voice strategy will indicate what voice arrangements are to be made, if any.

The voice strategy appropriate for an organization depends upon the values and attitudes of management and, if they exist, trade unions, and the current climate of employee relations. Strategic planning should be based on a review of the existing forms of voice, which would include discussions with stakeholders (line managers, employees and trade union representatives) on the effectiveness of existing arrangements and any improvements required. In the light of these discussions, new or revised approaches can be developed but it is necessary to brief and train those involved in the part that they should play.

STRATEGIC HRM IN ACTION

Employee relations at Capgemini UK

Capgemini UK is part of a global IT services company providing management consulting, outsourcing and professional services, with 112,000 employees across the world and 9,000 employees in the UK.

Capgemini's principal consultative mechanism is the 'forum', which includes both union and non-union representatives. The forum approach was established in 1999 using the works council model adopted by Capgemini in the Netherlands. This is seen as a problem-solving model encouraging two-way communication, as opposed to the more adversarial approach characteristic of consultation in France. Local forums have been established covering individual business areas; the UK National Works Council (NWC) is made up of nominated representatives from each of the local forums and an international works council operates from the global company headquarters in Paris.

SOURCE: CIPD (2011) *Employee Relations at Capgemini UK*, CIPD, London

Trade union recognition strategy

An organization may have to decide on a strategy for recognizing or de-recognizing a trade union. An employer fully recognizes a union for the purposes of collective bargaining when pay and conditions of employment are jointly agreed between management and trade unions. Unions can be de-recognized, although this is happening less frequently.

Employers in the private sector are in a strong position now to choose whether they recognize a union or not, which union they want to recognize and the terms on which they would grant recognition, for example a single union agreement.

When setting up on greenfield sites employers may refuse to recognize unions. Alternatively, they can hold 'beauty contests' to select the union they prefer to work with, one that will be prepared to reach an agreement in line with what management wants.

An organization deciding whether or not to recognize or de-recognize a union should take some or all of the following factors into account:

- the perceived value or lack of value of having a process for regulating collective bargaining;
- if there is an existing union, the extent to which management has freedom to manage; for example, to change working arrangements and introduce flexible working or multiskilling;
- the history of relationships with the existing union;
- the proportion of employees who are union members and the degree to which they believe they need the protection that their union provides;

- any preferences as to a particular union, because of its reputation or the extent to which it is believed that a satisfactory relationship can be maintained;
- if de-recognition is contemplated, the extent to which the perceived advantages of not having a union outweigh the disadvantages of upsetting the status quo.

STRATEGIC HRM IN ACTION

Industrial relations strategy at easyJet

EasyJet has to negotiate with 23 different unions – an unavoidable consequence of the large scale of its operations. But it is operationally challenging for HR. The strategy has been to agree a greater number of multi-year deals, which create stability for staff and the business. But as the HR director commented: 'The key thing is to create a relationship. Be honest with each other about what you can and cannot do.' It is also crucial to realize that issues which raise union hackles may not originate purely in the business. They could be driven by a central agenda in the union and the only way to ensure a balanced discussion is to maintain regular direct channels of communication with the staff, so that messages are not filtered through union reps alone.

SOURCE: *People Management* (2013) August pp 36–38

KEY LEARNING POINTS

- *Employment relations strategy defined*

  Employment relations strategy defines the intentions of the organization about what needs to be done and what needs to be changed in the ways in which the organization handles relationships with employees and, if any, their trade unions.

- *The employment relationship*

  The employment relationship is a largely informal and constant process that happens whenever an employer has dealings with an employee, and vice versa.

  Strategies for managing the employment relationship will focus on establishing overall intentions about how a constructive and co-operative employment relations climate can be developed and what approaches are adopted to achieving mutuality and trust.

- *The nature of employment relations strategy*

  Overall, employment relations strategy is concerned with developing the employment relationship (as discussed earlier in this chapter) in order to build stable and co-operative relationships with employees that minimize conflict.

- *Partnership strategy*

  A partnership agreement strategy aims to get management and a trade union to collaborate to their mutual advantage and to achieve a climate of more co-operative and therefore less adversarial industrial relations.

- *Employee voice strategy*

  An employee voice strategy will indicate what voice arrangements are to be made, if any. These can take the form of representative participation (collective representation through trade unions or staff associations or joint consultation) and/or upward communication through established channels (consultative committees, grievance procedures, 'speak-up' programmes etc) or informally.

- *Recognition strategy*

  An organization may have to decide on a strategy for recognizing or de-recognizing a trade union.

References

Boxall, P F (2013) Mutuality in the management of human resources: assessing the quality of alignment in employment relationships, *Human Resource Management Journal*, **23** (1), pp 3–17

Herriot, P, Hirsh, W and Riley, P (1988) *Trust and Transition: Managing the employment relationship*, Wiley, Chichester

Kessler, S and Undy, R (1996) *The New Employment Relationship: Examining the psychological contract*, IPM, London

Walton, R E (1985) Towards a strategy of eliciting employee commitment based on principles of mutuality, in *HRM Trends and Challenges*, ed R E Walton and P R Lawrence, pp 35–65, Harvard Business School Press, Boston MA

PART FIVE
The international scene

Strategic international HRM

Introduction

International HRM is concerned with human resource management in multinational enterprises. Its aim is to ensure that an international organization attracts, deploys, develops and engages the quality of people it requires to achieve its strategic goals.

International HRM is more complex than HRM in one country. Managing at a distance across international boundaries and in diverse environments is demanding. It is necessary to understand the different local contexts. This means that sensitivity to different cultures and different ways of doing business and managing people is necessary.

As Dave Ulrich (1998: 126) commented, faced with globalization, organizations must 'increase their ability to learn and collaborate and to manage diversity, complexity, and ambiguity'.

Strategic international HRM (SIHRM)

To deal with the issues mentioned above a strategic approach to international HRM is required. As defined by Schuler, Dowling and De Cieri (1999: 321) SIHRM deals with: 'human resource management issues, functions and policies and practices that result from the strategic activities of multinational enterprises and the impact on the international concerns and goals of those enterprises'.

The aims of SIHRM are to ensure that HR strategies, policies and practices are developed and implemented that will help the enterprise to operate profitably in a number of different countries and ensure that each unit can operate effectively within its context – its culture and the legal, political and economic factors that affect it. Sparrow and Braun (2007: 173) advised that: 'It is the utilization of organizational capabilities worldwide that provides multinational companies with competitive advantage.'

In this, the organization has to bear in mind the point made by Pucik (2007: 203) that: 'The global firm must manage the contradictions of global integration, local responsiveness and worldwide co-ordination.'

SIHRM issues

The fundamental strategic HRM issue for multinational companies is how to cope with 'complex cultural, geographical and constitutional pressures'; they have to 'enhance the ability of specific functions to perform globally' (Sparrow and Braun, 2007: 187–88). The specific issues that affect international as distinct from domestic HRM are the impact of globalization, the influence of environmental and cultural differences, the extent to which operations should be centralized or decentralized, and the extent to which HRM policy and practice should vary in different countries (convergence or divergence). The last two issues are of particular concern when framing international HR strategies.

Globalization

Globalization is the process of international economic integration in worldwide markets. It involves the development of single international markets for goods or services accompanied by an accelerated growth in world trade. Any company that has economic interests or activities extending across a number of international boundaries is a global company. This involves a number of issues not present when the activities of the firm are confined to one country. As Ulrich (1998: 126) put it: 'Globalization requires organizations to move people, ideas, products and information around the world to meet local needs.'

SOURCE REVIEW   The distinction between international and global HRM – Brewster, Sparrow and Harris (2005: 996)

Traditionally, international HR has been about managing an international workforce – the higher-level organizational people working as expatriates, frequent commuters, cross-cultural team members and specialists involved in international knowledge transfer. Global HRM is not simply about these staff. It concerns managing all HRM activities, wherever they are, through the application of global rule sets.

Research conducted over a number of years by Brewster and Sparrow (2007: 48) showed that the nature of international HRM is changing fast. They noted that among some of the larger international organizations: 'these changes have created a completely different approach to international human resource management, one we have dubbed "globalized HRM". Whereas international human resource management has tended to operate in the same way as local HRM but on a wider scale, globalized HRM exploits the new technologies available in order to manage all the company's staff around the world in the same way that it has traditionally managed staff in the home country.'

Environmental differences

Environmental differences between countries have to be taken into account in managing globally. As described by Gerhart and Fang (2005: 971), these include 'differences in the centrality of markets, institutions, regulation, collective bargaining and labour-force characteristics'. For example, in Western Europe collective bargaining coverage is much higher than in countries such as the United States, Canada and Japan. Works councils are mandated by law in Western European countries such as Germany, but not in Japan or the United States. In China, Eastern Europe and Mexico, labour costs are significantly lower than in Western Europe, Japan and the United States.

Cultural differences

Cultural differences must also be taken into account. Hiltrop (1995) noted the following HR areas that may be affected by national culture:

- decisions on what makes an effective manager;
- giving face-to-face feedback;
- readiness to accept international assignments;
- pay systems and different concepts of social justice;
- approaches to organizational structuring and strategic dynamics.

The significance of cultural differences was the influential message delivered by Hofstede (1980, 1991). He claimed that 'organizations are culture-bound' (1980: 372). Using worldwide data on IBM employees he identified four national cultural dimensions: uncertainty avoidance, masculinity/femininity, power distance and individualism/collectivism. One of the conclusions Hofstede reached was that the cultural values within a nation are substantially more similar than the values of individuals from different nations. This has been taken up by subsequent commentators such as Adler (2002), who asserted that Hofstede's study explained 50 per cent of the difference between countries in employees' attitudes and behaviours. But this view has been challenged by Gerhart and Fang (2005). They subjected Hofstede's findings to further analysis and established that at the level of the individual as distinct from the country, only 2–4 per cent of the difference was explained by national differences and that, therefore: 'Hofstede's study should not be interpreted as showing that national culture explains 50 per cent of behaviours' (Gerhart and Fang, 2005: 977). They also established from Hofstede's data that culture varies more between organizations than countries. In their view, cross-country cultural differences, while real, have been overestimated and may well pale in importance when compared with other unique country characteristics when it comes to explaining the effectiveness of HR practices. But they accepted that national culture differences can be critical and that insensitivity to national culture differences can and does result in business failure (as well as failures and career consequences for individual managers).

On the basis of research conducted in 30 multinational companies, Stiles (2007: 37) commented that: 'while national cultural differences were not insignificant, they were less important than we imagined; organizational culture actually had more influence on HR practice'. The conclusion from the research was that: 'To think there is one best way to manage human resources is simplistic and wrong, but the variation and contextualization of HR, at least for the companies we studied, owes little to national culture' (Stiles, 2007: 41).

Centralization or decentralization

As Pucik (2007: 201) declared: 'Many firms competing globally are being pointed in contradictory strategic directions. In order to survive and prosper in the new global competition, companies must embrace closer regional and global integration to cut cost and improve efficiency, while at the same time, meet demands for local responsiveness to increase local acceptance, flexibility and speed.' On the basis of his research he identified three strategic approaches to this issue:

1 A mega-national strategy, which means that the whole company operates in a centralized fashion. Worldwide facilities are centralized in the parent company, products are standardized, and overseas operations are used as delivery pipelines to serve international markets. There is tight central control of strategic decisions, resources and information. As a result, the competitive strength of the mega-national firm is its global integration, resulting in cost efficiencies. However, the firm's ability to respond to variations in local conditions is limited and the international operation can become bureaucratic and inflexible.

2 A multi-domestic strategy, which emphasizes local differences by decentralizing operations to their subsidiaries and local business units in order to be close to customers, in order to create a heightened sense of local accountability and to encourage more local innovation and entrepreneurship. But this can lead to an inability to compete on global terms with fully integrated competitors, slowness in responding to change and failure to benefit from pooled resources, including knowledge and management expertise. Decentralized companies meeting these problems tend to veer towards centralization until bureaucracy, lack of responsiveness and the inability to retain good people locally leads the pendulum to swing again towards centralization.

3 Dual centralized/decentralized strategy, which aims to benefit from both approaches. Firms adopting a dual strategy recognize that decentralization (local autonomy) and centralization (global integration) are not contradictory, but form a duality. They attempt to maximize the benefits from both approaches in order to achieve high integration while remaining locally responsive. This can mean following the old adage of 'think globally and act locally' and can get the best out of both worlds. But it is a hard strategy to implement. It requires managers with what Pucik calls a 'global mindset', who can behave and act in a way that recognizes the global nature of the firm and who can focus both on worldwide strategies and the need to encourage the development of local initiatives and allow a reasonable degree of local autonomy within a global framework.

Convergence and divergence

According to Brewster, Harris and Sparrow (2002) the effectiveness of global HRM depends on the ability to judge the extent to which an organization should implement similar practices across the world or adapt them to suit local conditions. This is a strategic decision that is an aspect of the choice between centralization or decentralization, as referred to above. The dilemma facing all multinational corporations is that of achieving a balance between international consistency and local autonomy. They have to decide on the extent to which their HR policies should either 'converge' worldwide to be basically the same in each location, or 'diverge' to be differentiated in response to local requirements.

SOURCE REVIEW   Convergence and divergence issues – Perkins and Shortland (2006: 33)

Strategic choices surrounding employment relationships may be influenced primarily by 'home country' values and practices. But those managing operations in one or a range of host country environments face the challenge of transplanting 'ethnocentric' principles, justifying the consequential policies and practices in their interactions with local managers, other employees and external representatives.

Brewster (2004) thought that convergence may be increasing as a result of the power of the markets; the importance of cost; quality and productivity pressures; the emergence of transaction cost economies; the development of like-minded international cadres; and benchmarking 'best practice'. Stiles (2007) noted that common practices across borders may be appropriate: 'Organizations seek what works and for HR in multinational companies, the range of options is limited to a few common practices that are believed to secure high performance.' Brewster, Sparrow and Harris (2005) think that it is quite possible for some parts of a HR system to converge while other parts may diverge. But there is a choice. The factors that affect the choice include the extent to which the unit is operating mainly at a local level, the strength of local norms, and the degree to which financial, managerial, technical and people resources flow from the parent company to the subsidiary. A further factor is that some international companies are much more prone to the exercise of central control than others, whatever the local circumstances.

Sparrow and Braun (2007: 170) identified three approaches to global HR strategy:

- The wholesale transfer of HRM policies and practices successful in the parent company to affiliates.
- The creation of HR systems with a maximum of adaptation to local context and conditions.

The transfer of best practice from wherever it may be found among affiliates in the organization.

Approaches to SIHRM

Bartlett and Ghoshal (1991) set out the following fundamental assumptions governing the approach to strategic international HRM:0

SOURCE REVIEW   Fundamental assumptions in SIHRM – Bartlett and Ghoshal (1991: 59)

Balancing the needs of control and autonomy, and maintaining the appropriate balance, are critical to the success of the multinational enterprise in being globally competitive, sensitive to the local environment, flexible and capable of creating an organization in which learning and the transfer of knowledge are feasible.

Strategic management is always about making choices and this is particularly the case in international strategic management. As mentioned earlier, the fundamental strategic choices are on the degree of centralization/decentralization and convergence/divergence to be adopted. Multinational companies have to make strategic choices on how to find and develop talented managers with a global mindset and how to make the maximum use of expertise by transferring learning across units in order to 'enhance an organization's capability to gain and use its knowledge resources' (Sparrow and Braun, 2007: 178).

The research conducted by Brewster, Sparrow and Harris (2005: 949) identified three processes that constitute global HRM: 1) management and employer branding; 2) global leadership through international assignments; and 3) managing an international workforce and evaluation of HR contribution. They found that organizations such as Rolls-Royce had set up centres of excellence operating on a global basis. They observed that global HR professionals are acting as the guardians of culture, operating global values and systems.

It was established by the Global HR Research Alliance study (Stiles, 2007) that global HR policies and practices were widespread in the areas of maintaining global performance standards, the use of common evaluation processes, common approaches to rewards, the development of senior managers, the application of competency frameworks and the use of common performance management criteria.

Generally the research has indicated that while global HR policies in such areas as talent management, performance management and reward may be developed, communicated and supported by centres of excellence, often through global networking, a fair degree of freedom has frequently been allowed to local management to adopt their own practices in accordance with the local context, as long as in principle these are consistent with global policies.

STRATEGIC HRM IN ACTION

Centralization/decentralization at Transco

Transco is a well-known European multinational corporation (MNC), operating in over 100 countries and employing more than 100,000 people. Having developed into a large and diversified MNC with operations widely dispersed on a global scale, Transco found that its size and structure meant that it had become a collection of semi-autonomous subsidiaries that, in turn, knew too little about what each other were doing. The weaknesses of this somewhat unintentional multi-domestic strategy came to a head and prompted a dramatic organizational restructuring effort whereby Transco consciously tried to become more 'global' both in its streamlining of core businesses and in its 'network' approach to managing its foreign operations. The restructuring was justified as an attempt to achieve greater synergies and organizational control as well as for financial and sustainability reasons. Accordingly, previously decentralized decisions about a range of issues were increasingly centralized at corporate and regional levels.

SOURCE: Sippola, A and Smale, A (2007) The global integration of diversity management: A longitudinal case study, *International Journal of Human Resource Management*, **18** (11), pp 1895–916

KEY LEARNING POINTS

- *Strategic international human resource management (SIHRM) defined*
  SIHRM is the process of planning how best to develop and implement policies and practices for managing people across international boundaries by multinational companies.

- *The aims of SIHRM*
  To ensure that HR strategies, policies and practices are developed and implemented that will help the enterprise to operate profitably in a number of different countries and ensure that each unit can operate effectively within its context.

- *SIHRM issues*

  The fundamental strategic HRM issue for multinational companies is how to cope with 'complex cultural, geographical and constitutional pressures' (Sparrow and Braun, 2007: 187).

  The specific issues that affect international as distinct from domestic HRM are the impact of globalization, the influence of environmental and cultural differences, the extent to which operations should be centralized or decentralized, and the extent to which HRM policy and practice should vary in different countries (convergence or divergence). The last two issues are of particular concern when framing international HR strategies.

- *Approaches to strategic HRM*

  Strategic management is always about making choices and this is particularly the case in international strategic management. The fundamental strategic choices are on the degree of centralization/decentralization and convergence/divergence to be adopted. Multinational companies also have to make strategic choices on how to find and develop talented managers with a global mindset and how to make the maximum use of expertise by transferring learning across units.

  While global HR policies in such areas as talent management, performance management and reward may be developed, communicated and supported by centres of excellence, often through global networking, a fair degree of freedom has frequently been allowed to local management to adopt their own practices in accordance with the local context, as long as in principle these are consistent with global policies.

References

Adler, N J (2002) *International Dimensions of Organizational Behaviour*, South-Western, Cincinnati OH

Bartlett, C A and Ghoshal, S (1991) *Managing Across Borders: The transnational solution*, London Business School, London

Brewster, C (2004) European perspectives of human resource management, *Human Resource Management Review*, **14** (4), pp 365–82

Brewster, C, Harris, H and Sparrow, P (2002) *Globalizing HR*, CIPD, London

Brewster, C and Sparrow, P (2007) Advances in technology inspire a fresh approach to international HRM, *People Management*, 8 February, p 48

Brewster, C, Sparrow, P and Harris, H (2005) Towards a new model of globalizing HRM, *The International Journal of Human Resource Management*, **16** (6), pp 949–70

Gerhart, B and Fang, M (2005) National culture and human resource management: assumptions and evidence, *The International Journal of Human Resource Management*, **16** (6), pp 971–86

Hiltrop, J M (1995) The changing psychological contract: the human resource challenge of the 1990s, *European Management Journal*, **13** (3), pp 286–94

Hofstede, G (1980) *Cultural Consequences: International differences in work-related values*, Sage, Beverley Hills CA

Hofstede, G (1991) *Culture and Organization: Software of the mind*, Sage, London

Perkins, S J and Shortland, S M (2006) *Strategic International Human Resource Management*, Kogan Page, London

Pucik, V (2007) Reframing global mindset: from thinking to acting, in *Strategic Human Resource Management*, ed R S Schuler and S E Jackson, pp 200–13, Blackwell, Malden MA

Schuler, R S, Dowling, P J and De Cieri, H (1999) Framework of strategic international HRM, in *Strategic Human Resource Management*, ed R S Schuler and S E Jackson, pp 319–55, Blackwell, Oxford

Sparrow, P R and Braun, W (2007) Human resource strategy in international context, in *Strategic Human Resource Management*, ed R S Schuler and S E Jackson, pp 162–99, Blackwell, Malden MA

Stiles, P (2007) A world of difference?, *People Management*, 15 November, pp 36–41

Ulrich, D (1998) A new mandate for human resources, *Harvard Business Review*, January/February, pp 124–34

International HRM strategies

LEARNING OUTCOMES

On completing this chapter you should be able to define these key concepts. You should also understand the considerations affecting strategy in the following areas:

- resourcing;
- talent management;
- performance management;
- reward;
- the management of expatriates.

Introduction

International HRM strategies are primarily concerned with resourcing, talent management, performance management, reward management and the management of expatriates. In each of these areas, except that of managing expatriates, the strategy will determine the direction in which the company wants to go, in the light of overall considerations relating to convergence or divergence.

There are, however, a number of HRM practices in which the parent company will play a major part. Workforce planning and talent management for more senior staff may be centralized, as may be resourcing decisions that affect the deployment of staff from the parent company or from other countries (third country nationals). The remuneration of senior staff and expatriates will certainly be centralized. While performance management systems will be administered by subsidiaries, the centre may want to ensure that the processes involved conform to what is regarded as best practice within the organization and provide the information required for talent management and staffing decisions. An international HR function may also be concerned with encouraging the actions required to promote multicultural working throughout the organization.

Resourcing strategy

International resourcing strategy is based on workforce planning processes, which assess how many people are needed throughout the multinational company (demand forecasting), set out the sources of people available (supply forecasting) and, in the light of these forecasts, prepare action plans for recruitment, selection or assignment.

Workforce planning may be carried out by the parent company HR function, although it will focus mainly on managers, professional and technical staff throughout the global organization, and is linked to talent management. Workforce planning for junior staff and operatives is more likely to be carried out by subsidiaries, although the centre may require information on their plans.

Resourcing in an international organization means making policy decisions on how the staffing requirements of headquarters and the foreign subsidiaries can be met, especially for managers, professionals and technical staff. Sparrow, Scullion and Farndale (2011: 42) emphasized that multinational companies (MNCs): 'increasingly demand highly skilled, highly flexible, mobile employees who can deliver the required results, sometimes in difficult circumstances'.

On the basis of their research, Paik and Ando (2011: 3006) suggested that: 'To effectively integrate and co-ordinate activities of foreign affiliates, MNCs need to maintain a higher level of control at headquarters. MNC headquarters want foreign affiliates to act as if they were the headquarters' agents. In this situation, MNCs are inclined to staff foreign affiliates with managers who understand and appreciate headquarters' directives.' However, they also noted that this policy may evolve to rely more on the local 'host' country staff, as headquarters learns how better to integrate activities of foreign affiliates to achieve global efficiency. Cumulatively, headquarters will learn more about managing in the host country and local practices, and will build relationships with local suppliers and recruit more local employees.

TABLE 21.1 Advantages and disadvantages of using PCNs and HCNs

Employment of:	Advantages	Disadvantages
Parent company nationals (PCNs)	• Facilitates control and co-ordination • Provides managers with international experience • Provides people with the best skills for the job • Promotes the dissemination of the MNC's policies and values	• Limits the promotional opportunities of HCNs • Expatriates may find it hard to adapt to the characteristics of the host country's culture and institutions • Expatriates may impose an inappropriate management style based on that of their parent company • The remuneration of PCNs and HCNs may differ • Lack of continuity • The host country may resent and even limit the deployment of foreigners.
Home country nationals (HCNs)	• Familiar with local culture, institutions and legal requirements • No language barrier • Provides continuity • Morale improved as HCNs see career potential • Fits local government policy for employing nationals • Reduces employment costs	• Unfamiliar with parent company's practices and systems • Dissemination of HQ practices more difficult • May not have the immediate skills required • More difficult to exercise control from the centre

Whichever orientation exists, an important strategic choice has to be made in staffing subsidiaries in an international firm between employing parent company or home company nationals or a combination of the two. Dowling, Festing and Engle (2008) listed the advantages and disadvantages of each approach, as shown in Table 21.1.

Additionally, or alternatively, a decision may be made to employ third country nationals (TCNs) in certain posts. These might be easier to obtain than home country nationals and could cost less. But as pointed out by Dowling, Festing and Engle (2008), they might not want to return to their own countries after assignment, the host government may resent hiring of TCNs, and national animosities would have to be considered.

International talent management

Mellahi and Collings (2010: 143–44) defined international talent management as:

> The systematic identification of key positions that differentially contribute to the organization's sustainable competitive advantage on a global scale, the development of a talent pool of high-performing incumbents to fill these roles which reflects the global scope of the multinational enterprise, the development of a differentiated human resource architecture to facilitate filling these positions with the best available incumbent and to ensure their continued commitment to the organization.

They suggested that enabling high-performing home country nationals to become senior managers improves the performance of an international business because: 1) it is able to respond effectively to the demands of local stakeholders; 2) it is legitimizing in the host country; and 3) it provides incentives for retaining and motivating talents.

The conduct of international talent management involves basically the same methods as those used in a domestic setting, namely, a pipeline consisting of processes for:

- *Talent planning*: defining what is meant by talent and establishing how many and what sort of talented people are needed now and in the future.
- *Talent pool definition*: on the basis of talent-planning data deciding what sort of talent pool is required. This would consist of the resources of talent available to an organization in terms of numbers, competencies and skills. It would include identifying pools of talent that possess the potential to move into a number of roles. This replaces the traditional objective of succession planning with its short-term focus on finding replacements for managers who leave. The talent pool is filled mainly from within the organization, with

additions from outside as required. The pool is not managed rigidly. It can be expanded or contracted as demands for talent change, and new members can be included and existing members removed if they are no longer eligible.

- *Identifying talent internally*: by reference to the definitions of talent pool, using assessments of existing staff to decide who is qualified to be included in the talent pool.

- *Recruiting talent*: bringing in talented people from outside the company to supplement internal talent and become additional members of the talent pool.

- *Performance management*: talent is not fixed and therefore needs to be reviewed regularly though performance management, which also provides information on learning and development needs.

- *Management development and career planning*: a continuous programme of developing the abilities of members of the talent pool and, so far as this is possible, planning their careers.

- *Assignment or promotion*: talent pool members are assigned to positions in headquarters or, as expatriates, in foreign subsidiaries. Alternatively, they may be promoted within headquarters or a subsidiary. Although in a fully formed talent management system the talent pool is considered to be the major source for senior assignments or for promotions, people not actually in the pool may still be eligible. If no one suitable is available in the pool then it may be necessary to recruit externally. Those assigned or promoted will still be included in the talent pool.

The global nature of MNCs makes talent management a particularly complex issue. Mellahi and Collings (2010) identified three reasons why global talent management often fails:

- Subsidiary managers may believe that it is in their interests to keep their own best talent rather than bring them to the attention of headquarters or other subsidiaries.

- Decision makers at the centre do not always have access to accurate information about the availability of talent elsewhere in the organization.

- Even when information is available, the sheer volume, diversity and, possibly, unreliability of the data hinders the centre's ability effectively to manage talent in subsidiaries.

Sparrow, Scullion and Farndale (2011: 48) commented that: 'The co-ordination of international talent management strategies in highly decentralized MNCs is more problematic due to greater tensions between the short-term needs of the operating companies and the long-term strategic needs of the business.'

> ## STRATEGIC HRM IN ACTION
>
> International talent management at HSBC
> HSBC has created a system of talent pools that track and manage the careers of high potentials within the international firm. After those employees have been identified, they are assigned to regional or business unit talent pools, which are managed by local human resources and business unit leaders. They are then selected initially for new assignments within their region or business and may later be given positions that cross boundaries. Managers of the pools single out people to recommend for the group talent pool, which represents the most senior cadre of general managers and is administered centrally.
>
> **SOURCE:** Ready, D A and Conger, J A (2007) Make your company a talent factory, *Harvard Business Review*, June, pp 69–77

International performance management

Performance management systems in subsidiaries covering home and third country nationals are the area of HRM where there is likely to be the most convergence. This means that a system based on the one used in the parent company is applied completely or partly worldwide. As Briscoe, Schuler and Tarique (2012: 347) observed: 'There are some valid reasons which suggest that... a standardized approach may be warranted for the sake of global integration, culture cohesiveness, fairness, mobility of global employees, and as a control mechanism.'

The trend towards convergence was confirmed by the Global HR Research Alliance, as reported by Stiles (2007: 39), which concluded that: 'In performance management we found little or no difference across the world. We witnessed a concerted effort on the part of group HR departments to maintain global standards supported by global competencies (at foundation, managerial, technical and leadership level), common evaluation processes and common approaches to rewards. It was difficult, therefore, to find many distinctive local practices.'

The effectiveness of international performance management is affected overall by the sheer complexity of international business and the distance separating headquarters and subsidiaries. Briscoe and Claus (2008) noted that a challenge is provided by 'the major differences that arise between host national perceptions and those of the home office regarding what was being accomplished and the circumstances under which it was being achieved'.

The particular issues affecting international performance management are the increased difficulty in influencing and controlling line managers; cultural differences; the problem of achieving consistent rating results; and variable levels of maturity among subsidiaries, which affect relative performance.

STRATEGIC HRM IN ACTION

FIGURE 21.1 International performance management at Standard Chartered

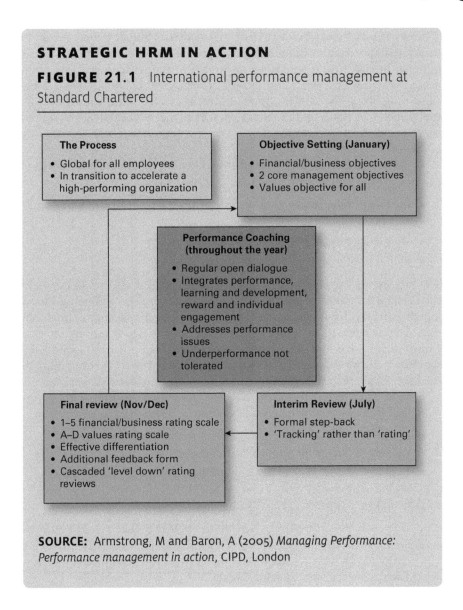

The Process
- Global for all employees
- In transition to accelerate a high-performing organization

Objective Setting (January)
- Financial/business objectives
- 2 core management objectives
- Values objective for all

Performance Coaching (throughout the year)
- Regular open dialogue
- Integrates performance, learning and development, reward and individual engagement
- Addresses performance issues
- Underperformance not tolerated

Final review (Nov/Dec)
- 1–5 financial/business rating scale
- A–D values rating scale
- Effective differentiation
- Additional feedback form
- Cascaded 'level down' rating reviews

Interim Review (July)
- Formal step-back
- 'Tracking' rather than 'rating'

SOURCE: Armstrong, M and Baron, A (2005) *Managing Performance: Performance management in action*, CIPD, London

International reward management

International reward management involves the management of all aspects of rewards in organizations operating worldwide, or at least in a number of countries. Traditionally, discussions of international reward strategies and practices have tended to focus on an elite of expatriate workers, sourced from headquarter locations and rewarded in isolation from local country staff. Today a diverse and complex pattern is emerging, requiring a more strategic approach than simply copying the practices of other multinationals.

International reward strategy is concerned with the development of an integrated approach to building reward policies and practices across international boundaries. It should be integrated in the sense that it takes into account the business goals and drivers of the parent company while at the same time fitting the strategy to the different contexts and cultures across the globe. The issue of the extent to which the reward strategy should be centralized or decentralized (convergence or divergence) needs to be addressed.

Baeten and Leuven (2010) listed the following main concerns affecting global reward strategy:

- the extent of centralization or decentralization of reward policies and practices;
- balancing corporate and national cultures;
- global benchmarking of levels of pay.

The factors that are likely to impact on international reward strategy are the corporate culture of the multinational enterprise, expatriate and local labour markets, local cultural sensitivities, and legal and institutional factors. A choice has to be made between, on the one hand, seeking internal consistency by developing common reward policies in order to facilitate the movement of employees across borders and preserve internal equity, and on the other hand, responding to pressures to conform to local practices.

Briscoe, Schuler and Tarique (2012: 297) identified the following options for establishing a worldwide reward system:

- Create worldwide salary levels at HQ with differentials for each subsidiary according to their differing costs of living.
- Base pay on local levels (usually excluding executives and globally mobile employees).
- Establish a global base per position where there is a global market for particular occupations or for senior managers and global employees.
- Set up two classifications for pay – local and national. All local nationals above a certain level are placed on the headquarters scale. The others are paid on a local scale.

STRATEGIC HRM IN ACTION

International reward strategy at General Motors

General Motors (GM) moves people around the globe frequently, because its products are designed and built on global platforms. The international philosophy of GM was expressed in the mantras 'One GM one global team' and 'Global perspective: local engagement'.

But different locations were using different levels of pay structures and job evaluation schemes. A 'leading change' programme involved compensation chiefs around the world. The global team, under the banner of the phrase 'Global compensation takes the approach that what can be should be':

- analysed the various strategies, structures and practices in place around the world;
- used corporate governance to decide what needed to be global, regional or local;
- identified 'best practices' in compensation to establish a common philosophy, tools and structure for the salaried workforce;
- engaged key stakeholders in the process;
- provided tools, support and education;
- created with the help of Mercer Consultants more than 200 benchmarks in 30 job functions and then slotted them into global salary grades.

SOURCE: Mercer Human Resource Consulting (2009) *A Whole New World*, Mercer, New York

Managing expatriates

The management of expatriates on international assignments is a major factor determining success or failure in a global business. Expatriates are expensive. They can be difficult to manage because of the problems associated with adapting to and working in unfamiliar environments and cultures, concerns about their development and careers, difficulties encountered when they re-enter their parent company after a foreign assignment, and questions about how they should be remunerated.

A strategy for managing expatriates can relate to the global assignment cycle described by Sparrow, Brewster and Harris (2004: 145), the three phases of which are:

- *Pre-departure*: planning the assignment, selecting the individual, administering the relocation programme and conducting preparatory training and development.
- *Assignment*: performance management, pay and benefits, family support and preparation for repatriation or reassignment.
- *Post-assignment*: retention by reintegrating returning international assignees into organizational career systems.

KEY LEARNING POINTS

International HRM strategies are primarily concerned with resourcing, talent management, performance management, reward management and the management of expatriates. In each of these areas, except that of managing expatriates, the strategy will determine the direction in which the company wants to go, in the light of overall considerations relating to convergence or divergence:

- *Resourcing*
  International resourcing is based on workforce planning processes, which assess how many people are needed throughout the MNC (demand forecasting), set out the sources of people available (supply forecasting) and, in the light of these forecasts, prepare action plans for recruitment, selection or assignment.

  Resourcing in an international organization means making policy decisions on how the staffing requirements of headquarters and the foreign subsidiaries can be met, especially for managers, professionals and technical staff.

  An important choice required in staffing subsidiaries in an international firm is between employing parent company or home company nationals or an appropriate combination of the two.

- *Talent management*
  Talent management is the process of ensuring that the organization has the talented people it needs to attain its business goals.

  The conduct of international talent management involves basically the same methods as those used in a domestic setting, namely, a pipeline consisting of processes for talent planning, talent pool definition, identifying talent internally, recruiting talent, performance management, management development and career planning, assignment or promotion.

- *International performance management systems*
  International performance management systems basically contain the following elements, which correspond to those found in domestic systems: performance agreement, performance management throughout the year, performance review.

  The effectiveness of international performance management is affected overall by the sheer complexity of international business and the distance separating headquarters and subsidiaries.

  The particular issues affecting international performance management are the increased difficulty in influencing and controlling line managers; cultural differences; the problem of achieving consistent rating results; and variable levels of maturity among subsidiaries, which affect relative performance.

- *Reward management*
  International reward strategy is concerned with the development of an integrated approach to building reward policies and practices across international boundaries.
  The factors that are likely to impact on international reward strategy are the corporate culture of the multinational enterprise, expatriate and local labour markets, local cultural sensitivities and legal and institutional factors.
- *Expatriates*
  The management of expatriates on international assignments is a major factor determining success or failure in a global business.

References

Baeten, X and Leuven, V (2010) Global compensation and benefits management: the need for communication and coordination, *Compensation & Benefits Review*, **42** (3), pp 392–402

Briscoe, D R and Claus, L M (2008) Employee performance management, in *Performance Management Systems: A global perspective*, ed A Varma, P S Budhwar and A DeNisi, pp 15–39, Routledge, Abingdon

Briscoe, D, Schuler, R and Tarique, I (2012) *International Human Resource Management*, 4th edn, Routledge, New York

Dowling, P J, Festing, M and Engle, A D (2008) *International Human Resource Management*, 5th edn, Cengage Learning EMEA, Andover

Mellahi, K and Collings, D G (2010) The barriers to effective global talent management: the example of corporate elites in MNEs, *Journal of World Business*, **45**, pp 143–44

Paik, Y and Ando, N (2011) MNC's competitive strategies, experiences, and staffing policies for foreign affiliates, *International Journal of Human Resource Management*, **22** (15), pp 3003–19

Sparrow, P, Brewster, C and Harris, H (2004) *Globalizing Human Resource Management*, Routledge, London

Sparrow, P, Scullion, H and Farndale, E (2011) Global talent management: new roles for the corporate HR function?, in *Global Talent Management*, ed H Scullion and D G Collings, pp 40–55, Routledge, London

Stiles, P (2007) A world of difference?, *People Management*, 15 November, pp 36–41

AUTHOR INDEX

Abell, D F   28
Adams, J S   18
Allvesson, M   51
Ando, N   28
Armstrong, M   1, 63, 64, 211

Baeten, X   254
Baird, L   43
Barney, J   40–41
Baron, A   63, 64
Baron, D   127
Bartlett, C A   243
Becker, B E   11, 12, 139
Beer, M   8–9, 96
Benson, G S   65
Boselie, P   11
Bourne, M   135
Boxall, P   6, 7, 11, 18, 27, 28,
    32, 41, 44, 137, 227
Braun, W   238, 243
Brewster, C   10, 239, 241–42
Briscoe, D R   252
Brockbank, W   12
Brown, D   155, 210–11

Caldwell, R   51
Cappelli, P   43
Carnall, C   87
Cascio, W F   156
Chandler, A D   27
Chatzkel, J L   106
Claus, L M   252
Coens, T   138, 156
Collings, D G   190, 250,
    251
Cooke, R   101
Coster, C   6
Cowling, A   175
Crawford, E R   163

Davenport, T H   120
Delery, J E   42
Dickens, C   84
Digman, L A   31, 45
Doty, H D   42
Dowling, P J   250
Dyer, L   38, 44, 52

Egan, G   149
Ehrenberg, R G   203
Eichinger, R W   204
Elias, J   106

Fang, M   239, 240
Faulkner, D   32
Flaherty, J   138
Fletcher, C   153
Fombrun, C J   8
Fouts, P A   126
Francis, H   12
Fredrickson, J W   28
Freeman, R E   125
Friedman, M   126

Gerhart, B   239, 240
Gheorge, C   134
Ghoshal, S   121, 126, 243
Grant, R M   63
Gratton, L   14, 38, 85
Guest, D E   8, 15, 17, 42, 162

Hack, H   134
Hambrisk, D C   28
Hamel, G   41
Hansen, M T   119
Harrison, R   203
Harter, J K   162
Heller, R   31
Hendry, C   6, 38
Herriot, P   229
Hillman, A   125
Hiltrop, J M   240
Hird, M   11
Hofsted, G   240
Holder, G W   38, 44, 52
Hope-Hailey, V   13
Huselid, M A   12, 139
Husted, B W   125, 127

Jackson, S E   9, 53
Jenkins, M   138, 156
Johnson, G   27, 32, 190

Kahn, W A   162
Kanter, R M   27, 32, 51

Kaplan, R S   135
Kearns, P   106
Keble-Allen, D   156
Keegan, A   12,
Keenoy, T   10
Keep, E   199
Keim, G   125
Kessler, S   227
King, Z   15
Kramer, M R   125, 126, 127

Lafferty, J   101
Lake D   53
Lawler, E E   87
Legge, K   7–8,
Lengnick-Hall, C A   38
Lengnick-Hall, M L   38
Leventhall G S   18
Levitt, T   126
Leuven, V   255
Lombardo, M M   204
Long, P   1

Mabey, C   31, 45
MacDuffie, J P   45
Macey, W H   162
MacLeod, D   201
McMahan, G C   61–62
McWilliams, A   42, 125, 126, 127
Manocha, R   105, 107
Marlow, S   20
Marsh, C   145
Marsick, V J   202–03
Martin, J A   31
Martin-Alcázar, F   9
Mellahi, K   190, 251
Meshoulam, I   43
Michaels, E   191
Miles, R E   44
Miller, K   19–20
Mintzberg, H   32, 44, 63, 64
Mohrman, S A   87
Moran, P   126
Murlis, H   211

Nahpiet, J   121
Nalbantian, R   107
Norton, D P   135

Osterby, B   6

Paauwe, J   44
Paik, Y   248
Patterson, M G   17
Pellant, A   192

Penrose, E   42
Perkins, S   242
Pettigrew, A   6, 31, 38
Pfeffer, J   42, 191–92
Porter, M E   43, 125, 126, 127
Prahalad, C K   41
Pritchard, K   90
Pucik, V   240–41
Pulakos, E D   154
Purcell, J   7, 15–16, 17, 27, 32, 89

Quinn, J B   31
Quinn-Mills D   40, 174

Reilly, P   14
Reynolds, J   201, 202, 205
Richardson, R   42, 45
Robinson, D   162
Rothwell, S   175
Russo, M V   126

Salazar, J   125, 127
Scarborough, H   106, 188
Schneider, B   18
Schuler, R S   9, 42, 53, 238
Sheilds, J   156
Shih, H-A   139
Shortland, S M   242
Siegel, D   126, 127
Sink, D S   134
Sisson, P   12
Sloman, M   203
Smith, R S   203
Snow, C C   43
Snyder, W M   121
Sparrow, P   31, 238, 239, 243, 248, 251, 255
Stephens, C   54
Stiles, P   240, 243, 252
Storey, J   6–7, 8, 10, 40
Stoskopf, G A   154
Strebler, M T   149–50
Strickland, A J   27, 32, 63
Syrett, M   51

Taylor, S   175
Thompson, A A   27, 32, 63
Thompson, M   17, 42, 45
Thorne, K   192
Trevor, J   89
Truss, C   10, 27, 162, 163
Tuttle, T C   1134
Tyson, S   12–13, 32, 52

Ulrich, D   12, 14, 17, 41, 53, 239
Undy, R   227

Walters, M   175
Walton, R E   229
Warren, C   237
Watson, T J   7
Wenger, E   121
Wernerfelt, B   40
West, M   17
Whipp, R   31

Whittington, R   30
Willmott, H   17
Windsor, D   125
Winstanley, D   16
Wood, S   65
Wright, P M   61–62, 64

Younger, J   192

SUBJECT INDEX

Accounting for People Task Force   106
agile working   144
Astra Zeneca   200–01

BAE Systems   196
best fit
   approach to   43
   and competitive strategies   43–44
   life-cycle model   43
best practice
   approach to HRM   42–43
   lists of best practices   42
blended learning   206
BT   218
bundling   45, 78–79
Business in the Community   127–28
business model   77–78
business model innovation   28
business partner role of HR specialists   56
business strategy   77, 108

Capgemini UK   231–32
change management   87
Chartered Institute of Personnel
      and Development (CIPD)   96,
      129, 143, 144–45, 163, 174 175,
      190–91
Children's Trust   90–91
communities of practice   121
Conference Board   162, 163
contextual model of HRM   9
Corporate Leadership Council   163
corporate social responsibility (CSR)
   activities   127–28
   defined   125
   developing a CSR strategy   129–30
   rationale for   125–26
   role of HR   129
   strategic CSR   126–27
CSR Academy   129
culture change   101

Deloitte   144
development   201
diversity and inclusion strategy   184
DSG International   220

easyJet   233
Economist Intelligence Unit   144
employee engagement
   defined   161–63
   and discretionary behaviour   203
   factors influencing   163–64
   importance of   163
   strategy   164–66
employee relations strategy
   approaches to   230
   concerns of   230–31
   defined   226–27
   nature of   230
employee resourcing, see resourcing
employee value proposition   225–27
employee voice strategy   231
employment relations climate   228–29
employment relationship   227–28
engagement, see employee engagement
e-reward   156
ethical dimension of HRM   18–19
European model of HRM   10
Expatriates, management of   255
external environment   16

fit   41
5-P mode of HRM   9
flexibility strategy   184
front-line managers, see line managers

Gallup   163, 164

Harvard model of HRM   8
heads of HR functions, strategic role of   55
high-commitment management   66
high-involvement management   65
high-performance management   65
high performance work culture   138–39
high-performance work systems   139–43
how people learn   204
HR advisors, strategic role of   56
HR analytics   66, 106, 111
HR architecture   11
HR business partners, strategic role of   56
HR directors, strategic role of   54–55
HR function role of   12

HR partnership role   89–90
HRM, *see* human resource management
HR philosophy   9, 12
HR policies   9, 12
HR practices   9, 12
HR practitioners, strategic role of   51–52
HR processes   9, 12
HR programmes   9, 12
HR strategies
    corporate social responsibility   126–27
    diversity and inclusion strategy   184
    employee engagement   164–66
    employee relations   226–27
    flexibility   184
    human capital management   107
    individual performance
        management   149, 156–57
    international HRM   247
    knowledge management   117–18
    learning and development strategy   198–99
    organization development   95–103
    organizational performance   135–37
    resourcing   171
    reward   209–11
    talent management   192
HR strategy
    defined   12, 62–63
    development of   71–80
    effective delivery of   86–88
    evaluation of   67–68
    formulation of   75–80
    implementing   85–90
    inside-out approach to development   73
    integrating business and HR strategy   77
    line managers, role of   85
    and organizational performance   145–46
    outside-in approach to development
        73–74
    overall approaches   65
    purpose of   124–25
    the 'say-do' gap   85
    specific   66–67
HR system   11–13
human capital management
    aims   106–07
    defined   105–06
    HR analytics   106
    link with business strategy   108–10
    measures   112
    metrics   106
    strategy   107
human resource architecture   6
human resource development, *see* learning
    and development

human resource management (HRM)
    context of   16–17
    contextual model of   9
    concept of   6–7
    defined   6, 7
    European model of HRM   10
    5-P mode of HRM   9
    goals of   7
    hard model of HRM   10
    Harvard model of HRM   8–9
    HR architecture   6
    HRM today   10–11
    Impact on organizational
        performance   17–18
    matching model of HRM   8
    models of HRM   8–10
    and motivation theory   8
    philosophy of   6, 7–8
    in SMEs   19–20
    soft model of HRM   10
    theories of   8
human resource planning, *see* workforce
    planning
human resource strategies, *see* HR strategies
human resource systems, *see* HR systems

IDS   163
Individual learning   203–04
individual performance management   148–49,
    see also performance management
internal environment   16–17
international HRM   237–38, 247
international HRM strategies
    performance management   252–53
    resourcing   248–50
    reward management   253–54
    talent management   250–52

Johnson & Johnson   101

knowledge management
    approaches to   119
    defined   212, 213
    process of   118
    sources and types of knowledge   118–19
    strategic issues   120–21
    strategy   117–18, 121

lean manufacturing   145
learning   201
learning and development, elements of   201
learning culture   200
learning and development strategy   198–99
learning needs, identification of   204

line managers
    HR role of   15–16
    and HRM   9
    and reward management   221–22
    role in implementing HR strategy   85
Lyreco   206–07

McKinsey   191
motivation theory   8
mutuality   229

organization development   96–100
    activities   96
    organization restructuring   145
organizational capability   138
organizational learning   202–03
organizational performance, management of
    approach to   134
    dimensions of management   134
    implementation of strategy   137, 138
    process of management   134
    strategic approach to   135–37

partnership agreement strategy   231
partnership role of HR in delivering
        strategy   89–90
people management   6, 7, 10
performance management
    activities   151–53
    as a continuous process   150
    defined   148–49
    implementation problems   155–56
    limitations of the performance
        management model   153
    nature of a performance management
        system   149
    principles of performance
        management   149–50
    strategy   156–57
performance management for individuals,
        see individual performance
        management
performance management strategy
    individual performance   148–57
    organizational performance   133–46
personnel management   6, 10

resource-based capability   203
resource-based view
    defined   8
    and HRM   8
    organizational performance strategy
        137
    and strategic HRM   40–41

resourcing
    bundling of   173
    components of strategy   173
    defined   171
    integrating business and resourcing
        strategies   172–73
    plans   178–80
    retention strategy   180–84
    and strategic HRM   171–72
    strategic resourcing   171
    workforce planning   174–77
reward strategy
    basis of   211–12
    characteristics of   211
    content of   215–17
    defined   209–10
    development of   219
    effectiveness of   220–21
    guiding principles   217
    and line management capability
        221–22
    problem with concept   222–23
    reason for   210–11

70/20/10 model of learning   204
SHRM, see strategic human resource
        management
SIHRM, see strategic international human
        resource management
smart working   143–44
SMEs, HRM in   19–20
social learning   204
stakeholder theory   126
Standard Chartered   253
strategic business partner   52
strategic change management   87
strategic configuration   44
strategic fit   41
strategic human resource management
        (SHRM)
    aims of   39–40
    best fit approach   43
    best practice approach   42
    conceptual framework of   40–45
    defined   1, 37
    and HRM   38
    and HRM strategies   38–39
    life cycle model   43
    nature of   37–38
    perspectives on   42
    problem with   45–46
    and the resource-based view   40–41
    strategic configuration   44
    strategic fit   41

strategic international human resource
      management (SIHRM)
   approaches to   243–44
   centralization or decentralization
      240–41
   convergence and divergence   241–42
   cultural differences   240
   defined   238
   environmental differences   239
   globalization   238–39
   strategic issues   238
strategic learning and development
   aims   199
   defined   198–99
   philosophy   199–200
strategic management   27
strategic resourcing   171
strategy
   characteristics of   28
   content of   28
   defined   27
   development of   30–32
   implementation of   32–33
   see also HR strategy
strategy maps   135–36

talent   190–91
talent management
   defined   189–90
   pipeline   193–95
   strategy   190, 192
'three-legged stool model' of HR   13–14
trade union recognition strategy
      232–33
training   201
training courses   205–06
transactional HR activities   12
Transco   244
transformational HR activities   12
traust   229

workforce planning
   approaches to   175–77
   defined   174
   demand forecasting   175
   hard and soft workforce planning
      174–75
   limitations   175
   link to business planning   174
   supply forecasting   176
workplace learning   204–05